Journeys through Rajasthan

Journeys through Rajasthan

From the 16th to 21st centuries

Edited by

Amrita Kumar

RUPA
PUBLICATIONS INDIA

It is good, good beyond expression, to see the sun rise upon a strange land and to know that you have only to go forward and possess that land – that it will dower you before the day is ended with a hundred new impressions and, perhaps, one idea. It is good to snuff the wind when it comes in over large uplands or down from the tops of the blue Aravallis – dry and keen as a new-ground sword.

RUDYARD KIPLING

CONTENTS

Foreword

Rajasthan, Rajputana, land of kings, bards, minstrels and enchanting folklore, a kaleidoscope of colour – my birthplace, my home and the seat of my ancestors. A land like no other, which conjures up all that the mind of an avid traveler can dream of and even more. The land whose history stretches back to the Indus Valley Civilization (archaeological sites at Kalibangan in Northern Rajasthan) and the lost river Saraswati, Mt. Abu, the seat of sages in the ancient Aravalli ranges, and Brahma's sacred lake of Pushkar. Even while straddling its magnificent past, Rajasthan embraces the present with effortless grace – momentous developments like India's first nuclear test at Pokhran, economic reforms, modernization of agriculture, and the IT revolution.

There is a couplet in Rajasthani – KÔS KÔS PAE PANI BADALE CHAR KÔS PAE BANI, meaning every mile the taste and depth of water changes and every four miles the dialects, signifying the diversity of Rajasthan. From the vast sandy stretches of the Thar desert to the tiger reserves and bird sanctuaries, from the eternal haunting beauty of its temples, forts and palaces to the earthen charm of its villages, Rajasthan encapsulates the magic of this rich cultural diversity and extraordinary spirit of its people, reflected in all aspects of their life and in the unhurried pace of organic growth and development. Above all, it was the special relationship between the erstwhile rulers of Rajasthan and the thirty-six communities of priests, merchants, agriculturalists, craftsmen and tribals that shaped this unique evolution of the modern state of Rajasthan.

The idea of this anthology is brilliant and timely. Amidst the profusion of coffee table books on Rajasthan, it fills an important vacuum by bringing together eminent writers from diverse backgrounds and varied views to share their personal experiences. Their stories are authentic, real, spontaneous, and a part of the story of Rajasthan – including the traditional and the modern, urban and rural, wealthy and impoverished – has evolved naturally out of their narrative. The addition of ancient accounts makes the reading more comprehensive and pleasurable. Indeed, it would be impossible to encompass Rajasthan within any single anthology but this volume is to be seen as an intimate set of revelations that a reader can easily relate to and would, I hope, inspire him to experience this unique land for himself.

HH Gajsingh II
Jodhpur

Introduction

Rajasthan is quite clearly a land of extremes where the jewels roll as much as the sands blow. Through its short, freezing winters and long blazing summers, it may have remained isolated and almost been forgotten. But its rather strategic location on the trade routes as also its proximity to the long-standing capital cities of Delhi under several different names (the 13th being New Delhi) ensured that Rajasthan was both frequently traversed and aggressed through history, just as it was kept under close watch from the imperial capitals. Could this balance of opposites then have been the reason to make Rajasthan among the most populated of the desert regions of the world that girdle the globe?

The official end of feudalism may well have been sounded in 1950 when nineteen gun-salute states, two chieftainships (Kushalgarh and Lava) and one *suba* or province (Ajmer) merged to form this state. Names like Raiwara, Rajwara and Raesthan were considered before it eventually came to be called Rajasthan! But the hierarchical aftertaste of feudalism continued for decades and can still be savoured in the language of 'hukum' and 'hazoor' or in the gestures of 'khamagani' uttered bent at the waist with open hands gathered from the outside in a more formal namaskar.

Rajasthan is also a historical example of why it is better to be ruled by one's own people, even when great differences of lifestyle may define this relationship, than by aliens. The Rajasthani people still offer a reverential devotion to their new political rulers and administrators unlike in the states where the British had governed. The latter may have been better governed, but naturally grew to be hotbeds of sedition and contention, with its people becoming more aggressive and agitational. This natural sense of courtesy in Rajasthan now serves the tourist industry – especially in the old world context of its heritage hotels.

Mythology

Rajasthan, this ancient land of Aryavrata, is linked to the macro vision of the cosmic creator, Brahma – for the Hindus consider his home to be in Pushkar. The oldest spiritual text, The *Rigveda* enumerates:

> *In the valleys of hills on the confluence of rivers,*
> *The wisdom of the Brahman [the 'absolute'] was born.*

The sacred lake at Pushkar is considered by Hindus to be among the holiest waters along with the much less accessible Manasarovar situated at 4,560 metres en route to Mount Kailash in Tibet, where Shiva supposedly resides. But what are the criteria which have earned Pushkar the epithets of *tirthaguru* (guru of pilgrim sites) and *tirtharaj* (king of pilgrim places)?

According to the Puranas, the eighteen compilations of Brahmanical mythological lore, there are four categories of pilgrimages for Hindus. In a hierarchy of descending order, these are: *daiva-asura-tirthas,* created by the gods, mainly by the male deities of the trinity – Brahma, Vishnu and Shiva; *asura-tirthas,* associated with the destruction of demons by the trinity; *arsha-*

tirthas, related with the austerities, penances and sacrifices of renowned seers and sages; and *manusha-tirthas,* holy places created by men – preferably the rulers of the solar and lunar dynasties.

Rated on these criteria, Pushkar stands unique and highest among pilgrimages because it qualifies on all four grounds. First, it was chosen by Brahma while both Vishnu and Shiva attended the sacrificial fire rite that he held for its creation. Second, the demon Vajranabha, who performed penance in the Meru valley to propitiate Brahma, was destroyed here by Pradyumna, the son of Krishna. Shiva also took the form of a goat to kill the demon Vashkali here. Third, the sages Agastya, Bhartrihari, Kanva/Kashyapa, Jamadagni, Vamadeva, Vishvamitra, Kapila, Markandeya, Pulastya and even Yama, the lord of death, are believed to have done penance in caves here. Fourth, the Pratiharas of Mandor, the Kachhwahas of Amber/Jaipur, the Hadas of Kotah and Bundi, the Rathors of Marwar/Jodhpur, the Sisodias of Mewar/Udaipur and the Marathas of Gwalior have all had a hand in building and repairing temples and *ghats* at Pushkar.

As a pristine oasis in the Thar desert, Pushkar must always have appealed to the weary traveller or warrior, and once the legendary Sarasvati river flowed here. The sanctity and necessity of flowing water can hardly be overemphasized because the Ganga basin figures most prominently in all the *tirtha* lists of the epics and holy scriptures:

Pushkaradhipati tirthani gangadhayasariasthata
(Pushkar occupies the highest place among the pilgrim sites as does the sacred Ganga among rivers)

However, one lull in the popularity of Pushkar is recorded in history. After the destruction and conquest of Ajmer at the end of the 12th century by Muhammad of Ghori, people lived in fear and insecurity. Conspicuous patronage, building activity and worship at Pushkar was revived and thrived only in the 18th century. After 1947 – and particularly after the privy purses were abolished – royal patronage has waned, and now the priests rely more on the largesse of common pilgrims.

Geology

A rocky diagonal dramatically slashes the sandy canvas of Rajasthan like a dry brushstroke. From Delhi in the north-east this diagonal descends south-west to the Gulf of Cambay. These are the Aravallis which came to exist as an enormously thick series of argillaceous rocks at the close of the Archean era. Geological terms which may sound reptilian to lay readers, do describe well the crocodile crests of the great synlinorium which occupy the central part.

When the sediments deposited by the pre-historic seas underwent upheavals, the sedimentary rocks stood up, slanted or vertical, in composite banded gneisses, slates, conglomerates and basal quartzites which were peneplaned and denuded in later ages. To the west and south-west of Rajasthan, these are often engulfed in sandy alluvium making the picture postcard clichés of dunes in desert sand.

Geologists believe that some fourteen million years ago Rajasthan itself emerged from the cosmic flood or the Tethys Sea, named after the Greek sea deity, wife of Oceanus. Seventeen kilometres east of Jaisalmer, one hundred and eighty million year-old petrified trees can still be seen, just as fossils continue to appear in Osian.

But it is the geological wealth of Rajasthan which makes it the Italy of India. Kota, Jaisalmer, Aandhi, Makrana – are all names of places as well as the brand names of stones that are mined there.

History

In India, age also means wisdom, but because of the fact of its location, history has also meant much bloodshed in Rajasthan. Being one of the most prosperous regions in the world till the 18th century, India became the cynosure of the Islamic kingdoms. Despite not being those naturally rich regions, Rajasthan along with Sindh (now in Pakistan), Thana (in Maharashtra), Broach (Gujarat) and the Punjab suffered the constant blunt of this external aggression.

Digvijay Singh writes: 'because in areas where their orders were accepted [Hyderabad, Rampur, Lucknow, Delhi etc] the Muslim rulers tried to convert as many Hindus as they could by sword, Jiziya or religious persecution (by breaking Hindu temples and psychologically pushing the Hindus into believing that theirs was a weak god).' Contrary to what the Udaipur historians have long said, Digvijay Singh goes on to assert emphatically: 'Presence of Rajput generals in the Mughal army was a blessing in disguise for the Hindu population as the Mughal army when headed by a Rajput general could not engage in wanton destruction of Hindu temples as well as mass conversion of Hindus to Islam. The perseverance of Hinduism in India by the Rajput sword against the entire might of the Islamic rulers is the most glorious achievement by a race in the annals of world history and everyone should know this fact.'

This sentiment is also echoed by James Tod in *Annals and Antiquities of Rajasthan*: 'What nation on earth could have maintained the semblance of civilization, the spirit or the customs of their forefathers, during so many centuries of overwhelming depression, but one of such singular character as the Rajpoot? . . . Rajasthan exhibits the sole example in the history of mankind, of a people withstanding every outrage barbarity could inflict, or human nature sustain, from a foe (Muslims) whose religion commands annihilation; and bent to the earth, yet rising buoyant from the pressure, and making calamity a whetstone to courage. . . . Not an iota of their religion or customs have they lost. . . .'

But history runs its own course. The Rajputs, Marathas and Sikhs had narrowed in on all sides when the Mughal Empire ran into decadence and decline. But who could have prophesied that from nowhere in the neighbourhood or even within India, but from the distant lands of Europe would come the maritime powers: the Portuguese, the Dutch, the British, French and the Danes, and that India would be colonized? William Wilson Hunter writes in *The Indian Empire, Its People, History and Products*: 'So far as can now be estimated, the advance of the English power at the beginning of the present century alone saved the Mughal Empire from passing to the Hindus.'

Many Rajputs feel once-removed from the demographic political rule today. Living in the past, they are nostalgic about the obeisance history once gave them – or more truly, one that they forced from their times when they held the reins. Though history knows only a forward march, books of history must do this retro-recording service so that the future knows the strengths of the foundations it stands on. It is to these Rajput heroes to whom this debt of cultural continuity in social and religious practice – or indeed the gift of life itself – is owed.

Arts

In Jaipur's Ram Niwas garden sits the now renovated Prince Albert Museum where lies one of the rarest carpets in the world depicting the 'char bagh', theme where the gardens are interspaced with water channels. It is all too easily imagined that this is an Islamic contribution to Indian culture but P.R.J. Ford, a great specialist of floor coverings writes in *Oriental Carpet Design*: 'One may call all Persian carpets "woven gardens", the artistic precipitate of the nomad's dream. But there is also an ancient tradition of weaving designs which directly imitate the special formal layout of the Persian garden. What is probably the most famous carpet in history had such a design. It was produced (in what technique is not known – probably kilim or felt, rather than knotted) for the palace at Ctesiphon of Chosroes (Khosroes) I, one of the last Persian emperors before the Arab conquests of the seventh century AD. It is reported to have been some 27 m (90 ft) wide and five times as long, and its fabric was embellished with silk and thousands of pearls and jewels. Chosroes used it on the floor in winter to "remind him of the spring". The Muslim conquerors tore the carpet to pieces as booty when Ctesiphon fell in 641; but the sacred aura of the garden was enshrined in the Koran, where the faithful are promised a Paradise containing "four gardens, beneath which waters flow". Although the "spring of Chosroes" clearly proves that the idea contained in the garden carpet is older than Islam, the description of the celestial gardens in the Koran will certainly have been drawn upon by later artists working on the design.'

It is not always easy to draw simple or quick conclusions in a land as historically aggressed and enriched as Rajasthan where

70% of the pilgrims who visit the Dargah at Ajmer are Hindus. Fortunately, they carry no historical memory of the defeat of Prithviraj Chauhan in 1192 at the hands of Muhammad of Ghori and of all the destruction of temples and the humiliation that followed. Any place of worship for a Hindu is quite simply the house of god! In this lies a certain ongoing wisdom of continuity.

❖

Those who have been even once to Rajasthan have their own love story to narrate. But they often tell it only to friends at dinner parties. Readers of this volume will certainly find a resonance in the travels of the sixteen writers who have experienced this historic land through the 19th, 20th and 21st centuries.

But those who have never been to the fascinating state of Rajasthan, can take this book as the beginning of a love affair. Even the real in this state is so unreal: so many landscapes from the travels always remain in the memory as photogravures and etchings, and so many evenings of dance and music still performed in the forts and palaces become miniature paintings brought alive again.

Aman Nath
May 2011

1

GOING HOME

Amrita Kumar in Ajmer, Nasirabad, Ashapur and
Todgarh, on to an imagined journey in the footsteps of
Tod and Kipling

June is the worst time to go to Rajasthan. The first thing that
hits me as I arrive in Ajmer is the heat, and vertigo, the feeling
you get after a train ride, of walking along a platform that's
moving like a treadmill. Sweat pours down my neck in rivulets
like I've broken a vein. Loudspeakers blast my blocked ears open
with high-pitched announcements of the arrival of the Shatabdi
on platform number six.

Ajmer Junction is the familiar synthesis of Gothic and Saracenic
you see in all small towns where the British settled, thick walls
and pillars now laced with paan stains. Outside the station auto
drivers, taxi drivers and seedy hotel touts are making a din, mostly
around the foreigners. In my confusion I settle for Babu. He has
bloodshot eyes and rubber chappals on his feet, the heels of
which appear to have melted away in the heat. His taxi's a white

Ambassador with the back seat higher than the front one so my head keeps hitting the roof and there's no leg room either because he's adjusted the front seat further back than it normally is. Why in this weather does he have a rug on the back seat? It's fluffy and ugly and ochre-coloured and it keeps shifting around and gathering folds under me.

I tell him to take me for a quick spin around Ajmer before we head for Nasirabad. I tell him I don't know the roads so he should keep telling me where we are which he interprets as my wanting to know everything about him, like his life were so inextricably intertwined with every street and *gali* of Ajmer that he has no choice. It's a small-town thing I think, the impossibility of perceiving a place as outside oneself and in a strange way and despite my annoyance, the distance between Ajmer and me begins to reduce as we go along and I begin to be grateful.

Ajmer is a dusty old town, a faded old painting in which the lines of demarcation have merged. In 1818, I recall, it had been sold to the British by the Marathas for a mere Rs 50,000, not enough today to buy one room in a New Delhi house. It's surrounded by a ring of low, bare, dun-coloured hills, the occasional *acacia* and *zizyphus* accentuating their emptiness. There's an astounding assortment of vehicles on the roads – cycle rickshaws, *phatphats,* obsolete cars, rickety buses spewing carbon monoxide, snaking between them girls in salwar kameez and helmets riding Lunas. Railway crossings too, tracks seemingly thrown across crowded roads by a maniac when actually it's the town that's arbitrary, a confusion of building styles, beautiful mildewed old structures squeezed between newer uglier ones.

We circle the Anasagar where I see a group of people with all sorts of instruments in their hands. I lean my head out of the car to see what they're staring at and I see that indeed the water has something in it, a blue-green algae like deposit. I'd read somewhere that the Anasagar was dying, being choked by sewage and agricultural effluents and that environmentalists were objecting to its obnoxious odour. Cyanobacterial bloom it's called, I think. Had the British stayed on might Ajmer have been a picturesque lake resort? Look what we've done to that lake and what do these people think they can do now? Can anyone bring a dead lake back to life? Dredge its stories out of its depths and return them to those who own them? But those stories had fled long before, taken refuge in the myopic recesses of old men's eyes where they changed shape and colour so no one can find them now.

From its opposite banks the lake looks different, large and comforting, stretching beyond what the eye can see to a haze of brown hills in the distance. It was on one of those hills that Prithviraj Chauhan once waged a battle. Strange how history returns to you a sense of the present. Perched on a crag is the whitewashed British Governor's house, high and lost and lonely, a touchstone to the fear inside that I might never find what I've journeyed here for.

We're headed for Martindale Bridge, right after which we hit the Ajmer-Nasirabad highway. It's as straight as a ruler, no detours anywhere. Highways are normally located at the periphery of a town as this one might have been except that the burgeoning population of Ajmer seems to have turned it from a thoroughfare into a muddled extension of the town so that on my left there's an eye hospital, on my right a row of mobile phone shops, smaller make-shift shops in between selling imitation Levi jeans and school bags, a petrol pump next to a row of vegetable shops, trucks queuing up outside, spewing carbon monoxide onto the vegetables, a government office in a combination of Rajput and Mughal architecture, newly built in pink sandstone and hard by an excessively tube-lit chemist's shop right next to an open air barber's shop under a *neem* tree, its clients unaffected by the din and the passers-by as if there were an invisible wall around them. In short, a hundred years after this magnificent highway was built by the British it's only a bird that could tell you it's a road. And despite it being straight as a ruler you could get terribly lost on it.

As the miles fly past I find myself thanking god for the British, for the magnificent roads they gave us, for their extraordinary ability to cut a metal swathe across impossible terrain. It's probably thanks to the highway that the terrain is not as impossible as it would have been a hundred years before. There's been a green revolution since, wheat fields and *bajra* and mustard on either side, and even the hills around appear to have softened from the way I imagined they would be, mellowed the way women do with age, sprouting a few hair on the chin, or is it that period before they die, when they assume the manner of adolescent girls? Of course I know there are other harsher parts of the desert where the Aravallis flaunt their age like tyrants.

Forty-five minutes later we hit the Nasirabad cantonment. It's completely deserted. Deep in the heart of these burning acres stands the beautiful ochre and white St Paul's Cathedral in perpendicular Gothic. In the calculations of the British was there a terrible misconception as to the significance of Nasirabad in the imperial scheme of things, or, was Nasirabad more important once than anyone remembers? What's a magnificent piece of England doing in a medieval Rajput town? It's the same air that all small towns taken over by the British bear – Batala, Meerut, Lakhimpur, Bareilly, Jabalpur, Jullunder, Beawar and more. Colonial structures quite charming when viewed on their own but juxtaposed with the chaotic Indian way, conveying the sense of a bully having rampaged through land that belonged to somebody else, snuffing out its life breath.

I get off the car briefly. Within the cathedral, along the walls on either side, are marble plaques commemorating officers and soldiers of the 89th Field Battery who'd died in the 1857 Mutiny. As I read the inscriptions I begin to believe the cantonment contains men of flesh and blood though I'd have to wait till twilight to see them because like the legendary witches of the Thar that's when the battalions would probably emerge, no blood on their fangs but heat boils suppurating inside their fatigues, running and marching and doing their drill.

Back on the highway I see in the distance the ramshackle outline of old Nasirabad, the part that existed long before the British came here. The highway ends here, right after a bus stop which, unlike the cantonment, is a beehive of activity, buses taking off every few minutes for Ajmer or Kishangarh and beyond. Through the mayhem of conductors ululating and banging the sides of buses to announce their departure and other buses rolling in through clouds of dust, the people on the tea stall benches appear like a study in still life, due in part to the enormous size of the brightly coloured *safas* of the men who sip their tea and smoke their *bidis,* their hands moving back and forth without their heads moving in conjunction, a phenomenon unique to Rajasthan and owing to the weight of those *safas* that render the heads beneath them immobile. Even the humblest of them looks like a king in this stance, bare legs under their muslin *dhotis* crossed at the knees like women, elaborately embroidered and sequined *mojris* on their feet like pirates' boats adrift.

A bumpy lane leads into the old town. I ask Babu to accompany me on foot. Beyond a point cars can't go as there's just one main lane here with a bazaar on either side, a sea of people choking the lane to make it appear narrower than it is, bright pink, yellow and olive green *safas* bobbing up and down in their midst, one foot higher than the turban-less heads, some turbaned fellows one foot lower, cruising along the lane on mobikes, fancy goggles on, gold earrings glinting in the sun. In between the old shops are posh new ones with shining linoleum counters behind which father, son and probably uncle or brother-in-law sit in a row, panels of gleaming taps behind them, white ceramic pots and sinks.

This old town was once connected through trade with the 16th century commercial mart of Bhilwara. Its character is a cross between a medieval village and a trading depot but as its two faces are not separated geographically you can't get a full sense of things as they were, or perhaps that's the way they always were, but it's a matter of lingering doubt because there are parts that look like they've come out of a blurred watercolour painting and then less than fifty yards away the harsh overwrought lines of workshops where old train compartments from Ajmer Junction are being hammered and reshaped into doors and windows, speak a different story – a puzzle of mismatching parts of varying vintage that no one seems to question, they simply flow with the tide, moving among cyclists, cows, vendors in happy disharmony.

Deep in the interior stand the old homes, *havelis,* of the merchants of Nasirabad, some at a precarious tilt and though they aren't more than three stories at the most they loom like skyscrapers in relation to the width of the cobbled paths that lead to them. Life would have been different here before the British came, their inner courtyards hiding women from the world, the sudden intrusion of male guests sending them hurtling into the *zenana* from where they peeped at them through fretted windows. In between these fairytale-like houses are ugly new ones, some doubling up as hardware and bicycle repair shops, and some *havelis* aren't really *havelis* anymore because they've given up their terraces, newly constructed rooms balancing on top of old ones. One of them is painted sugar pink and green, railings above embellished with round copper medallions engraved with a portrait of Queen Elizabeth, the same profile you see on English postage stamps. Layers upon layers of history choking each other to death.

I look for the Mission Hospital where my grandmother used to work. I locate it along a narrow lane. Standing on that lane you can't tell whether the hospital came first or the ugly hardware shops all around but it must have been the hospital because it has on either side of it large windows in an attitude of permanent shock as if they had expected to look out into the blue yonder. They're tightly shut, bolts jammed with disuse, green casement curtains drawn, but as I enter the hospital I see that none of this double barricading keeps out the constant hammering and sawing from the workshops that eventually balances itself out against the slow whirring of hospital fans, slung low on creaking stems that sway drunkenly over airless rooms. It's like everything else in Nasirabad that appears to balance itself out against something else and this is the charm if you can see it, old against new, ancient *havelis* against new houses whose windows and doors smell of train compartments, those buses back on the highway rolling in through clouds of dust against old men on benches frozen in time, the white heat of the sun against the cool of the desert nights, the hospital beating its own brave rhythm against the dying heartbeat of an ancient town.

Babu asks me if I'd like to see the railway station. I never imagined there was one. I thought Ajmer was it. So we take a bumpy road circumambulating the old town to its remote end where a small yellow-washed single-storied building stands amidst a dry field, quite isolated from the bustle of the bazaar and looking no more important than someone's house. A single metre-guage track, a single platform along which half a dozen people stand, no urgency about them, no sense of waiting for a train, as if they'd been standing there forever. Could they be here to kill time? Do people still exist on earth who have fun watching trains arrive on platforms? This is how railway stations should be ideally. One window, one sleepy head framed by that window, all the time in the world to be pleasant while answering a question or giving you a ticket. I hang around the platform for a while pretending I have a train to catch. The names of destinations are written in chalk in Hindi on a blackboard. I don't recognize them ... *Chaupat Khamb, Bagri, Indauliya* ...

I am tired and hungry. I ask Babu to take me back to the bus stop where I look for an *alu kachora*. I'm standing at a *dhaba,* the ashes of history flying all about me, I feel I'm choking on them and then it happens so fast. I ask a *dhabawallah* where Ashapur is, whether he knows where my grand uncle's hunting lodge used to be once.

'Udhar,' he says, pointing every which way towards the ring of low hills that surround Nasirabad.

'Udhar kidhar?' I say, not really paying attention. I am simply making conversation, trying to distract myself from the desire to faint. 'Anyway it's not there anymore,' I say.

And he says, *'Kyon nahin bai, bilkul hai!'*

Disbelieving, I confirm and reconfirm this with him and then wrapping my *kachora* hastily in a piece of newspaper, I look around for Babu. He's a few *dhabas* away. I call out to him, tell him to try and understand what the man means, waving to him to hurry up.

We take the road to Kishangarh. Within minutes Nasirabad recedes and fallow fields begin, in between sudden inexplicable patches of lush green and the odd *dhaba* with wooden benches outside, men in *safas,* legs crossed, doing nothing but gazing at the traffic. An hour down the road Babu swerves to the right again abruptly, plunges straight into a wheat field, into wheat stalks growing higher than the taxi. An involuntary scream escapes me. I fear Babu's lost control of the wheel until I realize we're on a narrow dirt path running right through the fields. The path is bumpy but Babu doesn't slow down, he negotiates clutch and brake superbly with his floppy rubber half-chappals and I hang on for life as we plunge and rise and gallop and shudder our way through those fields, dry brown stalks sweeping the windows, wheat dust turning the windshield and windows opaque.

As suddenly as they'd begun, the wheat fields end and we're in wide-open space. I lower my window; Babu lowers his as I turn around to marvel at how we emerged from that giant clutch of wheat intact. All signs of civilization have disappeared. In the hazy distance are the Aravallis, dark and low and brooding here, the sky above without a single cloud, like a scene painted by a child without the skills to create nuances. Flat and blank, yet terrifyingly eternal as if time itself began here, light years ago. Not a soul in sight, no farmers with aquiline features or *safas,* no women swishing along in fluorescent *ghagras,* only a terrible emptiness in which not a bird chirps, not a leaf stirs, there *are* no leaves here, only gnarled branches like overgrown bonsai full of silent, deadly thorns.

My back hurts. 'How long more do you think?' I say to Babu.

'We're here,' he replies and that could mean anything for Babu has no concept of time I've discovered but I ask him anyway because words seem necessary to break the silence we've entered, a ritual to stir those skies and those thorns to speak, to acknowledge our existence. I look up once more and that's when I see it, a greystone bombed-out shell of a structure in the distance, the vista and the structure appearing to have grown through time to resemble each other, a joining of hearts through shared isolation so that even the outline of the house creates hardly a blemish against the sky. Gigantic weeds along a boundary wall, one thorny *babool* leaning against a broken arch. I get off the car. Babu swipes the ochre rug off the back seat, follows me to the boundary wall where he spreads it out to form a seat. There is compassion in his gesture. It dignifies my sitting on a broken wall looking at an abandoned house.

I try and imagine how my grand uncle would have conducted his days and nights in this wilderness but it's all a blank. I climb off the wall and walk the four steps up to the porch of the house, straining my ears for sounds, for sudden movements. In the quiet of the desert a footfall is magnified a thousand times. A lizard falls pat at my feet, stares at me with its chinless face and marble eyes. Who knows, there might be snakes. On the wall of the porch is an orange palm, the Congress logo. Below it the words 'Vote for Makhan Lal'. Above the logo, cleaving to the roof, a large conical beehive, alive and buzzing. I swivel around on my heel, taking in the roof, the floor, the wall, the broken arches together in the manner of someone making a survey, hiding from myself the truth that I am afraid. One eye on the beehive, I lower myself on the top stair and survey the garden. It's a virus of nettles. They appear to be stacked in dead clumps but that's the way they grow here, hiding their roots, tumbling over themselves in haste. You could kill a man by throwing him face down on one, pick him up with a deliberate jerk so he leaves his eyeballs behind, impaled on those thorns like two shivering *hor d'oevres.*

Dusting my behind I pluck up the courage to enter the house. There are no doors or windows here. Probably stolen a long time ago, making this a house literally blowing in the wind. The ceiling appears strong though, there's no seepage, only splatter marks beneath the spaces where those windows once were. The walls are covered with graffiti, vulgar words, hearts pierced by arrows, Rakesh loves Sonia, assorted penises and breasts. High up are the old marks of mounts ripped off, on which heads of deer or *nilgai* might have hung. Two large rooms stand side by side, a fireplace each, back to back. On either side, smaller rooms, all with arched entrances, one arch split by a branch of the oleander that blooms within the house. Nature has reclaimed this forgotten house and it's I, not the oleander who intrudes. It's a small lodge on the whole, barely a two-minute walk-through but it smells of monument, of old parchment, of a hidden river flowing through its veins. At one end is a bathroom. I know it's a bathroom from its sloping floor, a drainage dyke leading to the outside but apart from this there are no taps, nothing in it. Everything is gone.

At the rear of the house an exposed stairway leads to the roof. Several steps are missing. Entwining the strap of my handbag around my neck and under my armpits to form a rucksack I start climbing on all fours. There's no other way to negotiate those terrifying spaces. I arrive at the roof from where I look around hesitantly for I am unused to horizons. The sun is a burnt orange ball. A hundred yards, two hundred, four hundred, the miles fly past in a haze, stunted *acacia, tamarix* and *zizyphus* against that ochre landscape, the colours and hues of this vast wasteland to a herd of *nilgai* in the distance, beyond the *nilgai* a dry lake bed, the bitter dregs of old marshland. I take a step backwards as I see Babu below looking around for me. He hasn't seen me climbing.

I look down at my feet to regain my balance. The floor of the roof is dark and grainy. I bend down and touch the old stone with my palm and then I lie down and press my cheek to it, stretch my arms out on both sides to enfold the house, the sleep coming upon me akin to death.

◇

Two hours later I come down the stairs clutching at the broken wall. I see Babu asleep in the car on the back seat. I jab his leg. He looks annoyed. He looked for me all over, he blusters, thought I'd wandered off somewhere until he discovered I was up on the roof. 'Are we ready to return to Ajmer?' he asks.

'We're not returning just yet,' I say. 'We're going into the mountains.'

'Which mountains?' he says.

I tell him to take me back to the Nasirabad bus stop first from where I pick up two packets of glucose biscuits for us. I try and understand from a *dhabawallah* the layout of the hills surrounding Nasirabad. He tells me if I'm to venture into the high Aravallis I need to head towards Beawar and Bhim first, from there follow the pass into the mountains. 'But you musn't go beyond Todgarh,' he tells me.

'Why?' I ask.

'The area's full of go-s,' he replies.

'What's a go?' I ask.

'A thousand-legged Rajasthani monitor lizard that flies at you,' he says, 'wraps itself round your neck and squeezes you to death. A hundred men can't pull it off.'

Babu is tightlipped. I persuade him to take me. I tell him we'll be back in Nasirabad by evening.

✧

Todgarh is two hours from Nasirabad. We pass many villages on the way. Unfamiliar names, impossible to remember so I jot them down ... *Sanva, Jawaja, Devata, Bagliya, Kukda, Jassa Kheda, Dhol Bhata, Godhaji ka Gaon, Dungaji ka Gaon* .... An hour into the drive the mica region opens up, once upon a time magnificent golden mountains, now ochre, denuded, the odd shard of mica winking at the sun. It was the richness of these mountains that enabled the Rajputs so long to struggle against invaders for they yielded a wealth of minerals as well as silver ... an older than old story, for Tod in the early 19th century had already found the caste of miners extinct. Nervously I tell Babu I'd like to stop when convenient for him, to pick up a few stray mica rocks as mementoes along the way but he acts like he hasn't heard me.

Past the mica mountains, the Aravallis begin to grow dense, rolling in several dark layers as far as the eye can see. The slopes are barren apart from cacti as tall as trees. As we near Todgarh I tell Babu we're not stopping here, we're going just a little further on until the motorable road ends. He brakes furiously. We sit in the car in silence for a minute after which he says I can go where I please, he's going back to Ajmer. I leave the car and start walking. He follows me, mumbling something about not knowing what's good for me. I tell him to return to Nasirabad if he won't come with me, park at the bus stand and wait for me while I wander through Todgarh and then catch the roadways bus back after which we could return to Ajmer together. I don't give him a chance to argue. I keep walking.

Todgarh is antique land. It's chief of a *tuppa* consisting of a hundred villages and hamlets though you wouldn't believe it, so hidden are those villages between crags and defiles. The road on which I stand is strong and beautiful, again thanks to the British. It's the same all over Rajasthan, metal roads where you would have expected no more than dirt paths. The town is poised elegantly over three hills, slopes demarcated into sections with short stone walls forming a steppe like effect. This would probably be to establish ownership of land and I wonder what for, as nothing appears to grow here, nothing but cacti. You can see from the bone structure of the people's faces here, their weather-beaten skin that they've faced terrible hardships. It's there in their eyes, in their stance, in the determination of their profiles although their features bear the nobility of kings and queens. The *safas* of the men are much larger here and more vivid than those you see in the plains, or do they appear brighter against that dreary landscape?

Through the shimmering haze of heat the houses appear to be balanced on top of each other, so steep is the rise of those hills, gaily coloured walls standing out among the more staid creams and greys, some probably centuries old but painted over generously, the thickness of the paint unable to camouflage their vintage, the unevenness of their walls, the lopsidedness of their *jharokas* and balconies. Most striking of all are the houses painted white with a touch of *neel*. They shine against that landscape with much the same effect here as stained glass has on Mission territory. Sprawled across the other two hills is an ancient fort built of stone blackened with age, quite clearly belonging to the pre-cement era, thin slates wedged together to uphold it through the centuries, the only sign of vulnerability being that whole sections of it dip in parts as if the fort were gently sinking into the hills. I ask some passing children whether they know who built that fort up there and they say Which fort? so similar in character is the fort to the hills, merging with them not just physically but in the minds of the people who see, and therefore don't see it daily. I rack my brain for the little history I know and I recall that Gurjaras, ancestors of the modern Gujars, had established themselves in these parts in the beginning of the proto-Guler period. In their struggle for survival the Huns of Central Asia who had invaded the northern plains and the Gurjaras came into bitter conflict and this battle for supremacy started the process of building fortified settlements. Could this fort have belonged to that period?

The glucose biscuits weren't enough. I am tired and hungry and acidic. I feel a pain shoot through my left side. The air is heavy and dust-laden, the sun grows dim, making the entire town appear like it were shrouded in cold on a winter's evening. I walk towards a *dhaba* and ask for a tumbler of water. The old man at the *dhaba* asks me what I'm doing here so I tell him I'm looking for the village my grandfather came from, a village called Dahirya, and could he guide me? He waves to a group of people in the distance. Four men and one old woman leave the group to collect around us. He passes my question on to them.

'Dahirya doesn't exist anymore *bai*,' one man says, 'nor the Dahiryas. There was a terrible famine in these parts in 1868 followed by a cholera epidemic and the British came and took away a number of people in bullock carts. Some went with them.'

'What about the rest?'

'Try the dunes towards Jaisalmer, at Sam,' one of them says. 'Maybe they returned to where they originally came from.'

'But they left the dunes centuries ago,' I say, 'I know for a fact that they migrated, built their village along the banks of a river.'

'What river?' the old man says, 'there was never a river here.'

'Of course there was,' says the old woman, 'and still is.'

The men break into laughter. One of them circles a finger round his head to convey she's senile.

She lashes out at him. '*Haramkhor*, born yesterday so how would you know?'

'And you were born ten thousand years ago by the looks of you,' he retorts.

'I tell you the river's there,' she turns to me, 'but only the pure of heart can see it, not these *haramkhor* disbelievers.'

Raucous laughter again. They begin to move away. The woman turns back and tells me in a whisper, 'Yes, it's true, they came to these parts,' so I ask her whether she knows where their village was and she points in the direction of a disordered heap of gigantic rock up ahead on which no one could possibly have lived.

I look around for a *tonga*. The pain in my side is growing. No one is willing to take me, no one but an import from Punjab called Ram Bhatinda, owner of a ramshackle *tonga* without a roof. He tells me he isn't a *darpok* like the rest, I shouldn't listen to their useless chitter chatter and that he's often travelled through these parts which he knows quite well.

'Where's your roof?' I ask him.

'I have a roof *bai*,' he replies looking hurt, 'but it will take me some time to fetch it. It's under repair.'

I decide to do without the roof and without further ado the two of us take off straight into the mountains, the afternoon sun of the Thar beating upon our heads. Very soon the metal road ends. We're on a dirt track now. The *tonga* dips and heaves, causing my head to shoot through the roofless roof. 'This is nothing,' he says smiling, 'wait till we get beyond the rock.'

'Is it very bad?' I ask nervously, the pain on my side moving in waves towards my chest.

'I have never been there myself but I hear it is like the road to hell,' he replies.

I am outraged. 'I thought you said you knew these parts,' I say angrily and he replies that no one knew these parts. 'You make sure we're back in Todgarh in two hours flat,' I threaten him and he replies that he'll get me back much before that or forego his payment.

By now I am powdered with dust and feeling like a dead leaf forced by the wind to take wing. The sun is up like an all-seeing eye that will not shut and I am losing my capacity to think. With nothing around me but rock and stone and the spectre of the high Aravallis looming ahead, I enter a dreamlike state. I imagine I see a sea in front of me, foaming billows arising, until I realize we're entering a large expanse of flat ground between two mountains, the wind playing with clouds of dust. An hour later we're in the middle of nowhere. The rock has vanished. It isn't behind me or in front of me. The pain in my side is acute. I begin to imagine I'll die in the wilderness with nobody finding me or claiming my body that would be feasted upon by wild animals. The pony looks unhappy too, his head hanging low and straining at the reins as if he wished to lie down so I order Ram Bhatinda to stop at once but he appears not to hear me. Lashing at the flanks of the animal, he strikes boldly on into the black heart of the mountains. '*Bewakoof!*' I yell at him angrily, even as the *tonga* jumps into and out of a large hole slantwise, nearly throwing me over.

Signs of life. We enter a narrow *ghati* on an incline, perpendicular cliffs on either side into which are carved a dozen niches containing figures of Hanuman, little *diyas* before them, one flickering gently. My spirits lift. Perched high on a cliff is what appears to be the abode of a *sanyasi* and a little further on the incline, on the right, a flight of stairs cracked down the middle on account of a large fig tree having taken root there. '*Taanga roko!*' I yell at the top of my voice at Ram Bhatinda who pulls at the reins out of shock. I hurtle off my perch before he changes his mind and head towards the stairs, ready to embrace whoever I might find there but there's nothing but an abyss on the other side and a gigantic pile of ruins frozen in time, the thorny *babool* growing luxuriantly out of broken walls and columns. Weeds crackle under my feet. Magnificent flights of stairs on all sides descend into the abyss and I realize it's a *baoli* below me, excavated out of solid rock, its high watermark clear evidence that water flowed here in abundance once. But the only signs of life are huge bats, flitting silently past the columns, and stray dogs, the same colour as the ruins, wandering over piles of debris with large dead eyes.

I return to the *tonga*. Ram Bhatinda is on the back seat now in a half recline, looking up at the thin wedge of sky visible through the narrow *ghati,* one bare leg poised over a bony knee, smirk across his face. I contemplate yelling at him once more, at the top of my voice, to turn the *tonga* around but that one lit *diya* has given me hope so I refrain and off we go again, through the *ghati* and deeper and deeper into the mountains, past wasted fields, the remains of deserted villages, roofless houses, according to Tod great cities in their day, now a spectre of desolation. We're in the womb of the Aravallis now, great black mountains of granite and slate behind us and in front of us, splintered pinnacles in the distance soaring to the sky. Forming dark lines along the crests of the mountains are more fort-like structures with bastions and parapets and towers, again quite clearly of the pre-cement era, brushwood scattered over the surface of dead walls, skeletal trees growing out of them. I know that the Afghans long prowled around these regions and would therefore have required some form of defense. Or could I be mistaking them for forts? Could they have been luxury resorts? Religion appears to have been of great importance too in these parts, evident from the abandoned temples we pass and little mosques with elegant, crumbling minarets. More niches and caves too, some Buddhist, some Hindu, some dating back to the time of the Jaina kings. No sign of the Archaeological Survey of India ever having laid foot here. We're on an excruciatingly narrow ledge along the girth of a mountain now and Ram Bhatinda says we must go single file. I climb out of the *tonga*. My head spins. I clutch a tree to regain my balance. Four hills surround us with a deep canyon of stratified layers of hard rock below. High on a hill in the distance stands a colonial mansion like a holiday retreat, dank and yellowed by age. Ram Bhatinda pulls at the rickshaw wearily. The sun begins to set, gently passing its veil over the roof of the mansion, illuminating it briefly. In a voice that doesn't sound like mine I call out to Ram Bhatinda that I'd like to return to Todgarh now whereupon he informs me casually that he won't travel by night. I am infuriated beyond belief. I order him to turn back but he says we would be stuck on the road in the dark and that it's wiser to go on and spend the night somewhere, though he didn't know where. But I won't travel by night, he repeats firmly. The pain in my side is worse. Strange new sounds permeate the silence of the desert. My hair stands on end as I remember something about animals and snakes burrowing deep in the ground to survive the heat of the Thar and then coming out around sunset. Finally we clear the ledge and emerge on the other side of the mountain onto a dry open field. 'I won't go on,' Ram Bhatinda announces here, so we ready to sleep on the ground under the stars and despite the growing sounds of the nether world in my ears I drift off.

✧

The next morning I look around me and I see that Ram Bhatinda and his *tonga* are gone.

I watch the sun rise for a while, hoping the two will materialize from behind a rock at any moment but when an hour passes in such expectation I realize I've been abandoned. I call out his name. I retrace my steps, walking back towards the ledge, casting my eye across the vista but there isn't a sign of him or the pony. I start walking along the ledge towards the *ghati* but an hour later I see no *ghati*, only mountains around me stretching to eternity. I continue walking in whichever direction my feet take me until I see something strange. The ridge in front of me is changing shape. It's melting and it's growing, it's changing colour and then swinging from its base as if it were as light as a feather and then returning to size and place, continuing to perform theatrics for several minutes. Far in the distance a huge dense wall of smoke rises and begins undulating in waves towards the ridge, covering it completely, turning and twisting over it like a giant paintbrush. The ridge grows peaks now, crowned with icicles, the next minute a dense mass of foliage, a moving collage that keeps changing until the smoke grows lighter and a ray of the sun scatters the image into a thousand parts, each part within a huge lens, dwarfing the shrubs of the desert, now turning them to giant size until eventually the whole scene starts to fade.

I imagine I'm losing my mind. Maddened by thirst, I stumble along in a daze, clutching my side, seating myself down on a rock now and again, sobbing from fear and pain. The sky is a cerulean blue; by noon the temperature well over a hundred degrees. A wind begins to blow, clouds of dust rising and swirling around me. I cover my nose and mouth to stop from choking. After raging and whistling through the mountains for two hours that terrible wind ceases. With a sensation bordering on madness I plod on, past mountain and plain, neither affording relief from the other. Just as I think I can walk no more I enter a cul-de-sac, a barrier of bare dismal rock that encloses my path like a wall on three sides. Bone weary, I lean against the rock, unable to sit down for the pain in my side that now appears to be causing a swelling. I feel a breeze cool my cheek. I straighten abruptly. When all around me is nothing but heat rising in waves, where could the breeze be coming from? I look around puzzled. I touch the rock. I find it is moist. Then I hear a sound, a chattering quarreling sound that appears to be coming from behind the rock. With the last remnants of energy left in me I heave myself up and begin climbing. Halfway up I change my mind but realize that descent would be impossible now for I hadn't thought of removing my shoes and if I lost my grip my head could split wide open so I continue climbing until miraculously I reach the top.

Drawing myself to a vertical position I look around me and I see that the world appears to be divided into two by that rock –

the desert behind me, an oasis in front, cool and shady, thick with gigantic banyan and mango trees. Far on the right is a rumbling cluster of ancient moss-covered tombs among which black-faced monkeys leap around in gay abandon. Shaking my shoes off I begin to descend, slipping again and again but quickly recovering on account of the new energy amazement has given me. The monkeys grow silent, staring at me with their button eyes until one of them takes a giant leap into the forest, his companions hurriedly following suit. Bleary-eyed now from exhaustion and as a result quite unafraid as to what I might find, I stumble towards the tombs. They appear to be tinkling gently. Again I imagine I'm losing my mind until I near the tombs and see little bells attached to their arched entrances, the only sound in that incredible aura of quietude. On the walls are painted solar deities seated in racing chariots and, carved into a twelve-pillared pavilion stunning sensuous sculptures. Every surface of the tombs is decorated, domed ceilings rich with elephants and horsemen and dancing figures. The air is hushed here, radiating a sense of eternity. I contemplate lying down, pressing my cheek against the cool stone ground when I hear the sound of water. It appears to be coming from behind the tombs so abandoning thoughts of rest, I encircle the tombs and come upon two large rocks between which flows a stream of water. But the sound I hear is greater than anything a little stream can produce so after dipping my hands in the water and splashing my face I follow the sound to another set of rocks and in the process find I am climbing a rather high mountain this time to which there appears to be no summit. Giant leaves flap against my legs, whisper and rustle against my cheek as higher and higher I go in pursuit of the sound and when I reach a defile of sorts I stop to catch my breath. Utterly worn by now it begins to appear to me almost a welcome prospect were I to fall off that mountain straight but just then that breeze begins to blow again, reviving me, and I stand up tall and survey the strange new world around me. Around me is a dense forest echoing with the screams of the peacock and the call of the partridge. I lean forward to take a look below and that's when I see it, a magnificent ribbon of silver hidden altogether among the hills, rushing and winding through a pass to a golden valley below, three miles wide, its margins aflame with the *dhak,* and through the trees and patches of light caused by the play of the sun I see people.

The pain in my side is unbearable now. I make an attempt to call out for help but my head feels light, my tongue and lips tight and swollen. I grasp the rock on which I am standing and feel myself sinking to the ground.

✧

'Lie down *bai,* you're tired,' I hear a familiar voice.

I'm in the Ambassador, ochre rug under me, speeding along the Ajmer-Nasirabad highway. It's dusk outside. Babu has his headlights on, they sway and swing like lanterns on the winding road. 'Where did you come from?' I ask him, sitting upright. 'Where did you find me?'

'What where?' he replies. 'Lying on the road in a dead faint, that's where ... you must have got heatstroke.'

'But that's impossible,' I say, 'I went into the mountains, I found Dahirya, I found the river.'

He starts laughing. 'You're a very brave *bai,* and very determined,' he says, 'but with too much imagination. In the two small circles I took around Todgarh where did you go?'

2

THE SINGER OF EPICS

William Dalrymple in Pabusar

The landscape, as we neared Pabusar, was a white, sun-
leached expanse of dry desert plains, spiky *acacia* bushes
and wind-blown camel thorn. The emptiness was broken
only by the odd cowherd in a yellow turban, patiently leading his
beasts through the dust, and by a long, slow convoy of nomads
in camel carts, pursued by a rearguard of barking dogs.

Once, as we turned off the main Jaipur-Bikaner highway,
we passed a group of Rabari women, in saris of bright primary
colours, resting in the narrow shade of a single, gnarled desert
tree; abandoned road-building equipment lay scattered all around
them. A little later, we saw a group of three Jain nuns in white
robes, with masks over their faces, pushing a fourth in a white
wheelchair through the open desert as the heatwaves shimmered
and slurred around them. Though it was winter, it was still very
hot, and a hot, dry wind blew in from the scrub, and through the
open car window, furring our mouths and setting our teeth on
edge, and gritting the seats of the car.

With me as we drove through this bleak land was my friend Mohan Bhopa, and his wife, Batasi (which means 'Sugar Ball'). Mohan was a tall, wiry, dark-skinned man of about sixty, with a bristling grey handlebar moustache and a mischievous, skull-like grin. He wore a long red robe and a tightly tied red turban. Batasi was somewhat younger than him, a silent, rugged desert woman of fifty who had lived all her life in the wilderness. As we drove, she kept almost all her face shrouded in a high-peaked red veil.

Mohan was a bard and a village shaman; but rarer and more intriguing still, he and Batasi, though both completely illiterate, were two of the last hereditary singers of a great Rajasthani medieval poem, *The Epic of Pabuji*. This 600-year-old poem is a fabulous tale of heroism and honour, struggle and loss, and finally, martyrdom and vengeance. Over time, it seems to have grown from a local saga about the heroic doings of a river-chieftain protecting his cattle to the epic story of a semi-divine warrior and incarnate god, Pabu, who died protecting a goddess's magnificent herds against demonic rustlers. The cow kidnappers are led by the wicked Jindrav Khinchi, whom Pabuji defeats and kills. Pabuji also protects the honour of his women from another villain, a barbaric, cow-murdering Muslim plunderer named Mirza Khan Patan, and wins a great victory over Ravana, the ten-headed Demon King of Lanka, from whom he steals a herd of camels as a wedding gift for his favourite niece.

When this 4,000-line courtly poem is recited from beginning to end – which rarely happens these days – it takes a full five nights of eight-hour, dusk-till-dawn performances to unfold. Depending on the number of chai breaks, bhajans, Hindi film songs and other diversions added into the programme, it can on occasion take much longer. But the performance is not looked upon as just a form of entertainment. It is also a religious ritual invoking Pabuji as a living deity and asking for his protection against ill-fortune.

The epic is always performed in front of a *phad*, a long narrative painting made on a strip of cloth, which serves as both an illustration of the highlights of the story and a portable temple of Pabuji the god. India has many other traditions of legends, stories and epics being told by wandering picture-showmen; but in none of the other traditions have the pictures been elevated to the status of an incarnate *murti*, equivalent in holiness to an image in a temple. The audience is primarily made up of the traditionally nomadic and camel-herding Rabari caste, for whom Pabuji is the principal deity; but other castes also attend the performances, especially the Rajputs of Pabu's own warrior caste.

As we drove through the seemingly empty desert landscape, Mohan pointed out features invisible to the untutored eye of an outsider: he said, on this side, where now there were just a few stumps, stood until recently an ancient *oran*, or sacred grove. It was holy to Pabu's ally and friend, the Rajasthani snake deity Gogaji, who also has an oral poem and a living cult in his memory. For centuries no one had dared to touch the *oran*, said Mohan, believing that anyone who stole the wood would be struck down by the snakes guarding it. But three or four years ago, loggers had come, chopped down all the trees and carted away the wood to Jaipur: 'If people are no longer bothered by the threats of Goga's snake bites,' he said, 'how will they fear the anger of Pabu?'

I asked if there were still any *orans* left sacred to Pabu.

'Yes,' he said. 'There is one close to our village. So far we've been able to guard the trees. People only pick the fallen wood for cremations. But who knows for how long it will be safe in times like these?'

Mohan went on to tell a story of how the Bishnoi caste, who believe in a very strict ethic of non-violence to all forms of nature, had managed to preserve their *khejri* trees from loggers sent by the Maharaja of Jodhpur. They had hugged the trees, he said, even as the maharaja's axe men were felling them. Three hundred had died before the order was finally cancelled, and people still gathered every year to commemorate their sacrifice. I asked how long ago this had taken place.

'Oh, not so long ago,' he said, shrugging his shoulders. 'About 320 years back.'

I had known Mohan and Batasi for about five years when I set off with them that morning from Jaipur. We had just done an event about the Pabuji epic to a conference, and were now heading in the direction of their village of Pabusar, which lay deep in the desert towards Bikaner.

Soon after I had first met the couple, in 2004, I wrote a long *New Yorker* article on Mohan, and after the piece was published, Mohan and I performed together at various festivals; but in all the time I had known and worked with him, I had never yet visited his home. Pabusar, he told me, was a small oasis of green in the dry desert, and was named after the hero of his epic; indeed the village supply of sweet water was believed to have appeared thanks to Pabuji's miraculous intervention. Now it was the tenth day of the full moon, the day of Pabu, when his power was at its height and he was unable to refuse any devotee. This time the epic was to be recited not in part but in full, at my request, and I was looking forward to seeing Mohan perform it.

On the lonely, potholed single-track road to Pabusar, the last leg of the journey, we began to meet other pilgrims who were coming to celebrate the modest village festivities which marked the day of

Pabu. Some of the pilgrims were on foot: lonely figures trudging through the immensity of the desert in the white midnight. Other villagers rode together in tractors, pulling trailers full of women in deep-blue saris. Occasionally, we would pass through a village sheltering in the lee of a crumbling high-walled fortress, where we would see other pilgrims taking their rest in the shade of the wells that lay beside the temples. As we drove on, the settlements grew poorer and the road increasingly overrun with drifting sand. The fields of dew-watered millet grew rarer and more arid; and the camel thorn closed in. Dry weeds heeled and twisted in the desert wind.

In the end, although the drive from Jaipur was less than 120 miles, it took nearly the entire day. The roads grew almost impassable with sand, and without four-wheel drive we slipped and slalomed our way, two or three times having to push the car up modest hillocks using sackcloth to give the wheels traction.

When we finally reached Pabusar, it was nearly sunset. The goats were being led home for the night, and the shadows of the milkweed bushes around the village were lengthening. It was the pruning season, and a few goatherds had climbed up the *khejri* trees to chop fodder for their goats, camels and cows. On the edge of the village I saw a lone woman in a yellow sari beating a *kikkur* tree with a long stick – not some Rajasthani folk ritual, as I had instantly assumed, but, Mohan assured me, merely an elderly goatherd trying to get the seed pods to drop for her hungry, bleating kids.

The village of Pabusar – Pabu's Well – was, like the roads around it, half-buried by drifting sand, and fenced around on all sides by dry-thorn bushes. We abandoned the car in a final sand-drift only a few hundred yards from Mohan's house, and walked the last stretch. Around the white shrine-temple to Pabu, beside a small water tank, a large crowd was already beginning to gather for Mohan's night performance of the epic. A brightly coloured *shamiana* had been erected next to it, and to one side a generator was chugging away like an old tractor. The farmers were in a relaxed mood, squatting in turbaned groups sipping chai and smoking beedis and playing cards. Their cows had been given their fodder, and, crucially for herders in a desert land, they had also been given water – the key episode and the climactic moment in the Pabuji epic:

> *O Pabuji, the cows' little calves are weeping,*
> *The cows' little calves are calling out to Pabuji.*
> *O Pabuji, may your name remain immortal in the land;*
> *O Pabuji, may your brave warriors remain immortal!*

Outside Mohanji's small but newly built concrete house – a mark of some status in a poor village of conical thatched huts like Pabusar – Mahavir, his eldest son, was waiting for us impatiently. In his hands he held the furled *phad*. Another of Mohan's sons, Shrawan, whom I had met several times before, was also standing by, holding his *dholak*.

We had been expected earlier in the afternoon and the two boys, who were worried that we would miss the evening performance, spoke in an agitated manner to their father. But Mohan just smiled and led me over to his pump, where we washed. We gulped down a glass of hot masala chai, handed to us by a daughter-in-law. Then, reverently picking up the *phad*, Mohan led the way to the small Pabu shrine that he had built in his compound. There he gave thanks for his safe journey and asked the blessings of the deity for the performance. Then, without waiting for dinner, we headed off, through the sandy lanes, on the short walk to the tent where he was to perform.

The temple was a simple village affair, but newly built in marble. It had a single image chamber containing an ancient hero stone showing the mounted Pabuji in profile, sword held high. The temple, tank, well and village of Pabusar were all inexorably linked, explained Mohan. One night, during a great drought, Pabu had come in a dream to one of the poets of the Charan caste in the area. He told the man to follow the footprints from his door, through the sand, to a distant shallow valley where, said Pabu, you will find a stone. Take that stone as your marker, continued the god, and dig down thirty hands deep and there you will find an inexhaustible supply of the sweetest water in all the Shekhawati. This hero stone was the stone in the dream, said Mohan. Once it had been built into the parapet of the well, but now, since the new temple had come up, it was worshipped as a *murti*.

While he talked, Mohan placed two bamboo poles in the ground and unfurled the *phad* from right to left. It was like a wonderful Shekhawati fresco transferred to textile: a great vibrant, chaotic seventeen-foot-long panorama of medieval Rajasthan: women, horses, peacocks, carts, archers, battles, washer-men and fishermen, kings and queens, huge grey elephants and herds of white cows and buff camels, many-armed demons, fish-tailed wonder-creatures and blue-skinned gods, all arranged around the central outsized figure of Pabuji, his magnificent black mare, Kesar Kalami, and his four great companions and brothers-in-arms.

While Mohan set up, I looked closely at the *phad*. The *durbar* and palaces of the different players of the epic were the largest images, with Pabuji and his warriors in the centre, and the courts of his enemies, Jindrav Khinchi and Ravana, at the furthest distance from him at the two extremities. In between, all Indian life was here in this wonderfully lively, vivid textile, full of *joie de vivre* and folk-artistic gusto. The *phad* has a teeming energy that seems somehow to tap into the larger-than-life power of the epic's mythology to produce wonderfully bold and powerful narrative images. It is also marked by a deep love of the natural world: dark-skinned elephants charge forward, trunks and tails curling with pleasure; pairs of peacocks display their tails, white doves and red-crowned hoopoes flit between mango orchards and banana plantations. Warriors charge into battle against roaring yellow tigers, swords at the ready.

The different figures and scenes were not compartmentalized, but were clearly organized with a strict logic. Like the ancient Buddhist paintings in the caves of Ajanta, the story was arranged by geographical rather than narrative logic: more a road map to the epic geography of courtly Rajasthan than a strip cartoon of the story. If two scenes were next to each other it was because they happened in the same location, not because they happened in chronological succession, one after the other.

Seeing me peering closely at the *phad*, Mohan said that it was the work of the celebrated textile artist Shri Lal Joshi of Bhilwara. His family had been making *phads* for nearly 700 years, and their images had more power than those of any other artist.

'Even rolled up, Joshiji's *phads* keep evil at bay,' said Mohan. 'The way he paints it, the involvement he has with the epic, gives his *phads* more *shakti* than any other. His *phads* have the power to exorcise any spirit. Just to open it is to give a blessing.'

Mohan explained to me that once the *phad* was complete and the eyes of the hero were painted in, neither the artist nor the *bhopa* regarded it as a piece of art. Instead, it instantly became a mobile temple – the *phad* – visited the worshippers rather than the other way around. It was believed that the spirit of the god was now in residence, and that henceforth the *phad* was a ford linking one world with the next, a crossing place from the human to the divine.

From this point, said Mohan, the *phad* was treated with the greatest reverence. He made daily offerings to it, and said he would pass it on to one of his children once he became too old to perform. If the *phad* got ripped or faded, he would call the original painter and take it with him to the Ganges, or the holy lake at Pushkar. There they would together decommission it, or, as he put it, *thanda karna* – make it cool, remove the *shakti* of the deity – before consigning it to the holy waters, rather like Excalibur being returned to the lake in the legends of King Arthur.

'It is always a sad moment,' said Mohan. 'Each *phad* gives great service, but eventually they become so threadbare you can no longer see anything. After we have laid it to rest, we throw a feast, as if it was the cremation of a family member. Then we consecrate a new *phad*. It is like an old man dying, and a child being born.'

Batasi was now cleaning the space in front of the *phad*, and lighting a clutch of incense sticks. Shrawan tightened the screws of his *dholak*, and began to tap out a small beat. A small *jyot* (lamp) of cow dung was lit by Mohan, and circled in front of the image of Pabu. Then he blew a conch shell, announcing that the performance was about to begin. The farmers of the village finished their card games and cups of chai, and began to gather around. It was already getting cold, the temperature dropping rapidly in the desert on winter nights, and several of the farmers pulled their shawls tightly around them, tucking the loose end under their chins.

Mohan then picked up his *ravanhatta* – a kind of desert zither, a spike fiddle with eighteen strings and no frets – and began to pluck it regularly with his thumb.

'We'd better make a start,' he said. 'The reading of the *phad* should begin not long after sunset. We have a long night ahead of us, and the flame of my voice only really starts to glow after midnight.'

❖

On the morning after Mohan's night recitation of the epic, the *bhopa* and I sat down on a charpoy outside his house. The bright sun of the day before had given way to massing cumulus, and a strange grey light played over the desert and the village. The sun was now the colour of steel.

Mohan had sung the epic until dawn, and had slept for only four or five hours before being woken by the visit of a neighbour, a family of bangle sellers who had dropped in for a chat. Now it was mid morning and we sat looking out at a very rare but highly auspicious event in Pabusar: clouds massing for the winter rains. Rarer still, a few drops were actually falling on the ground.

'We call this rain the *mowat*,' said Mohanji, smiling brightly. 'Even a few drops are wonderful for the wheat and grain. One or two showers will give enough forage and fodder for the sheep and the goats until the monsoon. Four or five showers and even the cows will be happy.'

'Aren't you tired?' I asked. 'You were performing all night.'

'Sleep doesn't bother me,' he said. 'We are friends of sleeplessness. I'll happily do another performance tonight. After all these years I'm used to it.'

✧

That evening, after sunset, Mohan continued his performance of the epic. The first night had taken the story up to the episode of Goga's wedding to Kelam. The second opened with the story of the she-camels.

Watching the epic performed in a village setting where everyone was familiar with not just the plot but the actual text of the poem was a completely different experience to seeing it done before the sort of urban, middle-class audience I had previously seen Mohan perform to.

The farmers and villagers were all sitting and squatting on a red and black striped durree under the awning of the tents, and were wrapped up against the cold with scarves and shawls and mufflers. Rather than sitting back and enjoying a formal performance, as the middle-class audience had done, the villagers joined in, laughing loudly at some points, interrupting in others, joking with Mohan and completing the final line of each stanza. Sometimes, individuals got up to offer Mohan a Rs 10 note, usually with a request for a particular song or *bhajan*.

Three generations of the family performed: as well as Mohan and Batasi, Shrawan was on the *dholak*, the eldest son Mahavir also joined in with his *ravanhatta*, and Mahavir's naughty four-year-old son Onkar, Mohan's eldest grandson, danced alongside his grandfather in a white *kurta-dhoti*. For three hours the family sang without a break, and the audience cheered and clapped.

'Because the *phad* is dedicated to our god Pabuji, we are never allowed to get up in the middle,' said the village goldsmith, who was sitting next to me. 'Until the *bhopaji* gets tired and stops for chai, we have to sit and listen out of respect – even until dawn.'

'But now that we have TV our children don't like to listen so much,' added Mr Sharma, one of the village Brahmins, who had earlier insisted on taking me away for what he called "a pure vegetarian dinner". 'The younger generation prefer the CD with the main points of the story. It takes only three or four hours maximum.'

The idea that the oral tradition was seriously endangered was something I had heard repeated ever since I first began reading about the oral epics of Rajasthan. The Cambridge academic John D. Smith did his PhD on the *bhopas* of Pabuji in the 1970s. When he returned to make a documentary on the subject twenty years later, he found that many of the *bhopas* he had worked with had given up performing, and instead taken up work pedaling cycle rickshaws or sweeping temples. They told him that fewer and fewer people were interested in the performances, while the Rabari nomads who were once the main audience were themselves selling their flocks and drifting off to the cities: 'Having lost their flocks,' he wrote, 'they lost their chief connection with Pabuji, who is above all associated with the welfare of livestock.'

Another, still more serious threat that Smith identified were the DVDs and cable channels, and their broadcasting of the great mainstream Sanskrit epics, which he believed had begun to have a 'standardizing effect on Hindu mythology, which will inevitably weaken local variants, such as the Pabuji story.' There is no question that TV and film are formidable rivals: when the *Mahabharata* was broadcast on the Doordarshan TV channel in the early 1990s, viewing figures for the series never sank beneath

75 per cent, and at one point were said to have risen to 95 per cent, an estimated audience of some 600 million people. Everyone who could stopped what they were doing to sit in front of whatever television was available.

In villages across South Asia, hundreds of people would gather around a single set to watch the gods and demons play out their destinies. In the noisiest and most bustling cities trains, buses and cars were suddenly stilled, and a strange hush came over the bazaars. In Rajasthan, audiences responded by offering *arti* and burning incense sticks in front of their television sets, just as they did to the *bhopa's phad*, the portable temple of the *phad* giving way to the temporary shrine of the telly.

Some *bhopas* had clung on to their tradition, wrote Smith, but in a bastardized form, singing snatches of the epic for tourists in the Rajasthan palace hotels, or providing "exotic" entertainment in the restaurants of Delhi and Bombay. Either way, Smith concluded that 'The tradition of epic performance is rapidly dying ... Thus a tradition that was still flourishing in the 1970s – though even then promoting attitudes that seemed to belong to a much earlier age – has almost completely lapsed.'

When I had first read this, its grim prognosis sounded all too likely. But sitting now in a tent full of enthusiastic Pabuji devotees, Smith's predictions seemed unnecessarily extreme and gloomy. During an interval in the performance, while Mohan stopped for a glass of chai, and Mahavir continued to entertain the audience with a Hindi film song, I asked Mohan what he could possibly do to hold out against Bollywood and the TV, and if he was worried about the future. Were the epics merely going to become stories watched on television and borrowed from video libraries? What could the *bhopas* do to save their audiences?

Mohanji shrugged. 'It's true there is increasingly a problem with ignorance,' he said. 'Here in Pabusar it is still fine. But in the towns and cities the younger generation know nothing of Pabuji. They don't understand the meaning. If they listen it's because of the music and dancing. They don't know the *hunkara* – the correct responses – and they are always asking for irrelevant songs: new *filmi* ones from the latest movie that have nothing to do with the *phad*. Earlier people just wanted a pure recitation of Pabu – nothing else.

'I am always trying to improve my singing,' he added. 'And for the younger generation I try to put in the occasional joke when people are getting sleepy. Nothing Bollywoodish or vulgar, just enough to grab attention in between scenes. It's not easy for people to concentrate for eight hours – though here in the villages, where there are no distractions, few get up while I am performing.'

I asked: 'Will the *phad* survive?'

'Oh yes,' he said firmly. 'It will. It has to. For all that has changed, it is still at the centre of our life, and our faith, and our dharma.'

This, it seemed to me, was the key, and the answer to the question of how it was that the Rajasthani epics were still living in a way that the *Iliad* and the other epics of the West were not. The poems had been turned into religious rituals and the *bhopas* had become receptacles for the messages of the gods, able to penetrate the wall – in India always a fairly porous wall – between the divine and the mundane.

Moreover, the gods in question were not distant and metaphysical beings but deified locals to whom the herders could relate and who, in turn, could understand the villagers' needs. The people of Pabusar certainly took care to propitiate the great "national" gods, like Shiva and Vishnu, whom they understood as controlling the continuation of the wider cosmos, but for everyday needs they prayed to the less remote, less awesome figures of their local god-kings and heroes who knew and understood the intimacies of the daily life of the farmers in a way that the Great Gods could not, like the needs of the cattle of the village. It is these local gods who are believed to guard and regulate the daily lives of the villagers.

'In this village, everyone still loves the epic as much as they ever did,' said Mohan. 'There really is very little difference from the response I saw to my father's performances when I was a boy. It's true that some of the old customs have gone: when I was growing up, for example, if a water buffalo delivered a calf, the first milk and the first yoghurt were always offered to Pabu. These days no one seems to bother.

'And then there is a feeling that Pabuji himself is a little more distant than he used to be. When I was Onkar's age everyone in the village used to hear the noise of Pabuji riding through the village at night, circling the houses and the temple, guarding us from demons and epidemics. But it has been many years now since I heard the sound of his hooves. I don't know why that is. Perhaps because we have less faith than we used to, or because we show him less devotion.

'But you asked about the *phad*,' he added. 'Yes, here at least the *phad* has survived. Everyone knows it.'

I asked why he thought that was.

'You see,' said Mohan, 'this village was founded by Pabuji, so we are all of us great devotees. We don't ignore the other gods: they are wonderful and powerful in their own way, and their own place. But here if we have a problem we naturally seek first the help of Pabu.'

'Especially if is a problem with an animal,' said Mr Sharma. 'That is what he is most famous for.'

'The great gods are here of course,' added the goldsmith. 'But Pabuji is close to us, and when we need immediate help it is more sensible to ask him.'

'Pabu is a Rajput,' said a man in a turban, who had also been listening in. 'We people who worship Pabu are comfortable with his company. Like us, he eats meat and drinks liquor also.'

'He understands us and knows our fields and our animals.'

'He is a god from our own people,' said Mohan. 'He is like us.'

'Not that the other gods are far away,' added Mr Sharma. 'Gods are gods. Whatever god you worship, he is close to you.'

'But it's like applying to the village *sarpanch*,' said Mohan, 'rather than asking the prime minister. Naturally we are closer to the *sarpanch*.'

I wondered whether this lack of a devotional following was the reason that the great Indian Muslim epic, the *Dastan-i-Amir Hamza* had died out: its last recorded performance was on the steps of the Jama Masjid in Delhi in 1928. The *Hamza* epic was always understood to be primarily an entertainment, and so had died as fashions changed. But the *bhopas* and their religious rituals had survived because the needs and hungers that they addressed remained.

'Will Shrawan take on the tradition?' I asked Mohan.

'Of course,' he said. 'He knows the whole epic. All he lacks yet is confidence, and a wife with a sweet voice. But he loves Pabuji, and he can see that it's a good life. When the gods are asleep' – during the monsoon season – 'I stay at home and look after the goats. In the other months, I travel with my *phad* wherever I want. There is still a lot of work for a good *bhopa* – all the castes around here still commission readings of the *phad* when they need something.'

Mahavir and Shrawan were now beckoning for Mohan to return to the *phad* to continue the performance. Mohan smiled, and held up a single finger to indicate that he would come in just a minute. 'For myself, all my life my heart has been bound up in the *phad* and its stories,' he said. 'I have never had any real interest in agriculture or any other work. Pabuji has recognized this, and has guarded us. We none of us have ever had a serious illness.

'Every day, I get up hungry in the morning,' he said, picking up his *ravanhatta*, 'but thanks to him, neither I nor my family ever go to bed on an empty stomach. Not everyone in the village could say that, even the Brahmins and Rajputs.

'It is Pabuji who does this,' said Mohan Bhopa, walking back to the *phad* and strumming the first note with his thumb. 'It is he who looks after us all.'

Postscript

About a month after my trip to Pabusar, Mohan and Batasi came to Jaipur and we did another event together, at the literary festival there. Mohan was in his usual sparkling, mischievous form, dancing as flirtatiously as an eighteen-year-old despite his advancing years. Then a fortnight later, back in Delhi, I heard he was dead.

After his performance at the festival, Mohan had complained to a mutual friend of stomach pains, and had been taken to the main state hospital in Jaipur. Advanced leukaemia was diagnosed within a week, but owing to some bureaucratic tangle, Mohan had been directed first to a small hospital in the Shekhawati, and then on to Bikaner. At each of these he had been refused treatment, for bureaucratic or financial reasons, and sent on to another place. It is the sort of thing that often happens to the poor and powerless in India. When he died, still hospital-less in Bikaner, ten days after the first diagnosis, he had received no medical treatment whatsoever, not even a painkiller.

His body was taken home, and he was cremated in Pabusar, with wood picked from the sacred *oran* grove of Pabuji.

In her widowhood, Batasi continues singing the *phad*, and has begun to perform with her eldest son, Mahavir, who had earlier given up performing for lack of a tuneful partner. The two, mother and son, now sing the *Pabuji ki phad* together, keeping the family tradition alive until Shrawan finds a suitable wife and succeeds in teaching her the *phad*, or perhaps until Mohan's grandson, Onkar, is ready to tell the tales of Pabuji to a new generation.

3

DYING TO LIVE

Pradip Krishen in Jodhpur

Dedicated to the memory of Prof. M.M. Bhandari
(Doct-saab) who shared his knowledge of desert plants and great learning
freely and generously

Roughly six years ago, in the rains of 2005, I was invited by the Mehrangarh Museum Trust to "green" an unruly, rocky wasteland of some 70 hectares adjoining Jodhpur's medieval Mehrangarh Fort, on top of the hill. It was already green, but it was August and I knew this was a short-lived trick and that as soon as the rains ceased and the moisture fled, the whole tract would quickly return to being bare and rocky. It was a daunting prospect. The area had suffered decades of disuse and was severely eroded. It was overrun by a horribly invasive, bullying shrub from Mexico whose seeds had been scattered over the entire city from an aeroplane nearly a century before. There was hardly any soil and the underlying crystalline rock, volcanic in origin, was many times harder and more difficult to work than tractable sandstone.

It didn't take genius to see that the only way forward was to draw inspiration from nature and plant the things that grow *naturally* in rocky parts of the Thar desert. Of course, we had first to tackle the Mexican invader and grub it out – but that's a story I'll come to in a moment.

What we set out to do, in a word, was to try and restore the landscape to a "natural state" with plants native to Marwar's rocky desert. We didn't really have any means of knowing what this area looked like before it was inhabited five or six centuries before, perhaps even longer. But it was reasonable to assume that it was once like other wild or semi-wild rocky terraces in the desert. Give or take the presence or absence of a few pantropical weeds. Using inference and a little intuition, it was possible to piece together an assemblage of plants that once grew here naturally. Our ultimate objective was to create a Park that would be like an outdoor museum of rock-loving plants from this particular part of the world. Ultimately we would build walking trails and an Interpretation Centre for visitors, but all that lay in the future. In the bargain, Mehrangarh Fort would gain from the aesthetic value of a green space surrounding the Fort on two sides.

People occasionally ask me why we chose to "go native". It's quite simple, really. Native plants, by definition, are pre-adapted to the extremely harsh conditions in our tract. Plants native to Marwar's desert rock are adapted by a few million years of evolution to eke out a living in hostile, water-deprived niches. They live and prosper in precisely the same soil conditions, partnering with the same micro-organisms, adapting to the water regime, climate and temperature gradients that we had in our Park-to-be. Scientists call them "lithophytes" – plants specially equipped to grow in rocky conditions. So it made perfect sense that our first aim was to search out and bring back lithophytes from the desert and then try and rehabilitate them. It quickly became clear that what I had to do first was to inventory Marwar's lithophytes and get to know them as best I could.

Making the inventory itself didn't turn out to be very difficult. The desert flora is well documented and the doyen of the botany of the Thar desert was alive and well and living in Jodhpur. When we started out, in 2005, Prof. M.M.Bhandari ('Doct-saab') was nearing eighty but still had an infectious enthusiasm and an eagerness to share his knowledge with someone like me. Doct-saab became a crucial ally.

Over the next few years, in between the business of grubbing out the invasive Mexican shrubs and planting new ones in their place, I seized every opportunity of making short forays into the desert. Rocky hills and terraces became special targets for exploration. But it's not possible to shut your eyes to the sandy wastes and dunes in Marwar and with Doct-saab's help and remote control we explored the sandy desert too. Doct-saab would sometimes direct our exploration from his home, drawing on memories of trips he had undertaken in the area thirty years previously – 'When you find the temple near Barmer, go behind it and start climbing a small hill. Within two-three hundred yards you will start to find some small crucifers. Look carefully. White flowers. Four petals ... like this ... with a touch of orange in the stem. That's Farsetia. This is the *only* place you will find Farsetia in India. Maybe it's there in Sindh, Pakistan, I don't know. But go, see if you can find it, then come and tell me.'

Sure enough. Slender *Farsetia micrantha,* less than knee high, a touch of orange in its stem. Clinging on, somehow, thirty years later in the pediment of a dry, wasted hill. The only place in India. Wow!

This is the story of Rao Jodha Desert Rock Park and how we got started. It's not a boast or an advertisement. I just want to share with you a brief account of how we went about it. I knew of no precedents, no one to turn to for advice. Maybe someone out there would like to restore a plot in the desert? ... Here's a precedent.

❖

Grubbing out the Mexican invader (*Prosopis juliflora*) was objective # 1. In Marwari they call it "baavlia" – the mad one. Probably because it's crazy enough to seek out such inhospitable places, where it hunkers down and digs itself in. Baavlia seems to require no water or nutrients in the soil. It discourages everything else from growing or prospering nearby by secreting toxic alkaloids in its root-zone. It is madly successful in an unlikely, maverick sort of way and fully deserves its Marwari epithet.

Taking baavlia out, we knew, was going to be a struggle. If you cut it at ground level, it sprouts with redoubled vigour. Digging down and pulling it out mechanically by its roots is difficult and expensive because of the nature of volcanic rock. Using chemicals to kill it is not feasible in a place where water runoff is collected and stored. So what to do?

We received busloads of cockeyed advice. 'Cut it less than an inch above ground and cover the stumps with green *gobar*.' Tried. Didn't work. 'Let goats nibble it – the stems will never resprout.' Goats don't eat baavlia leaves. Too toxic. 'Set fire to the plant on a full-moon night.' Didn't even bother with that one. (Would you?)

I searched on the net and read about a successful eradication programme in Botswana. The magic formula is that you have to reach down *at least* 14 or 15 inches below the level of the soil when you cut baavlia, because it has a subterranean budding zone in its upper roots, from where it resprouts. So that settled it – somehow, we just had to find a way to dig baavlia out.

Compressor-driven augers was what we tried first. Much too slow and expensive, and completely impractical because of the extreme hardness of the rock. Someone suggested we should try tiny, minuscule, controlled, charges of dynamite. We were skeptical but tried it anyway and watched in dismay as it shattered the crest of a little rocky knoll. These knolls and hills were an intrinsic part of the historic landscape that we had set out to conserve. Lesson learned. Dynamite just wasn't the answer.

Help came in the form of highly skilled rock-miners who call themselves Khandwalias (after the Marwari word for rock – khanda). Five centuries before, their ancestors had chiselled gigantic blocks of sandstone from the hill to make the magnificent Mehrangarh Fort. Would they be able to handle rhyolite, the volcanic stone that underlies the sandstone on the hill but is so much harder?

We invited Dhan Singh Khandwalia to show us what he could do and led him inside the Park. He chose a small baavlia no more than a foot and a half high. Around it, the rock seemed dourly monolithic with hardly a crack or faultline that we could see. Dhan Singh chose a really heavy, short-handled hammer, squatted on his haunches and looked away while he smote the rock. I thought he was looking away to shield his eyes from flying fragments of rock, but the hammer blow wasn't fierce and nothing flew. What he was actually doing was cocking his ear and listening intently. He rang the rock with his hammer at a few more places. Somehow, the sound the hammer made told him all he wanted to know about the underlying rock. Infra-sound. How it was interbedded. How far the underlying layer ran. Where to go in from, at what angle. And how deep it was likely to yield. He shook his head at me, 'Yes, I can go in here .... At least two-three feet.'

So we left Dhan Singh there to cut and chisel away. An hour later, he had carved open the rootzone, digging down about a foot or so. Some of the baavlia's roots snaked off into tiny crevices in the rhyolite and two short roots that Dhan Singh had pulled out were surprisingly two-dimensional, like ribbons. This was part of Baavlia's arsenal of adaptability. Ribbon-roots for linear crevices. Brilliant!

It had been hard work for Dhan Singh, digging down just 14 or 15 inches. But I had no doubts any more that he could reach down deep enough to get below the budding zone and demobilize the baavlia completely. We decided at that moment to hire a platoon of thirteen Khandwalias to be our permanent baavlia-removal squad. And pit-makers. Their job was to go down *at least* 18 inches (just to be sure), pull out the baavlia, destroy it and then create pits in the excavated rock to receive new plants. Go in as deep as is feasible, three, three and a half feet, we told them. It wasn't always possible to excavate so much, but we knew that these pits – even the shallow ones – could become receptacles for a whole suite of new plants.

Almost inadvertently, we had arrived at a decision *not* to create new places to plant in. Baavlia had already done the hard work and shown us exactly where it was possible for a plant to establish itself in this difficult terrain. Places with a modicum of soil. Micro-fissures in the rock that connected to micro-pockets of buried soil. Provided we could find a means of selecting appropriate plants for these niches, maybe this was all we needed to do? Follow baavlia's lead. It turned out to be one of the wisest decisions we made – to place new plants *only* where baavlia had been evicted from. No change of land use in our development plans.

❖

I remember standing on a small eminence looking at the Park three months after starting work. We had succeeded in excavating baavlia from a little less than a hectare of rocky land. The ground was now deeply pitted, like a piece of comic-book Swiss cheese. We wanted to try out slightly different mixes of growing media, so a team of donkeys and their handlers went back and forth tipping pre-mixed soil from side-hung panniers into new pits. A few pits were nearly four feet deep. Some were elongated, five or six feet long, following faults in the rhyolite. Many were less than two feet deep, where the Khandwalias had come up against more recalcitrant strata of bedrock.

At that moment, looking around, it was frightening – the land looked stripped, violated. We had succeeded it removing the scourge of baavlia from this little patch. What if we failed to persuade our new ensemble of plants to take root here? What if our confidence had been entirely missplaced? Would we look back and wish that we hadn't touched the baavlia in the first place? What if we had removed the *only* thing that was capable of growing in that difficult spot?

It took a few months before we started getting answers. Most of the plants that we put in had been grown from seed and were still small, at best about 9 or 10 inches high. As grasses and other ephemerals came up quickly in the wake of that first monsoon, our little nursery-grown plants all but disappeared from sight. For the first time in decades, it was no longer open season for goats and cattle and camels that used to enter freely looking for fodder – they had been walled out. The whole tract looked wanly beautiful even as the grasses started turning yellow in late October. We placed 2,600 plants in old baavlia pits that first year. We still had no real basis to know if these newly introduced plants would survive. We would soon find out.

✧

There are basically three strategies that plants use to survive severe drought. (Actually there are more than three – I'm simplifying a bit). Succulence – storing water in tissues (leaf, twig, trunk, roots, anywhere will do) like a cactus does – is a good tactic and is widely used. Reaching moisture deep in the soil by means of enormous, penetrative roots works well too, but you have to be a tree to be able to do this. It's not so easy being a tree in rocky deserts. By far the most successful strategy involves crass opportunism – choosing to live *only* in the short period when there's moisture around. This last strategy – life in the fast lane – is used by hundreds of desert plants and by a preponderant number of lithophytes.

Imagine a small, herbaceous plant that does not have succulent tissues nor the time (read: lifespan) to grow long enough roots. There's a small window in the year beginning with the first rains in July and lasting till late October or November, when the soil retains a bit of moisture and a small herb might be expected to survive. Just about. What it's been kitted out to do (evolution, always evolution) is to germinate in the rains, rush through its life-cycle so that it flowers and fruits inside the window of opportunity, dropping its seeds in the ground before dying out. These seeds – typically hard-coated, like a time-capsule – lie dormant in the soil, waiting many months for next season's rains.

If you think about it, it's a simple but perfectly adequate stratagem – *avoiding* drought, rather than *surviving* or *tolerating* it. These plants don't need specialised tissues or organs. They're just wily opportunists who live their lives breezily when conditions are good, and skip out as soon as it turns nasty. Leaving behind little time capsules that will perpetuate their genes when the rains return next season. A large number of desert grasses use this stratagem. So do about 200 other species of plants. Come to think of it, so do many toads and insects and a host of small critters who are not specially equipped to endure the harshest conditions.

Let's just call it "Dying to Live". It works beautifully, and it was up to us now to learn to accept and celebrate this epiphanic moment in the year when the ephemerals come back to life.

Once we understood this strategy, it became perfectly clear that we needed to find a way of balancing the perennials that we were placing in old baavlia pits, with the amazing explosion of seasonal plants that germinated with the first rains.

❖

The ephemerals could take care of themselves. They were superbly equipped to do so. We needed to keep tabs on our perennials to make sure that we were doing the right thing by them. It was crucial to try and learn what worked and what didn't.

We painted little flat rocks blue with bright yellow numbers, one for each pit. We recorded vital stats like how deep the pits were, what the site quality was (rocky or with some soil), what exactly was going into the pits by way of soil mixes and species of plant ... and so on. And then we held our breath.

By December, we went around and painstakingly recorded how these plants were doing. Some had perished – we needed to know why, though it wasn't always immediately apparent. "Nibbled by hares" or "dug up by wild boar" was a comment in the notesheet. "Not sure why" also figured. There were lots of question marks.

We got down to analyzing the results using Excel spreadsheets, which allow you to conveniently lump and sort your data. When we brought all the kummatth (*Acacia senegal*) data together, for example, it told us clearly that while most kummatths were doing alright, they weren't managing at all well in pits less than two feet deep. And that they showed a clear preference for a soil mix with a little less clay than we had initially thought. Lesson learned.

The Excel datasheets were equally eloquent about bordi (*Ziziphus mauritiana*) and dhok (*Anogeissus pendula*) and nearly all of the other introduced plants. Slowly, over the next two years of continuing to record pit-data, we learned most of what we needed to about placing our plants in the right situations. Survival rates improved. We were now choosing to plant particular species in pits of a certain kind based on what we knew about them. A large part of the guesswork was being filtered out of the planting scheme.

✧

Rao Jodha Park is now in its sixth year of development. That may sound like a long time but remember that out there, in the desert, time marches to an infinitely slow rhythm. In an average year, we contend with a growing season that is less than eight weeks long. If a small tree puts on five inches of new twiggy growth in a season, that's a triumphal result!

How long will it take before the Park looks and feels like a *natural* rocky landscape with mature plants? Oo, that's a difficult question. Seven years, I had suggested when we started out, to *begin* to see concrete results. Maybe another ten or twelve before there is a *substantial* accrual of plant growth and biomass. I really don't know. This is guesswork, even after so many years of watching it grow.

There are still imponderables. How will the rains behave in the next few climate-change years, while some plants are still struggling to find a foothold? Will we be able to win the support and goodwill of the people of Brahmpuri who live right next to the Park? – crucial, because they have the capability of undoing years of careful tending. Will the Park be able to count on continuity of management and support, all of which comes from the Museum Trust at the moment? How will the advent of visitors affect the Park when the gates open for the first time?

We are getting ready to receive our first visitors in the rains of 2011 and are still busy refurbishing a 16th century historic gateway in the City Wall for our Visitors Centre. There will be Field Guides and Plant Lists. Hopefully, Bird and Insect Lists too, in time. Reptiles. Amphibians. We want to start a small shop in the Visitors Centre that sells things related to plants and to Nature, made exclusively by people in Jodhpur. Livelihoods.

We want to tell stories. About the desert and lithophytes and strategies that plants use for surviving drought. About the best times to visit the Park and how to get to see what's really worth seeing. But I must stop. I promised – no advertising.

4

TWO DISCOVERIES

Aman Nath in Shekhavati and Neemrana

L ike hurried sand in a lazy hour glass.
Some forty years have passed racing about full throttle in
my adult present. And of these, some thirty-five I spent
wilfully sifting through the sands of Rajasthan in private discovery.
Even today, it seems that my days flow over with the bounty of
a clockwork which ticks two to a second. And so two lives have
been lived in one – or even three or four.

Today, I can brush away the cliché that history repeats itself –
for I believe that it simply has no more time to return in cycles.
But as a historian, I think, I see it speeding on, away from itself,
burying the past faster than it did. Now a decade of events pass
in one year, and a year of global achievements in a week.

All those amazing people that made this overlapping journey
through my lifetime, will slowly be layered over as certainly as will
I. This nostalgia of my travels can, at best be a partial un-layering.
I've raced ahead continuously occupying my present with many

preoccupations: chiefly reawakening or telling of others' pasts. But a lot depends on who tells each story, and how. This time it's me telling my own tale.

Shekhavati

Once upon a time, at the monastic Jaipur home of Poppy Dandiya, which sat diagonally opposite the Santokba Durlabhji Hospital on Bhawani Singh Marg, I met a charismatic young man called Surya Vijay Singh. Dressed in a crisp cotton shirt and khaki breeches, he wore a toothy smile below a prominent handlebar moustache. The retina of his single eye that I could see sparkled many a tale – the other was hidden behind a black eye-patch tied on a black shoestring over thick, matted hair. For want of an idea to spark a dialogue, I asked in jest if he were a pirate. 'No', he stammered quite seriously, 'I lost my eye as a child when playing with our servants' children.' And, in that one moment of embarrassment over my innocent insensitivity, lay the whole discovery of the region of Shekhavati.

The next day, my newfound friendly "pirate" better known as Sunny – and I, took a sweaty local bus from Jaipur's Sindhi Camp to head for Nawalgarh. We were going to swim in his "three swimming pools in the desert", which he had announced the previous day, and indeed, they did seem an attractive proposition in a Rajasthani summer. We had been dancing in the Dandiya garage to the Beatles, not sure if we were in a discotheque or in a sauna bath, when Sunny had first held out his cooling mirage of desert pools as a temptation. He had told me that we would go in a bus though his father was also driving on the same road to Nawalgarh – but in a car, as he needed to go earlier. Such a distanced formality was not known in our family. I would certainly have been in my father's car if we were headed at the same time for the same destination. But I had not known the Rajputs earlier on their feudal home ground, and to my surprise, more was to follow.

The journey was not pleasant with all the sweat produced in the synthetic factories that men wore on their skins. Women too, all bagged-up in black *burqas*, produced their own brand of feminine odour, with squealing kids more than just peeing in their laps! The conductor, surely an accomplished trapeze artiste from a local circus, leapt in clean sweeps over the seats from neck rest to neck rest, gliding with a single hand on the sweat-greased bar above; the other hand shuffling in the give and take of tickets and money. Fellini was being enacted everywhere, but sadly, it went unrecorded for the world.

Disembarking at the bustling bus stand in Nawalgarh, we made our way to a noble suburban villa with a circular drive around a dry fountain. It was called Roop Niwas and its 1930's architecture had rounded steps, which led to a shaded verandah circling the sitting room. This was both very passé and alluring in that memorable summer heat. A nimboo pani and a quick hand wash later, we were at lunch on a table for twelve. But we were only four, and so we sat rather formidably – but oddly I thought – quite like the four cardinal directions in a compass. Sunny introduced me to his grandfather Rawal Madan Singh and his father Kanwar Sangram Singh, who took the East and West positions at the long ends of the table. We took the North and South. For a long time no one spoke as the dishes were brought and laid towards the centre of the table. To break what seemed a hugely awkward and inactive silence, I began to pass the food both left and right from my vantage, central position. 'How long will he be staying?' the grandfather asked me, gesturing towards his son with his chin. So, I was obliged to become the go-between and ask the Kanwar Sahib 'How long will you be staying?' 'Two nights' he said to me barely looking up from within his 1950's goggles which continued to be worn in a rather dark dining room which had curtains drawn on all its four sides. Since the answer was clearly directed only to me, I echoed it forward: 'Two nights,' he says, and the Rawal Sahib nodded. This feudal lunch with much protocol, was my first of a kind. I continued to interpret and relay from father to son, or vice versa, in the same language, at the same table. Breaking this routine, the grandfather did address his grandson directly but only on a few occasions. Their relations seemed somewhat less formal and more convivial.

A siesta was inevitable when we disbursed – I to my large room where the bathroom had a tub in gloomy brown mosaic chips. The tap trickled water in an unused wash-basin stained with deposits. The heavy fan droned the weather prophetically, for the electricity was suddenly cut. I lay in that 47 °C stupor only Indian summers can bring upon people. Sunny entered my room with a casual 'Do you have some money on you?' Yes, I did, and he wanted to borrow some to send a retainer for two bottles of beer. I gave him twenty rupees, saying I didn't drink, but his thirst was great enough to cover ours, it seemed. When they did arrive, he guzzled both the bottles, then left for his room and snored. I walked out in the sun with a black umbrella given me by a retainer and my future lay ahead vapourised in a quivering but tantalizing mirage. Amazing beige *havelis* rose in the distance, their bases adorned in what seemed like a colourful border. On closer scrutiny, they were processions of elephants, horses and camels painted almost to their life-sized scale. Little did I know at this moment that all roads and dust tracks in Shekhavati would soon be criss-crossed each weekend with the wheels of my destiny.

The three pools of Nawalgarh were more truly one, and that too hadn't been used for a rather long time. The two others were reservoirs to water the gardens from. But at least my appetite for a new region had been properly whetted, and in sharing its magic Francis Wacziarg and I would devote our life and partnership to the restoration of ruins for a changed end-use.

❖

In Delhi, Francis had been trying to convince me that it was important to record on film, the fast-disappearing water systems of Rajasthan: the Persian wheel turned by camels, the large leather pouches bundled together with iron hoops – for electricity was getting to the villages, so drilling and pumps were inevitable. We had already done a trip with my twin brother Achal, to the villages around Bharatpur and done some haphazard filming. Now a more focused romance was to begin.

The term Shekhavati was not frequently used in 1977 when Francis and I began our research on the painted Marwari *havelis*. This historical region, now broken into two districts, was addressed by their current nomenclature: Jhunjhunu and Sikar – both being the district headquarters of the area they encompassed. More than five years later, when our book on the wall paintings of the Marwari *havelis* appeared, the Chief Minister of Rajasthan was Bhairon Singh Shekhawat. We called on him at his residence in Civil Lines, Jaipur, and showed him a first copy of the book. He seated Francis' little daughter Aude by his side as he turned the pages and admired the plates. He looked visibly very pleased as he announced. 'All this time people had thought Shekhawat was only a person, now they'll know it's actually a place after which we are named! I will try and come to your book launch.'

He never really came – and just as well, for that morning, we also visited Rajmata Gayatri Devi of Jaipur to ask her to our book release function, and she said with her typical élan 'I hope you haven't called any ministers! They are all like flies – they dirty the walls while they sit on them.' But the then Governor General O.P. Mehra was invited, and he came. My father and he had studied together at the Government College in Lahore, but later, when they had re-met in New Delhi and played golf together, the General seemed not to have got over his social unease for he used to live in a little home in a little alley. My father told me that in all his conversation O.P. needed to cover that past with his General's ceremonial stripes and medals – as if my father's ancestral bungalow The Willows, No. 11, Nisbet Road, Lahore, still seemed to cast its mottled shade upon him.

Francis was still with The Banque Nationale de Paris, commonly called The French Bank, and he commuted thrice between Delhi-Jaipur-Delhi in the week preceding our book launch in Jaipur, while I stayed back in my oval room at the Durlabhjis. On one of these trips he phoned me to say that his Amrita Shergill House had been broken into from the verandah and the only thing stolen was his Boleau movie camera. So that film on the waterways of Rajasthan was jinxed and never to be. Two spools of film still lie in their circular cans. But a book did happen and it opened Shekhavati to the world. G.D. Birla was very impressed and he wrote an open letter to the Marwari community to patronise it and learn about their heritage.

Today, it is so hard to imagine that only thirty-five years ago tourism was so nascent in India. The enterprising tourists who ventured to this distant land still believed that the whole Indian civilization could be cupped under one 17th century marble dome, which already housed Shah Jahan and his beloved Mumtaz Mahal! Besides Agra, Jaipur and Delhi were the two other points of the golden triangle. Only the really courageous dared to break free and go to Benares: to be voyeurs of dead corpses blazing and releasing Indian souls.

To drive *off* the known tracks in those days, was so easily *discovery* with a capital 'D'. Most weekends of those five full years filled our lives with many unwritten volumes of experiences, surprises, much learning, and some memorable discomforts too. *Haveli* after locked *haveli* opened its doors to us, mainly at the asking, but many on persuasion after their suspicion of our purpose was put to rest. We became regular faces with the locals. But despite the hundreds of *havelis*, there was simply no place to stay in the whole Shekhavati region. Our most miserable and sleepless nights were spent there: one at the Jeen Mata Temple in Ralawata where a priest kindly offered us a room with mattresses on the floor. We spent it wide awake with the rats, demarcating our sleeping area with two lit torches as a night boundary, so that they wouldn't cross over into our territory. Another, we spent in the millet fields near Sikar, sleeping on a cart tied to a tree, with four mosquito coils on each corner. We awoke with a smoky-fire as one of the coils had touched a sheet, and then when it began to rain, we were compelled to huddle under a thatched cow shack, where the mosquitoes also lived and dined – or wined! In another extreme, we parked between the *gaushala* and a *johra* at the entrance to Sethon ka Ramgarh and slept curled in our Ambassador car, one on the front seat, the other on the back. As the legs couldn't be stretched, we awoke in a mist-haze with a light frost cover on the car, our legs were stiff and frozen and we had to re-learn to walk. Once we were stuck in mid-day 50°C June on the sand track between Mandawa and Fatehpur, pushing our car till we were dehydrated and compelled to eat our two remaining oranges with their peels. Later, at the Bhartia *haveli*, a crowd gathered around, calling us CIA agents who were secretly mapping their land, till a kind Mr Saraswat asked us in and offered us some water. By contrast, in Lohargal, where Bhima supposedly cast his mace in a pit and which was not so easily accessible, we were rather well-received with tea and *pakoras*, when we opened our tripod to photograph the frescoes. Our equipment had convinced them that we were engineers from the Public Works Department, surveying their village to build a road! In Mandrela, seeing the same tripod and cameras, they asked Francis and me if we were Japanese and if the mis-guided American satellite to the moon which was to land on Earth on that day, wasn't going to drop on them. They were all so frightened that they were packing their bags to flee! At Bissau, we slept on *charpoys* in the outer court of the Fort which a Bania trader had bought to turn into a grain mill. When he had wanted to pierce the wall to get his trucks to enter and reverse directly, circumventing the convoluted medieval path, he told us that gold coins had poured out. 'You never find the gold when you look for it,' he had said in all seriousness. So we concentrated on our photography and research. In retrospect, our gold lay in our own enrichment and in the sharing of our "discovery" of Shekhavati with the world.

On one of our early discovery drives, we had met the mustachioed Praduman Singh in Mandawa, and mistaken him for a farmer, till his Mayo College English amazed and befriended us. At his asking, we called on his historian father Kanwar Devi Singh and his family in Jaipur. We showed them slides of the frescoes from their village and they all seemed surprised – even his painter son Randhir Vikram Singh had never noticed the frescoes in the land of his ancestors! Kesri Singh was still busy pushing files in a bank, while the least "Rajput" of the four brothers, Bhanu Pratap was setting up a garment unit. They had sold and rented all the precincts of their Jaipur home, as had most of the erstwhile nobility of the area. Over the next many years, we were to give them new eyes to see their strengths as we helped to build on them, so that their traditions would survive the onslaught and levelling of modernism.

We called on the octogenarian Jhabarmal Sharma who had written in Hindi the histories of two of Jaipur's biggest *thikanas* – Khetri (in 1922), and Sikar (in 1927). He was living history himself and we benefited greatly from our conversations with him.

Inspired by his writings, we made a roadless pilgrimage to the cenotaph of Rao Shekha-ji who had died in 1488 at Ralawata from wounds inflicted while fighting the Gaurs, who had insulted a woman of his clan. Wedged between two earth walls our tyres skid on the sands. It was warm and we left some flowers on a marble plaque with some money for whoever the caretaker of this wilderness may have been. We felt the pride of being wandering Shekhawats!

Back in Delhi, we met Raja Sardar Singh of Khetri, aged around 90, who seemed to be the last survivor from a period that he had clearly lived in and also seen draw to an end. He lived with a certain Lady Manning, having finally made his peace with his British colonisers only in bed. At 9 pm sharp, we met him at his grand Sardar Patel Marg residence, up an impressive spiral stairway. That, we were told, was his first working appointment, as he slept all day and worked only by night. He arranged for us to stay our first comfortable night in Shekhavati at the Sukh Mahal of Khetri and he told us to write him of our plans for his palaces which we discussed. These had partly been donated to the Ramakrishna Mission, for Swami Vivekananda had used them to stay there. We drafted a letter for a proposed museum of Shekhavati and then got involved with the creation of Intach. We formed its first chapter as well as organised a seminar in Mandawa with Sir Bernard Fielden of ICROM where Lady Wade Gery, the wife of the British High Commissioner played an important role. Since Raja Sardar Singh was an Anglophile, we wanted to involve the British Government and their expertise to create this Shekhavati museum. But before this could materialise, he passed away, and his home came to be administered by a trust.

Seven years had passed in this Shekhavati adventure. The restoration of the *havelis* and the revival of fresco painting was never to be as we had imagined it, but it did become an international destination.

Neemrana

These passionate years of Neemrana, and the subsequent "neemranification" of some twenty-three properties in other parts of India, may never have happened if it wasn't laid on a solid and intense self-education programme and foundation that we gave ourselves in Rajasthan. From 1977 till 1986 – when Neemrana Fort-Palace was acquired, the black road stretched and ribboned out each weekend before us. We had been bent upon befriending every pothole it seemed, as all the roads "less-travelled by" became our sole mission. The big roads carried the whole world but seemed to lead to nowhere new.

Every Friday after work I would pick Francis from his home in 19 A, Amrita Shergill Marg, or he would fetch me from my home, A-51, Nizamuddin East, and then we would leave New Delhi behind us for as long as our work would let us free ourselves. Our first trips into Shekhavati were from West Delhi via Rohtak, Bhiwani, Loharu and on to Pilani. Later, we would drive past Dharuhera, Rewari, Narnaul – and we were in Shekhavati from its Singhana entrance. After our usual circuits discovering new "painted" villages and towns from Surajgarh to Bissau, or Ratangarh, Ramgarh, Fatehpur, we would loop the entire historical kingdom of Rao Shekha-ji and return via Sikar to Shahpura on the Jaipur highway. This was some 500 km on roads and tracks. Sometimes, via the heart of the painted *havelis* at Nawalgarh, we would swing back up to Nim ka Thana and Kotputli to head back home on the only highway of that time. On longer weekends, we would do the more secluded Alsisar-Malsisar or Mahensar-Mandawa routes before venturing into the Aravalli hideouts of Lohargal and Chirana, to head for Jaipur. That was where much of our interviews were conducted. On those weekends we would record 700 km, driving alternately to share the load.

Returning on one such trip from Jaipur to Delhi, we let ourselves be guided by our rather pro-active destiny. As we sped the two-lane highway in an Ambassador car, our eyes had fallen a few times on the gigantic but sad ruins of Neemrana. It was only after a while of seeing it that once, when we were less hurried to rush home to Delhi, we ventured to take the Neemrana detour. It was late afternoon and the fortress glowed in the sunshine. We drove up a dust track to a dead point near a sleepy police station and parked under a *neem* tree. The rest we did on foot. Only camels seemed to climb up this track and their vacuum hooves must have been perfect to cushion away the rubble and sand beneath. We climbed up a circular stone-paved road to a large gateway. The gates were spiked and partially open like an alligator's jaws contemplating a prey, and we walked right in – to be consumed by our own eternity.

From a distance, the stark and barren ranges had glared back at the late afternoon sun, their ancient Vedic name, Adavala, now anglicized to the Aravallis. But inside, it was all dark and overgrown, even at mid-day. As we negotiated our way between heaps of debris, it hardly felt like day. The dark ramparts beside the entrance gateway had collapsed in pyramidal heaps, and where the iron girders, which had once held the roofs, had been sold or stolen, the stones hung down precariously like hooks of death from the sky. Instinctively, we headed towards the light, only to discover courtyard after courtyard. Every now and then, stairways and ramps led us up or down, and soon we were in a rather magical space that looked like an excavation from pre-history. And indeed, as we later discovered, it was the oldest section dating back to 1464 CE with a ruined temple to the Goddess Asavari. This was where goats were once sacrificed at Dussehra.

A stairway led us to the back, (what now leads up to the Manak Mahal) and we stood under a hacked *pipal* tree, overlooking a reservoir of dark water mosaic-ed with lichen. A deep defencive gorge ran along the entire back of the fort wall. Then we clambered down a slope to a broken bastion, from where we took the breach out, sliding down with the debris to a semicircular turret. We stood facing full west and watched the sun do its daily finale. That was a cosmic Neemrana moment touched by its own magic – and it still is. Today, the sunset tea at Neemrana, sipped over the entrance gateway by the chessboard of the Shatranj Bagh, has become legend. Twinings had chosen to film it as the most magical spot to have tea on. The sun is the same, still drawing its same smooth arch across the entire sky – only the audiences keep changing. This then, is the big theatre of life. Francis Wacziarg and I had known it then: it was not Benares, nor was it Jerusalem – but it was simply a blessed spot on planet Earth called Neemrana.

A fortnight later, we drove down to Vijay Bagh at the edge of Neemrana village where Raja Rajinder Singh lived ever since he had abandoned the crumbling Neemrana Fort in 1947. We waited in the verandah of that colonial bungalow built for the British Resident, whenever he visited. A small mirror in the hat and umbrella stand reflected the crumbling fort behind us. I couldn't but think of Shah Jahan exiled in the Agra Fort looking at the Taj Mahal reflected through a mirror inlaid in the wall. After the Raja Sahib had told us about his Chauhan descent, and how even before India's independence and democracy, he had moved out of his "royal" life to be a simple farmer below, he asked our help in disposing off the burden of his ruin. 'I can even give you a commission if you find me a buyer. For thirty years I've been trying to sell it to the Government to make a school or some institution,' he had said. The year was 1980, and the whole idea which seemed so outrageous, still needed to brew, ferment and mature, as our attempted revival of Shekhavati was still to occupy us for some years. Our book appeared in 1982 and the Shekhavati Vikas Nidhi took much of our time as we tried to set up a school for fresco painting with Kripal Singh Shekhawat (who had revived the Jaipur Blue Pottery with Rajmata Gayatri Devi), and with the generous Anjolie Ela

Menon, both of whom lived for a while in Mandawa. We got many looms from Panipat to weave woollen blankets and set up a centre for the women. But all this was too avant garde for the Mandawa family for whom, concentrating on their own fortunes was more important at that time. So we backtracked slowly.

The work on our second book, *The Arts and Crafts of Rajasthan*, took us several times to Jodhpur, Jaisalmer, Barmer, Udaipur, Tonk, Kotah, Bundi, and Sirohi – researching and photographing everything from palace and village ornamentation to crafts persons who worked in leather, iron, stone, wood, gold, silver and on the varied looms. We met Maharaja Bhawani Singh and Maharani Padmini Devi of Jaipur, Maharana Bhagwat Singh of Mewar, Maharao Umaid Singh and Maharaj Kumar Brijraj Singh of Kotah, Maharaj Hukam Singh of Jaisalmer, Maharaj Swaroop Singh and Rani Usha Devi of Jodhpur, Maharao Abhay Singh of Sirohi, Maharawal Yadavendra Singh of Samode and every visit, photograph and unlayering of their world became for us a lesson on many counts.

Rather than cajole and plead India's wealthiest community who had their joint ownership constraints to restore their ancestral Marwari homes, we thought we should perhaps demonstrate by example. In 1984 a small, obscure *haveli* in Khohar, a hamlet near Sohna in the Gurgaon district of Haryana, was purchased for a sum of Rs 30,000. Just after I drove out from the Sohna *tehsil* after registering the ruin, a man on the road was hitching a lift.

'They've finished her, finished her!' he said, when I stopped and rolled down my glass.

'Who?' I asked in wonder.

'Indira Gandhi,' he replied. 'She's been gunned by her own bodyguards.'

Havoc flowed on my return to Delhi. Trucks were burning and exploding in Jangpura as I turned to Nizamuddin, and the Sikhs were running for cover. We lost the lights on our gates as my father wouldn't let an unruly crowd enter and search our house. Our Sikh neighbours had hidden and slept the night with us.

Through the political upheaval that followed, we were busy with our first restoration project at the Khohar haveli. By 1985 it was ready to receive curious friends – Montek and Isher Ahluwalia, Rome and Sunita Kohli, Mani Mann, Martand Singh, Ajay and Shiromani Singh, Vikram Seth, Bim and John Bissell with the Moynihans, Michel Guy, Elisabeth Juppe and Gerard Depardieu. Rashna Imhasly brought her parents Kekoo and Khorshed Gandhi who had pioneered the showing of art in Bombay with their Chemould Gallery. Along with them, the best known contemporary painters of that time: Ram Kumar, S.H. Raza, Tyeb Mehta, Gulam Mohammed Sheikh, and Krishen Khanna also came and were enchanted. It was then that we knew that we needed to go back to the Raja of Neemrana.

The whole world wanted to visit and see the Khohar Haveli and there were clearly two kinds of people in Delhi society: those who had enjoyed the *haveli*, and those who were still to find a way to get invited or simply invite themselves there. The Taj Man Singh opened in New Delhi. Among its early functions was a fashion show by Yves Saint Laurent, and the launch in Delhi of our book on the painted *havelis* of Shekhavati. It was no coincidence that the Indian restaurant at the Taj was called "Haveli". This word of Persian origin had become fashion speak for the litterati, glitterati and chatterati. Anjolie Ela Menon, who had been involved through our Shekhavati Trust to revive the frescoes of that region, used her first-hand experience to paint as well as put patina on the walls of the restaurant while staying at my house.

But the ruins of Neemrana Fort-Palace were not quite the same scale as the small *haveli*. As a banker from New Zealand had calculated at that time, the *haveli* was 4,500 times smaller than the fort! Also, in this period between 1977 and 1986, much of the gentry had been to see Neemrana and shown interest in acquiring it: Jacqueline Kennedy with the Jaipur royalty, Biki Oberoi's architects and structural engineers, Nand and Jeet Khemka, Krishan Amla. Even though they had all been frightened by the state of the ruin and retreated, the price had gone up seven times! During the Emergency, three formidable couples – Rajiv and Sonia Gandhi, Arun and Neena Singh, Sanjay and Maneka Gandhi had also visited Neemrana with the young Priyanka and Rahul in tow. But someone had flung a stone at the beehives, and everyone was stung. Rajiv the pilot was stung high on his forehead and as Rahul fled the bees and ran on the breached ramparts, his parents had been stung by worry. A decade later, Francis Wacziarg met the same fate and was stung too. As his son Romain ran out towards the edge of the ramparts, his heart had sunk in syncope.

Finally, the Neemrana deal was signed on July 30, 1986, and it wasn't easy to decide where to begin. On January 1, 1987, Romi Chopra, a close friend phoned early in the morning to say 'You are in the headlines.' The *Navbharat Times* read 'Neemrana mahal mein Rajneesh ka haath', saying that Osho Rajneesh had a hand in the purchase of the Neemrana palace. He had just been ousted from the United States and was indeed seeking a desirable place for an ashram, but we had no connection. I had attended one of his lectures in the Mavalankar Auditorium in Delhi, and I was carrying the plastic coated file that had been given to me as member of the "press" from *India Today* since I looked after their arts pages. Someone had seen that on my car seat and mistakenly connected the two.

The clearing of the rubble and crumbled debris at the entrance of the majestic 15th century Neemrana Fort-Palace took some three months. It was not entirely difficult to find Kumawat masons who had, in a long ancestral line been building in stone and lime mortar. A camel had to be got, and a millstone too, to crush different materials into a lime slurry that would be as tough as stone when it dried. We didn't add the jaggery and lentils, which were proverbially added to the mortar, but the façade began to rise and one could see that its nobility and silhouette would be reborn to be handsome. When the decorative crenellations were carved in stone and finally fixed on the top, the building seemed to wear its lost crown again. Kilometres of cables snaked through the monumental ruin, with just as many plumbing pipes. Both brought life. Without electricity, the water which we had drilled in the rocks, couldn't be pumped up some 300 metres – and without water neither the humans nor the gardens could survive. Some four years passed.

One day, midweek in the winter of 1990, I had the visit of Raja Rajinder Singh Chauhan at my office in 12 Scindia House, Connaught Circus, in New Delhi, a floor above the office of Air France. He had been there once before with six jewelled gold buttons he had wanted to sell. Now he came with a very different proposition.

'You have to be in Neemrana on the 4th of February, Baby is getting married.'

'That's great news! She must marry from the Fort,' I said instantly.

'But that has been sold, it doesn't belong to me anymore.'

'Of course not! Historically it shall always be yours. We have only taken on the burden of extending its life. It would give us great pleasure if you used it for the marriage.'

Tears trickled down his cheeks with a speed hard to imagine, 'But then, only on one condition.'

'And what could that condition be?' I asked, intrigued.

'That you stand beside me at the wedding.'

'Oh! Then everyone will ask you who I am.'

He then stood up and held my hand warmly across the table, reassuring both himself and me and said 'My brother!'

Francis Wacziarg and I drove down on that fateful day of February with two friends from New Zealand. The entire *barat*, the groom's party, was staying at the half-restored fort. When we drove up to inspect the arrangements, we were told that it was for the first time since forty years that the Fort-Palace had been dressed with streamers and garlands of flowers. There was something poignantly Felliniesque about the décor. A mirror had been nailed by the Holi Kund and a guest was enjoying a sunny shave. A *dhobi* ironed the Rajput *achkans*, as colourful *safas* with long tails were being stretched and tied. We were a bit late so we rushed down to the bride's *kothi* in Vijay Bagh, which had received a fresh coat of whitewash.

As our green Gypsy arrived on the dusty track, a retainer recognized us. Rather than be made to wait outside with the other male guests who stood on a hard patch – once a tennis court by the rose gardens – we were ushered straight in to the *zenana*. When we hesitated, the Princess' mother came out in her petticoat and blouse to pull us in. 'You are the *Mamas* of the bride, the uncles,' she translated for Francis's benefit, unaware that he spoke fairly fluent Hindi.

We found ourselves in the central room where the two Ranis had displayed an impressive dowry. The elder Rani, a princess of Nagod in Madhya Pradesh, was giving away most of what she had brought in her wedding. The second Rani had come as a maid in the dowry but when her mistress couldn't oblige the Raja with an offspring, she had risen to the occasion and become his third wife. After some niceties, we climbed to the roof where strings of bulbs decorated the house to record the occasion for ourselves with photographs. Soon, we heard the band and with a dusty stream of cars, the bridegroom and his party had arrived. After felicitating everyone and giving our gifts, we didn't stay for the dinner, as is often customary for the bride's side of the party, to not add to the guest liability in numbers.

✧

Three years later, we got news of the Raja's demise in Alwar. His body was "seated" in a taxi and brought to Neemrana. This took a few hours. On arrival, they carried him in a procession and then the village gathered for the cremation, but the body had stiffened in its seated position.

By the ancestral cenotaphs of his adoptive parents, the Raja of Neemrana was cremated in a seated position facing the Fort still under restoration. His face seemed to have a cynical smirk frozen upon it: some strangers had adopted his liability as a passion: He too had once been adopted to this throne. Wasn't history quite a joke, finally?

In the January of the following year, my father passed away and the two Ranis came all the way to Delhi to mourn with my mother. They reminded her that the Raja Sahib had also passed away exactly one year earlier on January 6! That, as it turned out also happened to be the day when Romain Wacziarg, the only son of Francis, had been born. To think that all the three of them had a choice of 364 other days to choose for their entry or exit from this planet! In the synchronicity of this fateful numerical conjunction, I could only read destiny's message of positivism, of which we too had now become a continuing thread.

5

BURY MY HEART AT RAMBAGH

Gayatri Devi in Jaipur

Throughout he nearer we drew to Jaipur, the more terrified and unsure I became. I tried desperately not to show it, but Jai, my husband and Maharaja of Jaipur, understood how I felt, I think.

Although my two previous visits to Jaipur had been private and informal, I couldn't help being struck by the ceremonial grandeur of Jai's court. But now I was to see it in all its full-blown splendour, as Rambagh Palace prepared to receive me as the Maharaja's new bride.

We were received by my sisters-in-law and Jaipur relatives, the wives of the nobles and of the staff as Jai showed me my apartments. They used to be Jai's own suite, but he had had them redecorated by a London firm. I was enchanted. There was a high-ceilinged, airy bedroom all in pink, with pale voile curtains, pastel divans, and *chaise-longues*; an oval bathroom with the bath set in an alcove; a paneled study; and a large sitting-room filled with *objets d'art* from the Jaipur collection. Small jewelled animals, rose quartz and jade, and curved daggers with white jade hilts carved to look like animal heads with jewels for eyes were displayed in glass cabinets. Jade boxes encrusted with semi-precious stones in floral designs held cigarettes and heavy crystal bowls were filled with flowers. Jai had also remembered my love for the gramophone and had got me the latest kind, which could actually take several records at a time and turn them over.

Outside my rooms ran a marble veranda overlooking the central courtyard of the palace. There my maids from Cooch Behar took turns to wait and answer any summons from me. On the other side, a small hallway separated me from Jai's apartments, which had also been completely renovated and were now filled with ultra modern furniture.

The whole of that first period of my life in Jaipur had an unreal quality, and I found myself performing actions as if I were in a trance, changing my clothes over and over again, sitting dazedly in group after group of in-laws, acknowledging introduction after introduction to the wives and daughters of nobles and officials. I remember how oppressively hot the nights were in spite of the fact that the rains had already started. We slept on the roof under the shelter of a cupola, and I lay awake for hours unable to sleep. One night I heard the faint tinkling of anklets in the distance and Jai told me it was a ghost, but it turned out to be only the pods of a flame-of-the-forest tree rattling in the night wind.

On a day declared auspicious by the pundits, I was taken on the ten-minute drive to the immense City Palace, a bewildering complex of interconnecting courtyards, pavilions, secluded *zenana* quarters, men's apartments, audience halls, weapons-rooms, large and small sitting-rooms, dining-rooms, banqueting chambers, offices, and so on and on. It was the official home of the Maharaja of Jaipur. I travelled there in a curtained *purdah* car escorted by Jai's personal bodyguard, the Bhoop Squadron of the Kachhwaha Horse, mounted on superb matching black horses and dressed in white tunics, breeches, black boots, and turbans of blue and silver, with silver cockades.

From the moment I entered the City Palace I was fascinated by it. Lying at the heart of the old walled city, it is almost a town in itself, with gardens, stables, and an elephant yard surrounding the many buildings and spreading over more than thirty acres. Like the town outside it, the City Palace was built in the first half of the 18th century in pure Rajputana architecture, with elegant scalloped arches on slender columns and latticed marble screens, with galleries and delicate wall-paintings. The whole place had a dreamlike feeling, each courtyard with its surrounding rooms producing another surprise.

Sometime later after all the ceremonies were over, Jai led me through the magnificent and imposing public courtyards and halls, which I would not have been allowed to see alone because they were all on the men's side of the palace. From the first courtyard, with its hall enclosed by high yellow walls, we entered the council chamber with its own courtyard, coloured entirely in pink. From there brass relief doors, nineteen feet high, opened into the *durbar* hall. Another door from the *durbar* hall led to an audience pavilion, more like a huge veranda, where the decorative murals and the doors inlaid with ivory were masterpieces of local craftsmanship. This in turn, overlooked the walled garden, in the middle of which the temple of Govind Devji or Lord Krishna, stood. Jai told me that traditionally all the maharajas of Jaipur governed the state in his name. And so we wandered on, from courtyard to courtyard, from pavilion to gallery to chamber to hall to garden, until I could only think that this was all a setting for some fabulous fairy-tale.

The *zenana* quarters were divided into a series of self-contained apartments. Mine, decorated in blues and greens was much like the others, with a little square courtyard and a private *durbar* hall hung with blue glass lamps, and inner rooms opening off it. I later came to know it far more intimately, as we went there for every ceremonial occasion, sometimes staying as long as a fortnight.

✧

Understandably, the pleasures and discoveries that I remember best from my early years in Jaipur were those I shared with Jai. Sometimes he would take me exploring on horseback or by car. He owned a number of forts in the country around Jaipur City, and we often went to one or another of them for a picnic. One trip I remember particularly vividly took us to the 18th century fort of Nahargarh built high on a hill overlooking the city. From there we rode along the crest of the rocky hills that surround Jaipur to another fort – Jaigarh – about 500 ft above the Palace of Amber. It had a great watch-tower scanning the plains to the north, and it was here that the fabulous Jaipur treasure was housed, closely guarded by one of the state's warlike tribes. Nobody but the Maharaja himself was allowed to enter the tower or to see the treasure. I waited outside the menacing walls while Jai went in. But true to tradition he never described to me what the treasure was like, and the only evidence I ever saw of its existence was the beautiful jewelled bird, with two large rubies for its eyes and an emerald hanging from its beak, which stood on the drawing-room mantelpiece at Rambagh.

From the verandas of Rambagh I had often admired a small fort, Moti Doongri, which was perched high on a rocky outcrop, its delicate crenellations scattered with bright bougainvillaea. From a distance it looked like an exquisitely fashioned toy. One morning Jai took me up there, and when I told him how much I liked it, he simply said, 'Then it's yours,' and Moti Doongri became my own special possession. Jai had the interior renovated for me, and we often escaped there from the formality and panoply of Rambagh to have quiet lunches or dinners, often alone, sometimes with friends. I always associated it with a particular warmth and intimacy.

Big-game shoots were organized at Sawai Madhopur. The first one after our marriage remains particularly clear in my memory. Jai had built a small shooting-lodge there, close by in the hills south-west of Jaipur, which was dominated by the famous fort of Ranthambhore, its battlements and walls spreading for miles. While Jai and I stayed in the shooting-lodge, our guests were accommodated in a camp even more elaborate than those I knew from my childhood, with tents fitted out with every comfort.

The shooting, too, was quite different from Cooch Behar. In Jaipur we didn't shoot from elephants but from raised platforms, *machans*. The game was just as plentiful: tiger, panther, bear, blue bull, *sambar*, and many sorts of deer. Much later we were to entertain Lord and Lady Mountbatten of Burma there, and the Queen and Prince Philip, too.

For impromptu weekends we often went to Ramgarh, a comfortable country house which Jai had built by the side of a lake surrounded by hills. It was an ideal spot for picnics and boating.

And then, as a recurring theme in our lives, there was polo. As soon as the rains were over, polo began and every other day there were practice games on the Jaipur polo-grounds, considered among the best in the world. In the late afternoons, after the heat of the day was over, I used to drive out to watch Jai playing or practicing. I always took my knitting with me and sat in the front seat of my car, with the top down, gazing out at the polo-ground and the graceful wheeling of ponies and riders and keeping my hands busy with wool and needles in a feeble attempt to calm my nerves and anxieties at the danger of the game. Even through my tension, I couldn't help seeing – almost with renewed surprise each time – what a beautiful game it is, and how the elegance of the movements of horse and players, perfectly synchronized, raises the whole performance from a sport to an art.

❖

The first festival I attended in Jaipur was Teej, celebrated in honour of the goddess Parvati, consort of Lord Shiva. The festival was one of particular significance in the *zenana* because in the stories of Hindu mythology, Parvati had meditated for years and years in order to win Lord Shiva as her husband. Accordingly, the unmarried women prayed to Parvati to endow them with a husband as good as Shiva, while the married women begged that their husbands should be granted many more years of life so that they could "always be dressed in red" – rather than the unrelieved white clothes of widows. We three Maharanis were supposed to perform the ceremonies of prayers and offerings in the shrine in the City Palace. But on that first occasion, Jai's other two wives were out of the state and I was told that I must enact each part of the ceremony three times, once for First Her Highness, once for Second Her Highness, and finally once for myself.

After the prayers in the City Palace, the replica of the goddess was taken out of the *zenana* and carried in procession through the streets of the town. To watch the spectacle, the *zenana* ladies were led by the palace eunuchs through a labyrinth of dark tunnels and passages and up and down ramps to a gallery that overlooked the main street on the north-west side of the palace. We must have had to walk for over half a mile, twisting and turning behind the eunuchs through the half-lit maze. I lost all sense of time and direction and was conscious only of the rustling sound of silk and the tinkling of anklets as we hurried along. When we finally emerged, I saw Jai sitting in state in another pavilion surrounded by his nobles. Through the lacy, carved marble screen of our own pavilion, we could get a clear view beneath us of a spacious arena made for elephant fights, a favourite sport of the old Rajput chiefs. This arena was being used by the townsfolk as a fair-ground and was crowded with sightseers, some of them city people but most of them peasants from the villages in the countryside surrounding Jaipur.

It was an exuberant and joyful sight. There were swings, merry-go-rounds, a big wheel, and endless rows of stalls selling trinkets, sweets, and little clay dolls, and mixed with the good-humoured jostling of an Indian crowd, everyone dressed in their best finery for their visit to the palace, children tearing about, yelling with excitement on this holiday. All of us gasped with admiration as on one side of the arena, the Jaipur cavalry gave a meticulous display of jumping and tent-pegging, while on the other a desert tribe of military ascetics performed a whirling sword dance of incredible dexterity. The elephants were lined up, their *howdahs* draped with sumptuous satins and velvets; the soldiers stood in perfect ranks, their silver trappings and uniforms brilliant in the sun; and all around them was the bustling mass with their bright turbans and multi-coloured dresses.

I watched enchanted for almost an hour. Then a signal was given, and I rose with the others to be led back through the windowless passages into the *zenana*. Meanwhile the men led by Jai, visited the temple and later gathered in a pavilion in the City Palace gardens to enjoy their drinks and be entertained by musicians and dancers.

When the image of the goddess was finally returned to the palace to be enshrined for another year, I again performed the prayer ceremony. On that first day all the palace ladies except the widows, had worn red. On the second day, we all wore green. We were peering through the screened galleries overlooking the streets to see the crowds and the gaiety. The pavement merchants spread out their wares, especially little clay models of Shiva and Parvati that were in constant demand. Groups of women sang songs to entertain the passers-by, and one of the songs, I was told, praised the Maharaja's new bride, who had brought rains to the parched countryside. I was glad that at least one section of the public, for however unwarranted a reason, liked me.

In all festivals the Maharaja played the central role. Dussehra was the most important festival for Rajputs and as the head of the Kachhwaha clan, Jai paid reverence to the arms and vehicles of war which included carriages, bullock-carts, horses, and elephants. Along with the other ladies of the Jaiput court, I watched these ceremonies from behind windows of latticed stone and kept quiet about my great pride at the public figure that Jai presented. After the ceremony Jai drove in a golden carriage, drawn by six white horses, to a special palace three miles away, used only for the Dussehra *durbar*. The public ceremonies were perfectly organized, magnificent in appearance and deeply reassuringly impressive to Jai's subjects. The procession was led off by troops, cavalry, bullock-carts, and camels, all accompanied by military bands, followed by Jai's personal bodyguard riding their matched black horses preceding Jai's own carriage. Behind him came the nobility on horseback, wearing brocade costumes, their horses grandly caparisoned. (Some of them were not very good riders, and there was always a great deal of laughter and teasing among us *zenana* ladies as the procession passed our windows.) All along the royal route Jai received a tremendous ovation and people crowded every window, balcony, or look-out point to watch him and shout, '*Maharaja Man Singhji ki Jai!*' 'Victory for Maharaja Man Singhji!' as he approached.

On the darkest night of the year which falls by the lunar calendar late in October or early in November, Diwali, the Hindu New Year is celebrated. In Jaipur, the palace and the whole city were illuminated, looking like a fairy-tale fantasy. The hilltop forts above the town were also lit up, and seemed to be suspended in mid-air. Beneath them, against the hills themselves, an outline of the goddess Lakshmi, the giver of wealth, was picked out in lamps, while in the city all the palaces, public buildings, and private homes were decorated. Rambagh and the City Palace blossomed with thousands of tiny lamps – clay pots holding oil and wicks – and, in the City Palace courtyard, dancing girls performed. Jai paid a ceremonial visit there, dressed in a black jacket and a black and gold turban, and, attended by his nobles, he offered prayers to Lakshmi while the dancing and singing continued, climaxed by an extravagant fireworks display.

Jai always invited guests for the Diwali festivities and persuaded them to play games of bridge or roulette, or any form of gambling to usher in the New Year. We ladies didn't join them. All of us dressed in dark blue, the colour appropriate for Diwali, watched the fireworks from another terrace and later returned to Rambagh for a large family dinner followed by our own private display of fireworks.

To me the loveliest of all is held a couple of weeks before Diwali, when the moon is at its brightest and a *durbar* is held outdoors to celebrate the festival of Sharad Purnima. Nothing much happens, but at this *durbar* Jai and his courtiers would all dress in the palest pink, their swords and jewels glittering in the moonlight. To me it seemed an extraordinary, almost ethereal scene, engraved forever in my memory.

Holi, which in Cooch Behar had been merely the expression of high-spirited delight in the arrival of spring, with people throwing red powder at each other, in Jaipur turned out to be more ceremonial. That first Holi after our marriage Jai rode through the streets on an elephant, followed on this occasion by Bhaiya, who was visiting us. As they rode through the streets, Jai and Bhaiya were sitting targets for the townsfolk who crowded the rooftops, windows, and balconies. Jai, ready for what he knew was coming, had equipped himself with a water-hose with a compressor to shoot on the crowds and make them keep their distance. In later years Holi became far less dangerous as we played in our own gardens, but the occasional accurate shot still hurt as much and the stains were just as permanent.

With all its strangeness, its delights, its worries, its embarrassments, and its joys, those first months in Jaipur taught me the duties and responsibilities, the pleasures and restrictions of being a maharani of an important state. It also showed me that it was possible to be lonely surrounded by people, yet happy even in the enveloping shroud of *purdah* life.

More simply, I suppose I was growing up. I might have muddled along for years, enjoying special occasions, often finding myself bored or at a loose end in my daily life, surrounded by luxury but with no interior furnishings for what I suppose I should call my soul, not seeing enough of Jai, fretting when I wasn't with him, making do with whatever company I could find in the *zenana*, unable to appreciate fully the deep satisfactions that such a life could offer.

But the war, once it got started in an active way, demanding the co-operation of India, changed my life as it changed so much more.

◇

While the war brought all kinds of restrictions to many people, to me in Jaipur it brought a certain measure of freedom. Jai encouraged me to work for the war effort, and I started at once by attending Red Cross work-parties at the Ladies' Club. I met all sorts of women there: teachers, doctors, and wives of government officials. Their company was far more stimulating than that of the *purdah*-ridden palace ladies, and besides I felt that, in however indirect a way, I was backing up the people closest to me who were taking an active part in the war – Jai, of course; Bhaiya, especially vulnerable now that the Japanese were advancing into Burma; and Indrajit, on active service abroad.

Jai's second wife Jo Didi and I organized work-parties to knit and sew for the Red Cross at Rambagh for the more orthodox ladies, and I even managed to persuade some of the women in the City Palace that knitting prosaic things like socks and sweaters was not below their dignity because it was all helping their Maharaja. Besides this kind of sedentary work, I put in much of my effort into raising money by organizing plays and fetes at the Ladies' Club in order to buy all sorts of amenities for the Jaipur State Forces in the Middle East.

With energy still to spare, and with rather more confidence now that my war work seemed to be successful, both financially and socially, I started to take over the running of the household at Rambagh. It was Jai's suggestion when his English Comptroller left to join the army that I should do so and I realized that although I had lived mainly in Jaipur ever since my marriage, I hadn't concerned myself at all with how everything was managed but, like everyone else, had simply enjoyed the high standard of comfort provided. There were something over 400 servants at Rambagh, and while Jai wanted to eliminate unnecessary extravagance, he had a military eye for detail and expected everything to be perfectly run. The guards at the nine gates, for example, were inspected at regular intervals. All the gardens had to be impeccably maintained. At various points throughout the palace, groups of boys were posted to prevent the many pigeons from causing damage to the buildings.

What surprised me most, however, was the extravagance of the store-rooms in Rambagh itself. When I looked into them for the first time, I was flabbergasted. It was like some fantastic parody of Fortnum and Mason's. Everything was of the best quality and ordered not just by the crate but by the dozens of crates, 'to make sure, Your Highness, that we don't run out,' explained an attendant, seeing my amazement. There was enough to last us for years – wines, spirits, liqueurs, cigarettes, tea, biscuits, shampoo, Christmas crackers, and so on and on – all beautifully arranged and labeled. Half of the things must have been there for years, and there was an appalling wastage of perishable articles.

When I asked for the names of the people who had access to the store-rooms, I found that there wasn't the least attempt to keep track of who helped himself to what. The palace had been supplying all the staff, the guests, and ADCs and their families and anyone else who happened to want something. For Jai, when I told him, it was the end of at least one illusion. For years he had been touched by a small act of thoughtfulness at any party he attended in Jaipur – his hosts always provided his favourite brand of Egyptian cigarettes, by no means easy to obtain. He now learned, as a result of my researches, that the cigarettes came straight from his own store-rooms. Jo Didi, too, was shocked that the Evian water which she liked and which was specially imported for her, was also regularly drunk by her maids and even by the governess's dogs.

The extravagance in the kitchen matched that in the store-rooms. The point at which the chef for Western food finally realized that I was serious about eliminating senseless waste and stopping the purloining of palace stores for private use came, ridiculously enough, over the recipe for *crème brulee*. Jai had invited his new Minister for Education and his wife to lunch and he wanted the meal to be a simple affair for just the four of us. Clearly, the chef didn't know that I had some education in domestic science and decided, apparently, that I would be easy to hoodwink. He ordered two pounds of cream for his *crème brulee*. Horrified, I pointed out that so much cream would spoil the dish, but he replied grandly that for the Maharaja no amount of cream was too much. When I insisted, he reluctantly gave in, and from then on all our nine cooks – four for English food, five for Indian – paid attention to my orders.

Anyone who arrived at the palace, and that could mean dozens of people every day, was always offered a drink by the ADCs. In the hot summer months, iced coffee was the most popular choice. We had our own farm and dairy, but another of my maddening early discoveries was that our own milk was being watered down because there wasn't enough to meet the demands of the ADCs' room. When I insisted that such open-handed extravagance should stop because it was most unsuitable in wartime, I became, of course, highly unpopular. The servants took their revenge by purposely interpreting my orders overzealously. When the Home Minister arrived one day to see Jai and asked for a glass of iced coffee while he was waiting, he was pointedly informed that 'Third Her Highness has forbidden visitors to be offered drinks with milk.' Similarly, when the English governess asked for more lavatory paper, she was told she must wait until I returned from a shoot and could sign an order, as I had given instructions that no supplies of any kind should be given out without my consent. It was, however, some satisfaction to me that in spite of all the resentment I caused, I managed in one year to cut down expenses in Rambagh by at least half – and that without making any particular sacrifice in comfort or hospitality.

I knew that I was the object of a lot of criticism and that after the old days of endless unchecked lavishness in the palace, many people resented my way of running things, but as long as Jai was pleased with me I didn't much care what the others thought.

❖

In spite of personal tragedies and Jai's military duties during the war years, we kept up our contacts with other princely states. When he was in Jaipur, entertaining took up a good deal of our time, and the visit of a princely family still had to be conducted, as far as circumstances permitted, with a good deal of ceremony.

In those days no maharaja, unless he was a close relation on an informal visit ever arrived with fewer than thirty attendants, and often there were many more. There was always at least one of the ministers of the state government, the head of His Highness's household, several nobles, ADCs, valets, ADCs' valets, and even valets' valets. Commodious as Rambagh was, there was often not enough room for everyone, and the lawns on each side of the palace were covered with tents to accommodate the visitors. During the Jaipur polo season in March, the Rambagh grounds became a permanent camp, and the state guest-house which had rooms for over 200 people was filled as well.

We also paid visits to other states. Frequently we went to Jodhpur, the family home of both Jai's first two wives, where the Maharaja was extremely kind to me and accepted me as another daughter. Jai was very fond of him and called him 'Monarch' with all the laughing affection in the world. He took me to watch the pig-sticking, the dangerous sport of spearing wild boar from horseback, for which Jodhpur was well known. Once we went out into the desert to shoot imperial grouse. I remember how pleased with myself I was for shooting thirty-five birds, only to learn later that no one else had got less than 200. But the Maharaja scolded Jai for equipping me with a sixteen-bore, which he said was too big for a bird shoot, and presented me, himself, with a splendid twenty-bore which I cherish to this day.

In 1943 we were invited, together with the Jodhpur royal family to pay a formal visit to Udaipur, considered the foremost Rajput state, whose Maharana takes precedence over all the other Rajput princes. It was the first time I had ever been there, and I was looking forward to seeing its historic sights, such as the Lake Palace, which is built in such a way that it appears to be floating on the water or the great, fortified and ancient capital of Chittor. But I hadn't been prepared for the sternness of the *purdah* that all ladies were supposed to abide by in Udaipur.

When we arrived at Udaipur station, the railway carriage was shunted into a special *purdah* siding, where the Maharani was waiting to greet us. Immediately we were made aware of how completely we were to be sheltered from the public gaze. In Jaipur our *purdah* cars now merely had darkened glass in the windows replacing the curtains of earlier years, but in Udaipur we discovered that we were expected to go about in a car with heavy wooden shutters, enclosing us in a blind, airless box.

When we went on a trip on the lake, our boat was tightly veiled with curtains, and the camera that I had brought with me turned out to be both useless and a source of some embarrassment. On the boat ride I had cautiously lifted a corner of the curtain and tried to take a picture. This rash act must have reached the ears of the Maharana, for later, on our departure he presented me with an album of photographs. My own special ordeal came when the ladies were asked if they would care to have a shot at a wild boar. The Maharani of Jodhpur and Jo Didi wisely declined but hadn't time to signal me before I accepted with enthusiasm. They then told me that the honour of Jaipur would suffer dreadfully if I missed, and this seemed far from unlikely, since wherever we went we were surrounded by at least fifty women jostling and chattering. It all made for a period of suspense because I had to score the first time. Regardless of the dictates of politeness, I brazenly pushed myself well to the fore of our party and to my relief felled a heavy tusker with my first shot.

I remember those wartime state visits with particular clarity because with the end of World War II, it became plain to us and to all the other princes of India that great changes were imminent for the whole of India, and for us especially. Indian independence was already taking shape, and we were gradually realizing that in the new order the princely states would no longer be able to retain their old identity.

Maharani Gayatri Devi of Jaipur (1919-2009) was once rated amongst the most beautiful women in the world by *Vogue* magazine. She loved polo, cars and *shikar* but, moving beyond the conventional role of a Rajput princess, she became a champion of women's rights, shocking the conservative Rajasthan of her time by condemning the *purdah* system. In 1943 she established the Maharani Gayatri Devi Girls' Public School in Jaipur. To her credit also goes the revival of the dying art of blue pottery. After the abolition of the princely states, she took to politics.

6

THROUGH A GLASS, DARKLY

Sanjay Singh Badnor on Rajasthan's royal legacy

For now we see through a glass, darkly, but then face to face:
now I know in part; but then shall
I know even as also I am known.

I Corinthians 13

I was seven years old in 1972 when the princely order of India came to an abrupt end. Prime Minister Indira Gandhi had introduced a bill in parliament to abolish the titles, privy purses and other privileges accorded to the maharajas. Though I wasn't directly affected, my mother's family who hailed from the princely state of Pratabgarh certainly was. Although the privy purse and the titles of my maternal grandmother, the Rajmata, and that of my uncle, the Maharawat of Pratabgarh, were taken away, everybody around us continued to address them in the same manner. Ironically, even in all the subsequent correspondence from the government they continued to be addressed as 'Your Highness'.

But yes, definitely and rather suddenly, their lives underwent a drastic change. Be it a family wedding or other celebrations, austerity measures were adopted and all the events became low-key affairs sans the trappings of royalty.

Over the past four decades I have observed the transition, captured and documented it through my lens. However, what I believed to be an era that was fast fading into oblivion is surprisingly making a comeback. It is being utilized to the hilt to sell India to the foreign tourist. The Rajasthan state tourism department too relies strongly on the Maharaja Factor, their flagship 'Palace on Wheels' – the hugely successful luxury train – being marketed solely using the royal pitch. Festivals, royal ceremonies and rituals are all being celebrated with greater pomp and show, largely for the benefit of the tourist. Once dismissed by the new Republic of India and referred to as the 'erstwhile order', today the custodians of our royal traditions are back to being addressed as Maharaja or Maharani, without the prefix.

Meanwhile, in the decades following 1972, the princes began realigning themselves with newer roles whether it was business or tourism or politics. A majority of the princes in Rajasthan successfully converted their palaces and stately homes into heritage hotels. They began rubbing shoulders with the common man, becoming more acceptable to the public at large. Their unconditional loyalty to their former kingdoms and subjects tilted the balance in their favour. This often makes me wonder about something a 19th century essayist, Walter Bagehot, once said about royalty: 'Its mystery is its life; we must not let in daylight upon magic.' In the case of Rajasthan both daylight and magic walk hand-in-hand.

Maharaja Brigadier Bhawani Singh of Jaipur at the City Palace on his birthday. The rulers of Jaipur belong to the Kachhwaha clan of Rajputs who trace their ancestory to Kush, son of Rama. Bhawani Singh was its last recognized ruler. His passing away in April 2011 marked the end of an era. (Top)

In 2002 Bhawani Singh adopted his grandson to be his heir. Thus, on April 27, 2011, the thirteen-year-old Padmanabh Singh was crowned the next Maharaja at Jaipur's City Palace. (Left)

The lifestyle of the former princes is now emulated by India's Rich and Famous, be it collecting vintage cars, playing polo or constructing modern day palaces. Rajasthan as a wedding destination is also much sought after today. Industrialists, politicians, NRIs, Bollywood stars and even Hollywood celebrities fly down to the desert state to celebrate their weddings in their own flamboyant manner. The Liz Hurley-Arun Nayar wedding at Jodhpur, the Chatwal wedding at Udaipur, and the Russel Brand-Kate Perry wedding at Ranthambore are cases in point. The vintage cars seen on the left are part of a collection owned by Shriji Arvind Singh Mewar. The interior is of the Imperial Suite at the Shiv Niwas Palace Hotel in Udaipur.

A gathering of royals at the marriage of Yuvaraj Shivraj Singh, son of Maharaja Gaj Singh II of Jodhpur (2nd from left). The articulate and soft-spoken Eton and Oxford educated Gaj Singh is hugely popular and respected for having struck the right balance between tradition and modernity. Anointed the 38th Maharaja of Jodhpur in 1952 at the tender age of four, he is virtually worshipped even today by the people of Jodhpur who address him as "Bapji". His contribution towards promoting tourism in the state is significant. He has also been instrumental in starting a mammoth potable drinking water project in his erstwhile Marwar region that has won him a million hearts. Representatives from over sixty royal houses attended the wedding of his son, making it the largest royal congregation in recent times. Seated on his left is Maharawal Brajraj Singh of Jaisalmer and on his right are King Gyanendra Shah of Nepal, Maharaja Ranjit Singh Gaekwar of Baroda, and Maharana Mahendra Singh of Udaipur.

Shriji Arvind Singh Mewar, 76th custodian of the House of Mewar, is today a savvy businessman, hotelier, and cultural entrepreneur. He has conceptualized "Eternal Mewar", a unique heritage brand exemplifying hospitality, cultural preservation, philanthropy, education, sports and spirituality. It is entirely due to his efforts that today the city of Udaipur has successfully been catapulted as an international tourist destination. He is also Chairman and CEO of the HRH group of hotels that has over fifteen properties spread across Rajasthan. With him here are his son Lakshyaraj Singh and his son-in-law Dr. Kush Singh Parmar.

7

WHERE ON EARTH AM I?

Jug Suraiya in Pushkar, Udaipur, and on the
Palace on Wheels

'Why on earth do we travel?' Many people have asked
this question. And I think that there are as many
answers to it as there are travellers.

I was a traveller long before I knew I was. As a young boy in
Calcutta, I would walk along the streets and avenues and bylanes
of the city. I would pass decaying mansions, elegant bungalows set
in shaded gardens, teeming tenements. As I walked by, I would
look in through open windows, catching stray glimpses of what
was within: A naked light bulb; a crystal chandelier; a man in a
singlet sitting at a table, lost in thought and cigarette smoke; a
child holding a headless doll; a beautiful woman looking at her
face in the mirror. I would invent stories about the people who
lived there, and what my life would have been like if I had been
one of them. No, I wasn't a voyeur, a word I had never heard of
at the time. I was just a storyteller recounting to myself the many
narratives that might have been me.

Physicists say that the universe we inhabit is only one in an infinite series of universes, not out there in distant space, but only a heartbeat away from us in a different dimension. Each time we open a door, pick up a book, start a conversation, we give rise to a countless progression of universes where we left the door shut, picked up not this but some other book, stayed silent rather than spoke. The world we know is only one of an infinitude of narratives of which, unaware, we are a part. I would like to think that what we call travel is a faint echo of that never-ending story of which we are both the narrators and the subjects.

Camel Ahoy!

I'd have made a lousy Lawrence of Arabia. Ask Paploo. Paploo was the first – and I hope the last – camel in my life. It was 1991, and I was on a desert safari in Rajasthan.

But if Paploo gave me a hard time, in the end I got my own back on him. Thanks to a creature even scarier than Paploo. A creature with wings ...

I'd walk a mile for a camel – in the opposite direction. That was what I'd have liked even with Paploo. If he was going south, I would have liked to be bound for the north. That's what democracy is all about and it was fine for me. Except that I was supposed to be riding Paploo, an exercise that would have been facilitated considerably had the two of us been travelling towards more or less the same point of the compass. But camels, as I was beginning to learn, have a mind – and a method of locomotion – uniquely their own.

Till I had made the acquaintance of Paploo some hours earlier, camels had been for me ships of the desert that pass in the night, strictly non-union cast members strayed off the sets of a remake of *The Return of the Sheikh*. Now I was sitting on one, more or less (less more and more less) and feeling like laundry left over from *Lawrence of Arabia*.

I was on a camel trek along the fringe of the Rajasthan desert, billed as the definitive adventure experience ("Real Sand Safari for Rs 50 per day only ... fooding, experienced driver etc ... contact Aswin") for those who have seen and done it all already, from rafting in the Zanskar valley to taking a postprandial constitutional in the Hindu Kush. I haven't done either, but I had felt I could hack it. That was before I met the beast.

We had long left behind the tent city of Pushkar. A flyblown speck on the map, 160 km from Jaipur, Pushkar buzzes to life on the first full-moon night in November when throngs of Hindu devotees from all over the country flock to take a pre-dawn dip in the village lake, considered sacred to Brahma.

The camel and cattle fair that coincides with the religious festival is considered sacred to Thomas Cook. Overnight, the desert blooms with the rainbow efflorescence of a thousand tents that spring out of the sand to house visitors. It is a high, wide, and handsome affair, of the kind that Rajasthan is so good at when it tilts back its colourful turban, gives an extra twist to its moustache, and gets down to the serious business of marketing ethnic exuberance.

Jazzy neon jinks in time to the strains of amplified Hindi pop blaring over the fairground. On a raised platform, a hermaphrodite in a tinsel sari does a Michael Jackson number to drum up customers for the lurid splendour of the "Maruti Sarkus". A dancer with seven water-pots balanced on his head twirls past a sign proclaiming "Best spaghetti in Rajasthan – recommended by Italians!"

And everywhere there are Paploo-clones. Camels – smelling of ancient sofas left in the rain – undulate by, plastic flowers in their supercilious nostrils and paisley designs painted on their scrawny rumps like registration numbers on motor vehicles.

Rampal had sidled up to me with a seductive 'Psst! Cheap camel ride,' while Paploo cocked an inviting eyebrow at me as though to say: 'Come on, make my day.' I had succumbed, and here I was on my camel odyssey, the rolling dunes stretching away to infinity.

The quietness was as tangible as the afternoon heat. Much more than the mere absence of sound, it was a vibrant element pregnant with metaphysical significance, a comma in the syntax of suspense. The suspense revolved around the question as to when Paploo and I would part company, unintentionally on my part. While some of Paploo moved clockwise, the remainder of him seemed simultaneously to move anticlockwise. It was like sitting astride a maverick mobile corkscrew. Every now and then, Paploo would detour and snake out a serpentine neck to help himself to hors d'oeuvres from a passing thorn bush, making our progress even more erratic.

'Say *'Hat, hat, hat!'* to him,' admonished Rampal, my friend, philosopher, and camel guide. I dutifully enunciated the mantra, without noticeable effect. 'Kick him in the ribs,' advised Rampal. This seemed a rash familiarity, but I essayed a tentative nudge with my heels.

Paploo broke wind comprehensively. At first I interpreted this to be an aid to propulsion – jet-age travel by camel class, so to speak. But it turned out to be no more than a general philosophical observation and we plodded on towards the dunes that seemed as distant as ever. I hung on grimly, steeling myself with the foreboding that the worst was yet to come.

An eternity later we reached the rendezvous where the car waited to take me back to civilization. With a final eructation, Paploo knelt and I tumbled into Rampal's waiting grasp. 'How was it?' he grinned wolfishly. 'It was nothing,' I replied lightly. 'Now I go to Jaipur where I am wait-listed to catch the indefinitely postponed Indian Airlines flight home.'

Rampal's face under his ten-gallon turban paled at the very mention of this ultimate, edge-of-the-brink safari to end all safaris. Even Paploo looked stricken. And as I drove away into the sunset I had the satisfaction of knowing that in recompense for my aching limbs I was leaving behind an aghast camel who, if ever we met again, would walk a mile for me – in the opposite direction.

The seventeen-minute saga

Rajasthan, ancient land of chivalry, is resonant with romance. I was witness to the birth of one such legend, backdropped by the splendour of the Lake Pichola at sunset.

It was a timeless saga that had to be made in precisely seventeen minutes. And so it was. Thanks to the man from London. With a little help from a motley crowd of onlookers who had their own interpretations as to what the tamasha was all about.

The blood-red sun hung like a burnished shield over the crest of the Aravalli hills, turning Lake Pichola into a sheet of crimson. Slanting sunbeams caught the jade-and-amber crystals topping the pinnacles of the palace on the lake – errant shooting stars from the turquoise sky. The towering ramparts on the bank glowed gold in the alchemy of light. Red and gold – apt hues to evoke the legend of Rajputana, Land of Kings, steeped in war and splendour and tales of Rajput valour as it defied Mughal might.

It was here that Maharana Udai Singh shifted his capital from embattled Chittor and, in 1559, founded Udaipur, the city named after him. A hard gallop away is the pass of Haldighati where, in 1576, the flower of Rajput chivalry led by Maharan Pratap Singh was cut down by Akbar's army under Man Singh. It is said that the sough of arrows was like wind through a field of corn and the clash of steel woke echoes in the distant hills.

But the man from London had things other than ancient battles, won or lost, on his mind. He was busy mounting his own campaign. 'Seventeen minutes,' he said. 'That's exactly how long the dusk lasts here at this time of year. I've timed it.'

And in seventeen minutes he had to capture the essence of his story which, in its way, was as much a contemporary romance as had been the sagas celebrated by minstrels in the far pavilions of the past. He was making an advertising film for an international brand of cigarettes. The story, like all good stories of all climes and ages, was simple. It featured the Man: tall, handsome, a patrician presence dominating boardroom or social rendezvous. The Woman: wife of the Man, beautiful, immaculately groomed, a charming consort to her husband. The Driver: spotlessly uniformed, loyal, a trusted family retainer. And last but far from least, the Car: a gleaming symbol of power and success, worthy successor to Chetak, Rana Pratap's legendary steed.

The Car had posed daunting problems of logistics to get on location. Brought up from Bombay by a driver (not to be confused with the Driver) it had undergone several adventures, including an encounter with a wayward buffalo, before reaching Udaipur. Smarting under some imagined slight, the driver, who looked like an out-of-work Hindi-movie heavy, had turned bolshy and had been heard muttering vague but dire threats that caused the man from London to fear he would sabotage the Car, or the film, or both, given half a chance. Crew members had been alerted to keep a close eye on the malcontent.

But now everything was finally set. The cameras, perched in turrets where archers must once have crouched, were ready to roll.

The Car, with the Driver at the wheel and the Man and the Woman in the rear seat, was to be shown winding through country roads in the tawny twilight. Headlights blazing, it would roll down the incline in the dusk, to the jetty where a canopied boat waited. The Driver would open the rear door and the Man and the Woman would get into the boat, in which a hamper would also be placed. The boat would arc out to the illuminated Lake Palace, its silvery wake glowing in the gathering dark. The final shot would show the Man and the Woman, he in dinner jacket and smoking, she in evening gown and radiant, silhouetted against the last ember glow of sunset. Crescendo of music, fade out.

It was beautiful, it was effective, it was neat. It was designed to make you feel that if you had the good taste to smoke the cigarette being promoted, like the Man you too might find yourself with a lovely and loving companion, being driven around a picture-book landscape on the ritziest set of wheels this side of a punk-rock superstar's dreams. The tapestry of association was deftly woven, twining the silken strands of a resplendent past with the crush-proof texture of today.

Trouble was it had all to be wrapped up in seventeen minutes. Seventeen minutes might sound a lot for a sixty-second film. But takes, retakes, and re-retakes gobble up time. Of course, the sequence could be shot in instalments over several sunsets. But it was generally felt that if executed in one fine swoop the exercise could have a graceful spontaneity lacking in a piecemeal endeavour.

So seventeen minutes it was.

The job wasn't made any easier by a large and curious crowd that had collected to watch the shooting. Word had buzzed around the honeycomb of lanes in the old city, and fiercely moustached old men in huge white turbans, women in dazzlingly bright *ghagras* and blouses, balancing water-pots on their heads, and children scampering like spinning tops had swarmed to the lakeside. Tourists, Indian and foreign, swelled the motley throng. Several vendors set up stalls selling tea and peanuts. A *dhobi* laden with bundles of laundry stopped to watch, and a man trundling a block of ice on a handcart parked his vehicle in a corner.

'How are we going to control this lot?' the man from London asked no one in particular.

The crowd hummed with conjecture and comment.

'Is that Sean Connery?' someone asked, spotting the Man and obviously thinking of *Octopussy* that had been filmed in Udaipur some time ago.

'No, no. It's a Hindi movie.'

'That does not sound like a Mercedes engine,' said a skeptical German voice, referring to the spluttering of the generator concealed in the boot of the Car to power the camera for close-ups when the vehicle was in motion.

'It's all an election gimmick, yaar.'

'*Arre nahin,* I tell you it's got something to do with family planning.'

'Please, get back! Get back, please! Lights! Action!' The man from London seemed everywhere and nowhere at once.

The floodlights blazed, the Car rolled down the slope, the camera whirred. The crowd fell silent, spellbound by the making of illusion. But what was real? The watching crowd, the glowing mirage of the palace on the water, the shades of the past beating like pigeons' wings in the thickening air?

Philosophical musings were jostled aside by slapstick as the tracking camera picked up the *dhobi's* bundles of laundry. The man from London shouted, 'Cut! Get those flaming things out of here.' A couple of crew members fell over themselves in the welter of haste and bedsheets to remove the offending objects.

The Car and the camera rolled again. The light sank like sand in the hourglass of dusk. The first stars spangled the indigo sky, vying to upstage the lights of the palace. The first shot was over.

The second shot was hurriedly set up: the Car on the quay, the boat and palace in the background. The models got out to stretch their legs while the lights and the camera were being positioned. 'Let's go,' said the man from London. The Driver opened the Car door for the Woman. Suddenly, a figure reared up in the back seat like a malevolent jack-in-the-box. It was the mutinous driver who had taken the opportunity of the crew's distraction to lay claim to his dispossessed Car by sneaking into it for a quick lie-down. With the man from London snapping at his heels, he was herded from the set, shambling with sheepish villainy.

The camera rolled for the final shot. The Driver handed the Woman and the Man out of the Car and into the boat. The boat curved away from the jetty towards the glittering palace, its wake a gleaming scimitar on the beaten silver of the lake. In the timeless hush before the curtain-fall of night, the puttering of its outboard engine might have been fading hoof-beats galloping into a happily-ever-after sunset.

The seventeen minutes were over.

The crowd, stirred with the sigh of night breeze, began to drift away, voices echoing on ancient stone.

'He was very handsome, no?'

'Yes, she was lovely.'

'You can't tell me that was a Mercedes engine.'

'Wish they'd asked some of us to join in. I wouldn't have minded at all.'

'What was it all about, anyway?'

In answer, the *dhobi* picked up his bundles and walked away, and the man with the handcart looked at the puddle where his ice had been and in which the lights on the quay were reflected in a Cheshire-cat smile.

Rites of passage

In February 1991, we took the seven-day Palace on Wheels (POW) railway tour through Rajasthan. It was a historic trip, in more ways than one. The Gulf War broke out the morning after we began our journey. Which was to be the last journey of the old POW; the original railway coaches in which we travelled have been put into museums and replaced by modern, air-conditioned coaches. One up for comfort, two down for romance.

We had a ticketless passenger on board. Sawai Madho I of Jaipur. Called Sawai (one and a quarter) because according to folklore he was so large (seven feet, 500 lbs) that you could have made one and a quarter maharajahs out of him instead of just one.

On the new, sanitized POW, old SM, as I got to call him after our trip together, wouldn't have stood a ghost of a chance.

Sawai Madho Singh I, formerly of Jaipur, was not amused. All right, so his successors and other fellow princes have been derecognized since his elevation to an even higher sphere. But that's no excuse to expect him to cram his spectral bulk, all seven feet and 500 lbs of it, into a cabin which could do double duty as a waistcoat if they let out a couple of buttons. How's a fellow to breathe, let alone move, in this trim-fit casket? Call it a "Palace on Wheels"? Heads should roll.

Squeezing past old Sawai Madho's ghostly dudgeon, I survey the tiny, two-bunk coupe that Bunny and I are going to travel in for seven days. It must, I reflect, have been pretty hard paneer being a maharajah. Or, for that matter, an avatar thereof in the form of a modern-day tourist bent on being taken for a royal ride down the tracks of history.

Outside, on the Delhi Cantonment platform, liveried staffers in red turbans are ushering garlanded passengers into the Palace on Wheels, which, in the initial stage of its 2400-km odyssey, will be pulled by the turn-of-the-century steam locomotive, the Desert Queen.

'Oh, my Gad!' wails a New World voice. 'They've got Indian showers in the bathroom!' Intrigued by what the voice obviously believes to be some ingenious form of indigenous torture, I peer into a pink-tiled bathroom equipped with a Western-style WC, wash basin, electric geyser. And a steel bucket and mug, presumably the "showers" in anguished question. Beside me, SM gives vent to a wraith-like snort, but whether in amusement or indignation, I cannot tell.

Back in the lounge area provided in each coach (ours, CT-7, was built in the Ajmer workshop in 1911 for the viceroy, so what SM is doing as my self-appointed fellow-traveller I don't know, but there he is) the saloon captain, R.S. Tewari, and his assistant, Shiv Ram, introduce themselves with old-world courtesy. They will be looking after our needs for the duration of the journey. The one-km-long metre-gauge train, Tewari explains, has twelve passenger saloons like ours, all built for regal VIPs in the mid-19th century or early 20th century. Each coach sleeps twelve passengers in two-berth and four-berth cabins. Each coach has two loos, a service area and a private lounge, done in period style. Of a total capacity of 100, the train is carrying eighty-six passengers, almost all foreigners. Not a bad payload, all things considered. Our coach has a Danish party of four, the Jansens; Vir and Rekha Rawlley; Bunny and myself. And of course, SM.

Escorted to the dining saloon (tiny crystal chandeliers, silken napery, red carpet) we are given an excellently cooked and immaculately served meal of Indian and Western fare, which somewhat mollifies SM. Back in CT-7, Bunny opts for the bottom bunk, so I take the top, even narrower. POW begins to roll. And sway. And pitch. And roll some more. I drift into uneasy sleep, am startled awake by a violent shudder. Is it a stray Scud strike from the Gulf War, or an errant B-52? No – only SM turning over in phantom repose. I fall back into fitful slumber.

Day Two

Jaipur. Tewari asks if we slept well. SM and I growl disclaimers in chorus. But at the entrance there are caparisoned elephants *salaaming* welcome with their trunks, more garlands, wailing *shehnais,* whining *sarangis,* all effectively drowning out the busybody fiddling with a transistor blathering about some war, somewhere.

We board a sightseeing bus. Anil Malik, the affably energetic senior manager who has been with POW since its inception in the early 1980s, bids us welcome. POW, he says, is not about luxury; POW is about history. And history often proves to be a bumpy ride, a memorable but less than entirely comfortable rite of passage. SM nods in lugubrious agreement.

With clockwork precision we are whisked through the sights: Hawa Mahal, City Palace, Amber Fort, Nahargarh. Then it's back to POW – where Shiv Ram waits to pour us a nightcap and ask after our day – and to the realization that sometimes the journey is the destination, that to travel historically is better than to arrive.

Not even SM's snores can wake me that night.

Day Three

Chittor. Sunlight on a broken column. Weathered stone that bore blind witness to Padmini's beauty which, reflected in a mirror, maddened Alauddin Khilji and led to the destruction of the citadel. War and repentance in Polaroid snapshot. SM shakes his head sepulchrally at the slings and arrows of outrageous Eros.

Romance, uncrossed by stars or adverse signals, also blossoms on POW. Anil Malik tells us of two young American passengers who, carried away by the staccato serenade of the steel tracks, exchanged moonlit rings at the Taj Mahal and married each other shortly thereafter.

This time around too, there is romance in the air. Maria Louisa seems to be carrying a torch for saloon captain Tewari, and blows him flying kisses across the length of the lounge, much to the amusement of her parents and the consternation of SM who does not approve of such forward behaviour. However, there is no imminent expectation of wedding bells ringing again, thanks to POW. For one thing, Tewari is already happily married. For another, Maria Louisa has yet to celebrate her fourth birthday.

But two impromptu birthday parties do take place on board, amidst a polyglot chorus of congratulations around the cakes presented with compliments of the management. SM joins in the celebratory sing-song in a horrendous French accent. I fear he is catching the infection of cosmopolitan camaraderie which is doing the rounds.

Day Four

Udaipur. The Lake Palace Hotel glinting like a jewel set on the burnished steel of Lake Pichola. Not far away is Haldighati. The silent hills resound with the legends of Rana Pratap.

The guide explains that the Udaipur rulers called themselves maharanas, a cut above maharajahs, not to mention lowly rajas. In a huff, SM stalks off to read about his own family history in the comfortable library attached to the elegantly appointed lounge-cum-bar on POW.

The whistle blows and we are on the move again through an increasingly arid landscape. Desert dust trickles in, parching throats and keeping the bartender busy. SM raises an ironic eyebrow at such effeteness. Venture across the wastes of history and yet jib at the sands of time? Forsooth!

Day Five

Jaisalmer. The fort rising like a golden mirage out of the desert. A copperplate script of camels etched against a blood-red sun. The old *havelis* veiled in carved stone as delicate as a fall of lace.

And in the evening, flickering bonfires illuminate Rajasthani folk dances in which everyone joins, egged on by POW manager Emmanuel Johnson. SM leads the conga line, foot-stomping and hand-clapping with the best of them, as though to the disco born. Maybe this new-fangled democracy business has its points after all.

Day Six

Jodhpur. The brooding hulk of Mehrangarh Fort, its craggy face pocked with the ancient cicatrix of cannon fire. The sprawl of the town far below, like a dizzy throw of blue-tinted dice. The echoing coolness of Umaid Bhawan Palace with its feast of princely memorabilia and equally lavish buffet lunch, of which SM has three helpings. All this and haggling for handicrafts too. At only US $130 per pax per day? Cheap at the price. Even for mere mortals and other commoners.

Day Seven

Bharatpur bird sanctuary, followed by Fatehpur Sikri, Akbar's dream city that had everything but water, a lack of which caused him to desert it a scant seven years after it was founded. Then Agra and the Taj Mahal. Because it is there; the ultimate picture-postcard, entrancing monument to monstrous egotism.

We stay on board, to be taken for a guided tour of POW by SM. All the coaches are equally splendid but some are more equal than others. Like the resplendent Bikaner Saloon, for instance, as SM grumpily admits. He cheers up a bit, however, when we assure him that the two Jaipur coaches are almost as nice.

There is a wistful air of valediction. For soon, not only will we be bidding farewell to POW, but the train itself will be taking its last bow. When this season ends, come the end of March, the old POW will be replaced by a new, streamlined, air-conditioned, dust-free version, currently being built in Madras. It is hoped that the updated POW, which will continue to be run by the Rajasthan Tourism Development Corporation, will extend the current schedule of twenty-six weekly round trips between October and March. The new train will certainly be more comfortable.

As we get down at Delhi, I hear a resigned sigh behind us. We turn to look, but it's only the Desert Queen emitting a last puff of steam.

8

WHEN I SAW LAXMI

Bittu Sahgal in Ranthambhore

This exquisite, small tiger reserve rewrote the natural history of the tiger in the 1980s and showed the world the extent of India's understanding of, and commitment to, large carnivore protection. Today, the park is a popular tiger destination, but it was not always that way. And without strong corrective measures, it may not stay that way.

December 1981: Laxmi sat less than five metres from us on the narrow dirt road leading away from Jogi Mahal towards the exit gate. Two, three, five … ten minutes … and still no sign of her budging. Our delight at finally spotting Ranthambhore's most-loved tigress, after a five-day search, began to turn to mild concern. Not because she was doing anything worrisome, but because she was now … fast asleep.

Long before Ranthambhore had become the kind of fashionable tiger-fest it now is, long before officialdom decided that Jogi Mahal (the quiet, basic but extremely beautiful, red sandstone forest rest house at the base of the Ranthambhore Fort) was off limits to all but government-approved VIPs, this forest was an alternate home for my wife Madhu, myself, and our daughters Miel and Tara.

This is why we had budgeted just forty minutes for the 14 km drive to the Sawai Madhopur station, to catch our train back to Mumbai. The "last day in Ranthambhore" routine was by now a practiced art: a short morning round (spent in silence amidst Raj Bagh's ruins), a lazy breakfast with *langurs* and tree pies for company, hurried packing, a last swing on the banyan tree for the kids before the family piled into the open jeep for the twenty-minute ride to the Sawai Madhopur Station ... with fifteen minutes to spare to catch the Punjab Mail back to Mumbai.

Of course, we had not reckoned with the five-year-old-and-in-her-prime Laxmi. Mistress of all she surveyed, she licked herself, lay on her back, glared at the *langurs* calling furiously from a nearby banyan tree ... only to flop down *again* to sleep.

Sure that we would miss our train, I whispered to my happy kids that we had just been invited to extend our holiday and that I would personally visit their Principal to explain that their delayed return to school after the holidays was the fault of a tigress. Just then, after a fifteen-minute nap Laxmi got up, stretched, yawned ... and disappeared into the grass. Much to the disappointment of our girls, we caught our train at the Sawai Madhopur station with three minutes to spare.

It was my seventh straight year in Ranthambhore. Not a year has gone by since without a "pilgrimage" to the park. But that trip in 1981 was extra special. I had brought with me the first issue of *Sanctuary* magazine to present to the late Fateh Singh Rathore. Ranthambhore's first Field Director, Rathore was the man whose mission to save tigers had motivated me to start the magazine that took over my life.

Standing out in stark contrast to the biological desert that is Rajasthan, Ranthambhore is like a balm, its soothing effect palpable the moment one enters the outer portals of the massive stone ramparts of the fabled Ranthambhore Fort. Constructed to protect kings, the battlements now defend another threatened monarch – the tiger.

The magic begins the moment you get off your train (the preferred mode of travel for most visitors) ... for the pace of life alters as the sights, sounds and smells of rural India take over. The Sawai Madhopur station is virtually as the British left it – red brick and mortar, complete with arches and columns, a touch dirtier and more crowded, perhaps.

I love everything about Ranthambhore. I discovered long ago that it has everything: wildlife, culture, history, religion and (with some luck) heart-pounding excitement.

Five minutes into the gate, as you crest a rise on a shady road, the incredible Ranthambhore Fort looms large and is every bit as impressive as the brochures promise. The park itself sprawls languidly across 824 sq km of contiguous, dry-deciduous forests where the rolling Vindhya and craggy Aravalli Hills meet. This forest supports one of the best-known populations of *Panthera tigris*, the royal Bengal tiger in western India.

The fort, occupied for years by Raja Hamir, lent its name to the tiger reserve. A Hindu battlement, it has seen a series of Muslim rulers try, unsuccessfully, to lay siege to it, including Allauddin Khilji in 1301. The army of the Mughal Emperor Akbar camped here (1558-1569) and the *Akbar Namah* records the menu that the generals were served when they ate under the famous banyan tree, which you can still sit under, at Jogi Mahal.

The park used to be the hunting preserve of the maharajas of Jaipur and many tiger shoots took place here, including an infamous visit in the early sixties when a tiger was set up to be shot by Queen Elizabeth II. Ranthambhore earned sanctuary status in 1958 but only after Project Tiger was launched in 1973, did it really receive the protection it deserved. Placed under the care of Fateh Singh Rathore, by the eighties, the park had earned itself the distinction of being one of the world's best-known tiger forests. And Fateh Singh became a legend in his lifetime.

In his words: 'The best way to find out if a tiger forest is doing well is to check whether its streams, lakes and rivers are healthy. Only then will forest life thrive.' This is what I saw happen in Ranthambhore down the years, as once-dry pools, streams and rivulets began running full all year round. This helped indigenous plants to re-establish themselves. A major side-benefit of this return to health was a groundwater-recharge-service that helped restock farmers' wells in downstream villages.

As with most popular wildlife destinations, most of the "hardcore" action tends to take place in the core, but that is also where hordes of tourists congregate on their "must-somehow-see-a-tiger" drive that kicks up as much dust as it does anticipation. Left to my own devices, I prefer the slower option; driving along the back roads to the distant outposts of Lahpur and Anantpura. I also love driving in the buffer areas to check out the nearby Keladevi, or Sawai Mansingh Sanctuaries. Often I find the greatest pleasure in just sitting atop the ramparts of the fort, where the aerial view is great and the birding even better.

At the eastern limits of the Aravallis, Ranthambhore's rolling hills are clothed with dry deciduous flora, with dhok (*anogeissus pendula*) trees dominating the landscape. Pipal (*ficus religiosa*), banyan (*ficus benghalensis*) and the odd jamun (*syzygium cumini*) groves underscore the fruiting diversity of the park, which is a "must visit" destination on the itinerary of most professional birding organisations around the world.

No trip to the forest goes unrewarded. It might just be a lone sambar stag or female deer suckling a fawn that you see, or perhaps large congregations of deer and wild pig gorging on the aquatic vegetation at Raj Bagh. Heads fully submerged in the water, the deer have often fallen prey to marsh crocodiles. The reptiles can grow to over four metres in the three shallow man-made lakes – Padam Talao, Raj Bagh and Milak Talao – around which most of Ranthambhore's wildlife is concentrated. Here you can spend hours in the company of waders and waterfowl, including snipes, grebes, godwits, sandpipers, geese and ducks. Large and median egrets can sometimes be seen hitching a ride on the backs of half-submerged sambar deer, picking parasites off their backs. The tiger reserve is also a raptor haven.

Visitors cannot stay in the park after nightfall, but early morning and evening drives through Lakarda, Semli and Bakaula often provide the most exciting experiences with hyenas, sloth bears, leopards or tigers. As you make your way out of the park, be sure to look up at the silhouette of the Ranthambhore Fort, within whose walls, residents say, leopard sightings are frequent. And if you dawdle soon after leaving from the Jogi Mahal exit gate at sundown (it's permitted), you might chance upon a ratel, Indian hare, common palm civet or Indian porcupine. Even if you don't see it, you might hear the Eurasian eagle owl or the brown fish owl. Over the years, scores of tourists have even reported seeing tigers and leopards on this dusk drive that belongs to humans during the day and the big cats after dark.

Here's my list of what you could hope see at Ranthambhore:

Mammals: tiger, leopard, sloth bear, ratel, dhole, Indian fox, hyena, caracal, jungle cat, ruddy mongoose, common palm civet, Indian porcupine, sambar, chinkara and nilgai.

Reptiles: marsh crocodile, Indian monitor, Indian rock python, Indian rat snake, common krait, common wolf snake, common kukri, Indian cobra and Indian flapshell turtle.

Birds: long-billed vulture, Bonelli's eagle, rufous treepie, brown fish owl, dusky horned owl, Eurasian eagle owl, painted partridge, Indian peafowl and bronze-winged jacana.

Plants: *anogeissus pendula, prosopis cineraria, acacia nilotica, phoenix sylvestris, sterculia urens, pongamia pinnata, syzygium cumini, ficus religiosa, ficus benghalensis, diospyros melanoxylon, lania coromandelica, ziziphus mauritiana, caparis sepiaria* and *adhatoda vasica* (weed).

9

FATE IN THE BALANCE

Prem Shankar Jha in Bharatpur

2010

If you are sitting in wintry London or New York and planning to visit India the chances are that you will visit Delhi, and having got there, visit Agra, the Taj and Fatehpur Sikri. If you are not a run-of-the-mill tourist, you may go 18 km further and spend a day in Bharatpur. Or if you are a dedicated bird watcher, you may spend a week. For the Keoladeo Ghana Bird sanctuary is 'One of the finest bird parks in the world, a reserve that offers protection to faunal species as well. [Apart from] Nesting indigenous water birds as well as migratory water birds and waterside birds, this sanctuary is also inhabited by sambar, chital, nilgai and boar. More than 300 species of birds are found in this small wildlife park of 29 sq km of which 11 sq km are marshes and the rest scrubland and grassland.'

So says the official guide. Birdwatchers like David Behrens, who first visited Keoladeo in 2001, are even more enthusiastic:

'Imagine a park with thousands upon thousands of birds' he writes. 'Everywhere you look there are ducks, geese, cranes, herons, pelicans, kingfishers, egrets, cormorants, kites, eagles, hawks, falcons, vultures, owls, hoopoes, drongos, mynas and robins – with brief noisy interruptions by the coming and going of the seven sisters – jungle babblers. This is not a silent park. Imagine parakeets as common as sparrows; dawn that starts with the piercing trumpeting of sarus cranes and evenings announced with the mocking howls of jackals and deep raspy hoots of the dusky eagle owl calling to its mate. Chitals abound with stately racks; sambar bucks are seen sparring in jest and the large ungainly nilgai with their funny black and white socks are seen grazing among the cranes. That was my introduction to Keoladeo Ghana National Park – a park that ranks as one of the best waterfowl preserves in the world and [is] also known for its wintering of the rare and endangered Siberian crane.'

Web listings like these keep bringing thousands of Indian and foreign nature lovers to Bharatpur year after year. There is only one problem. There are no birds. There are no marshes. And now most of the trees in the drylands are also gone. The sanctuary is dead. All that is left is an elaborate fiction – the grin of the Cheshire cat that lingers on after it has vanished.

Tourists who ask what happened to the marshes are told by their guides and rickshaw peddlers that the rains were poor this year so the marshes received very little water, which soon dried up. The unspoken implication is that things will be normal if they come another year. This allows the tourism industry and the Indian government to keep its websites unchanged and the travel agents happy but it is a blatant lie. For the marshes are not created by the monsoons, and do not depend upon them for water. And in 2009 Bharatpur had been dry for not one but seven years.

The Bharatpur wetlands were created circa 1750, by Raja Surajmal Jat, the warlike founder of the Bharatpur kingdom who built a dam, the Ajan Bund, at the confluence of two local rivers, the Banganga and the Gambhir. So long as the state was ruled by the Maharaja nothing impeded the annual flow of water into Bharatpur during the monsoons. But some time in the seventies the Rajasthan government built small dams on both rivers for irrigation. This pitted the sanctuary against the farmers and put a question mark over the future of the sanctuary.

The scales got further loaded against the sanctuary by the fact that agriculture and irrigation come under the Rajasthan government while forests and conservation come under the central government. As a result, from the seventies the centre has had to ask the Rajasthan government to release water for the sanctuary every July after the monsoons set in. When the monsoons were poor, or the prospect of rain was uncertain, the park became the first casualty. Despite this, since monsoons tend to be poor on an average only once every four years, and the water was seldom totally denied, the park limped along. The annual visitation of migratory birds slowly shrank, but since no one could estimate how much of this was caused by ecological changes like the increasing use of pesticides, or by losses inflicted by hunters during their long flight from Europe, the slow attrition did not catch the eye of the media.

But even the attenuated marshlands and the thinning inflow of migratory birds is now history. With a single year's exception, the marshes have been dry for the last seven years, because, beginning in 2003 the Rajasthan government ceased to open the sluice gates on the dams in the two rivers in July. The reason was not the monsoons but politics. When the BJP came to power in Rajasthan after a landslide victory in 2003, and the time came for the water to be released in July, the farmers in the irrigated areas went on a fast and said that they would rather die than let the sluice gates be opened. Vasundhara Raje Scindia gave in, and then kept on giving in year after year till the BJP lost the elections in 2008.

So with no water, the park has died. Only ornithologists can explain the full cycle of death, but as an annual visitor to the park since 1982, I have seen its most salient features unveiled by inexorable degrees before me. When there is no water in the marshes in August the magnificent painted storks with their black wings, white breast, orange beak and a Jackson Pollock splash of radiant pink on the abdomen, which are even more emblematic of Bharatpur than the Siberian crane, do not come to roost. Nor do the adjutant and open billed storks, the spoon bills, and several varieties of ibises, for all of them build nests for their eggs only in the branches of trees that stand in pools of water, for this is the only sure way of keeping their chicks safe from snakes and other marauders while they are away foraging for food.

The absence of water has also driven away the grey and purple herons, who, in their statuesque stillness, had replaced the great sarus crane as the sentinels of the Indian paddy fields and marshes, after the latter started to die out because of the effect of pesticides upon their eggs. Needless to say, with no water, snake birds, cormorants, coots, dabchicks, purple moorhens and scores of lesser species whose multitudes I had taken so much for granted twenty years ago that I would barely spared them a glance, were almost totally absent.

And of course the huge flocks of migratory birds, the teals, pintails, widgeons, gadwalls, red headed pochards and shovellers, and the rarer mallards are nowhere to be seen.

Till the spring of this year the forest, at least, had remained unchanged – 29 hectares of dense growths of *acacia, prosopis* and other varieties that thrive in semi-arid regions. But last month even these were gone. On entering the gates of sanctuary, I stopped aghast. In place of the canopy of trees that used to limit visibility and tell us that we had at last come to a patch of land that had not been ravaged by man, there was only sun-baked, dust-white land dotted with scrub and punctuated by an occasional tree, under a glaring yellow sky.

'Where have all the trees gone?' I asked my guide. 'They were all cut down about eight or nine months ago. They were *prosopis juliflora*. It is a thorny, fast growing tree and it was choking the growth of other species. Birds don't sit on it, and occasionally a doe or a fawn injures itself when it steps on a fallen branch. The forest department took the decision to cut them all down in order to give other species of flora a chance to grow.'

'But *prosopis juliflora* is not an exotic species like lantana,' I expostulated. 'Could the forest department not have thinned them to create space, or cleared them from another area deep in the sanctuary to test the impact this had on the growth of other species?' To this I received no answer.

But I did notice one change that the lack of cover had brought about. Birds were now no longer roosting close to the lone road in the sanctuary. One had to look for them with binoculars in the November haze. Last month I had to scour the tiny ponds of water close to the road and around the Keoladeo mandir, that had been created by the government's dozen or so tube-wells, to see a single pair of brahminys, a single pair of sarus cranes, half a dozen ibises, a pair of coots and at last, when I had almost given up hope, a lone duck, sitting so far away that I could not make out anything more than that it was some kind of teal. I saw a black-necked stork at 200 metres. There were no purple moorhens, no spoonbills, no bronze winged or pheasant-tailed jacanas. I saw one darter, and lovingly filmed a single water hen which seemed to be the only bird that had not rediscovered its fear of man.

In the newly minted grasslands stood trees with large, old untidy nests – a reminder of the fact that last year, the first after five dry years, when an extraordinary monsoon in Rajasthan brought water back into the marshes, some painted storks had at last come back to nest in them. But this year, once again, there was not single new nest, and a tomblike silence enveloped a park that used to be raucous with the croaking cries of young storks demanding to be fed. 'The storks came in August,' my guide explained, 'but when they saw no water they flew away.' It was the same story with the ducks and geese. 'Last week we had a flight of bar-headed geese, but they flew around us and continued southwards.'

All of that tragic afternoon my mind kept going back to the eighties and nineties, when I would sit on the Sapan Mori Bund and wait for the birds to come down on the water a few yards from me and start feeding as if I did not exist. I remembered bitterly cold early mornings when I would go out on the Ram Bund to take a boat into the heart of the sanctuary, to watch the painted storks feed their young, and find myself two metres from a bronze winged jacana, in the middle of a thousand tufted pochards, or ten yards from a black-necked stork roosting on an island. I kept remembering being awakened by the hoarse throated cries of sarus cranes – those life-long lovers – that patrolled every open field in the sanctuary in pairs, and the way I used to wait, with straining ears, to hear the long, flute-like double whistled call of the Siberian cranes, one of the most beautiful sounds in the world, which I shall never hear again.

For the Siberian cranes are gone. When David Behrens enthused over them, one last pair was all that was left of the fifty or so that used to come in the sixties and the dozen or more that still made the perilous trip from Siberia in the early eighties. I saw this pair one last time in December 2002, feeding contentedly in the marshes beyond the temple. Then they came no more. It is believed that on their way back to Siberia one of them fell prey to a hunter in Afghanistan or Uzbekistan. The other, one presumes, died of grief. Today, however, you can still see them in all their splendour on the Bharatpur website.

Tragically, as Bharatpur has edged closer to death its fame has continued to grow. In 1985 it was declared a National Heritage site by UNESCO. In the nineties it came to be known as the best place to see the Siberian crane. In the last decade Bharatpur town has flowered. There are luxury hotels set in beautiful, historic gardens. The food has steadily improved both in quality and variety. It is now a marvellous weekend getaway from Delhi. But not for those who wish to see birds.

Postscript
March 2011

In July 2010, after a gap of seven years the Rajasthan government finally opened the sluice gates on its dams and allowed water to come to the parched, and now grassy, former marshlands of Bharatpur. The reason, once more, had less to do with ecology than politics. In 2008, the Congress won the state assembly elections in Rajasthan so once more, the same party ruled the centre and the state. The Rajasthan government did not open the gates in 2009 because the country suffered its worst drought in more than fifty years, but generous rains in 2010 allowed it to fulfil its commitment to the Sanctuary once more.

Bharatpur still did not get more than half of the water it needed and a good part of even that was soaked up by the parched canal and grasslands of what had once been the marsh. But the park authorities were able to flood a quarter of the wetlands. So, at last the birds came back. The most noticeable were the painted storks. For the first time in five years the raucous cries of the young storks filled the air as they demanded food from their parents. As before, spoonbills, adjutant and open billed storks also made their colonies along with the painted storks.

In the drylands of the park, which had been stripped of their covering of *prosopis*, green saplings of *acacia* and other indigenous trees have begun to push their way up towards the sun once more. 'In another five or six years we will have tree cover once again,' a forest ranger remarked to me with satisfaction.

The return of water to the marshes has triggered a furious burst of growth of aquatic plant species. The water in the sanctuary is covered by a thick, almost unbroken, coat of green algae, a highly nutritious food for the birds that nest and feed in and around them. The plenitude of food will attract more birds next year and still more the year after. Left to itself, therefore, nature will restore the balance between flora and fauna in the park. The Siberian cranes will never come back: their annual, much awaited arrival is now a part of history. But the park authorities are in search of eggs from which to hatch Siberian cranes within the park. If they succeed and the cranes are able to breed, Bharatpur will one day have Siberian cranes again, only they will no longer come from

Siberia. But they will at least have saved this beautiful, hauntingly melodious bird from extinction.

But all this still lies in the future. That future will not happen if Bharatpur does not receive its full quota of water every year. The question mark that hangs over this has not been removed. The only way to do this is to meet the needs of the farmers who now rely on the waters of the Karoli dam through tube wells. These underground aquifers upon which these will have to depend will be replenished by the seepage from the marshes. But the central government is still placing its bets upon ferrying water from the Chambal river in pipes, from more than a 100 km away.

10

THE NOWHERE PEOPLE

Royina Grewal on the open road

Since more than half of Rajasthan is made up of arid wasteland which cannot sustain settled populations, nomadism continues to be a way of live for many thousands of people. Whenever I have met any of these people, I have been drawn to them, but I was particularly inspired by the nomadic Rabari herdsman who arrived at my home in Patan one day to deliver my surprise birthday present: two camels!

The herdsman had been on the road for months, and his quest for fodder would keep him on the move for several more. Constantly faced with the reality of drought, he had no option but to wander. He spoke longingly of his desert homeland: the vast expanses, the silences and the muted beiges and browns that are so soothing to the eye, unlike the strident greens of other places.

'The desert is like a beautiful woman,' he said dreamily, 'whose beauty and purity shines through. She does not need ornaments of greenery.'

The Rabari's reminiscences triggered off a flood of memories, for as a child I'd had an almost obsessive fascination with the desert. I had eagerly listened to adult conversations about the desert encroaching on Delhi, when trees had been planted feverishly and green belts established to arrest its progress. The shifting desert became for me a real, living entity, a menacing creature that men sought to entrap in greenery. My obsession had persisted even after my marriage. I was entranced by Ajit's description of a trip he had once made to Jaisalmer, when the road he had taken had been obliterated by the desert: dunes on the left of the road in the morning had shifted to the right by evening.

My imagination was stirred further when a group of Gaduliya Lohars came into our region. These nomadic blacksmiths travel through Rajasthan in beautifully worked metal carts, stopping off to tend to the needs of the villages they pass. To me they symbolize the quixotism of the Rajputs. Originally the armourers of Chittor, famed for the strong, sharp blades they forged, they abandoned the legendary citadel after it was conquered by the Mughals, swearing never to return until it was recaptured. At Independence, the Gaduliya Lohars were offered land and the opportunity to settle, but most preferred their wandering life. Now, many years later, they regret their decision. If they were settled their children could go to school, but their numbers have multiplied and it is too late to make good the promised land allotments.

The Gaduliya Lohars' camp site, squeezed into a vacant piece of land between the road and our village, was crowded with their distinctive carts, every surface covered in handworked brass. The carts were home to nearly thirty families, and had been used to travel around the country for generations. There were *charpoys* in many of them, and they were surrounded by goats, dogs and bright-eyed children.

Guler Singh was working the bellows beside the cart closest to the road, his seamed face shaded by an intricately coiled red turban. He wore an old plaid shirt, a fluid *dhoti* and lots of jewellery: brass earrings, necklaces of shining glass beads and a large beaten-brass bangle. He barely looked up at me as he worked on the griddle he was making over glowing coals. From time to time he puffed energetically at his bellows, studying the flame and the colour of the iron, and when both were perfect he signaled to his very pregnant wife to pound the iron with a huge mallet. Iron rang on iron, until he stopped her with a sign and heated the griddle some more. She pounded again, and the process continued until both were satisfied. Only then did Guler Singh acknowledge my presence.

'It was a crucial stage,' he apologized, straightening up painfully. 'The heating must be just right, and so it was vital that I concentrate on the exact colour of the coals to gauge the temperature. I have to be confident that what I produce is of fine quality. We still pride ourselves on excellence, even if we no longer make swords and spears and shields and arrow shafts.'

He paused, squinting at a match as he lit a *bidi*. 'Now we make axes and ploughshares, agricultural implements and household utensils,' he said wryly. 'It's a far cry from our days of glory but at least we survive.'

But I knew that the living they made was far from adequate. With the increasing use of mass-produced, factory-made implements and utensils, few people now bought their wares.

'Is it not time to return to Chittor?' I asked. 'Your ancestors' vow is history. Can't it be set aside?'

Guler Singh drew himself erect. 'The word of a Rajput is a pledge for all eternity,' he declared fiercely.

Time was money and food for the family, I realized, and so I reluctantly made my farewells.

'Why don't you come back and visit us later? Guler Singh suggested. 'Nights are best, because we are free from work.'

'But come within the next couple of days,' his wife warned me, 'because then we leave for Tijara.'

An idea began to form in my mind, and I asked if I could travel at least part of the way with them. 'In our carts!' they laughed incredulously. I persisted and they finally agreed.

I arrived on the designated day to find their carts being loaded into small trucks. 'What on earth is going on?' I asked Guler Singh's wife.

'We're moving,' she said, 'as we discussed. Now which truck are you going to take?'

I spluttered with confusion. 'But where are the bullocks ... the bullocks to pull the carts?'

'What bullocks? They're far too expensive for the likes of us. And they've got to be fed, you know, and that too costs money. That's why we have the trucks. Now, choose which one you'd like.'

I stood by, stupefied. This wasn't the journey I had wanted to make. Bullock carts in trucks! An entire way of life was passing and we didn't even know it.

❖

In Chittor, I wake to the sound of a passing train and am reminded of the caravans that once passed through this region. 'Many of them were Banjaras,' Dev, a friend of a friend who has offered to show me around town, tells me over breakfast. 'Many important trade routes passed through Chittor, and Banjara caravans creaked through this land for centuries.'

'What characterizes the Banjaras, and almost all nomadic people, is their strong cohesion,' Dev continues. 'I suppose they have only each other to rely upon.'

Listening to Dev, it occurs to me that the Banjaras' personal bonds reinforce their identity, and are their anchor in the absence of physical roots. I had always maintained that much of the enjoyment of travel comes from the absence of responsibility and commitment; perhaps the human condition cannot survive without such ties after all.

Dev interrupts my thoughts: 'The Banjaras are said to be the ancestors of Europe's Gypsies.'

I snap to attention.

'Some years ago I met a scholar here who was researching the connection. Anthropologists have established that the Gypsies moved out from north-west India in waves and were in Persia by about the 11th century. Apparently their spoken language, Romany, originates in Sanskrit and also has close connections to various Rajasthani dialects. There are many words in common.'

Dev tells me that he knows some Banjaras who have settled close by and we decide to pay them a visit. Dev's idea of "close by" is at least two hours away, and we drive endlessly, swooping up hills and gliding down into fertile valleys. A river flows beside the road, its sparkling blue waters framed by white sand, dark rocks and distant hills.

He fills me in on the Banjaras as we drive. They often hid their money and valuables along their route, in a small pit in the forest or in a hollow tree trunk; frequently, knowledge of the location of a Banjara's cache would die with him, and hidden treasure continues to be discovered all over Rajasthan, especially in the area around Chittor.

Some Banjara tribes supplied the commissaries of great armies, carrying grain on their bullock carts. Others traded in salt from the great salt lakes between Udaipur and Jodhpur; the people of Rajasthan once preferred its flavour over sea salt, but now no one wants it any more, preferring to buy refined salt in packets instead. Unable to move with the times, these less affluent tribes have had difficulty finding alternative employment. Some sell trinkets to the villages; others have wound up as labourers working for a daily wage at construction sites all over India.

As we draw up in front of the hamlet, I notice a girl in her early twenties combing her hair with sensuous enjoyment. There is a boldness about this girl, an absence of false modesty, and a vibrant sexuality. An older man comes out of one of the houses; he recognizes Dev, and greets him loudly. The girl hastily draws her *odhni* over her head and disappears. Kishan Ram is a hearty man, with a coiled moustache and a turban. We are lucky to find him, as he has only just returned from Gujarat. He purchased eight cows and bullocks and sold them in a village near Chittor for a hefty profit.

'A long journey,' I remark.

'That is nothing,' says Kishan Ram. 'In the old days, armies campaigned the length and breadth of India. And they required supplies: grain, ghee, fodder for their animals and thousands of items for personal use. So we were on the move the year round, procuring and delivering supplies. There was no railway, you understand,' he explains carefully, as though speaking to a child, 'the railway came later. We used to carry goods from Karachi in the west to Kanyakumari on the very tip of the peninsula.'

'A dangerous life,' I comment.

'We are a brave people,' he shrugs, 'completely unafraid. Even thieves and robbers are afraid of us.'

'For additional protection,' Dev adds wryly, 'many Banjaras persuaded bards to travel with them. Even the most villainous brigand would never harm a *charan*, who was regarded with an almost superstitious awe.'

In a culture where the written word was uncommon, every detail of life was stored in the memory of the bard, whose interpretation of events could either exalt a man to the heights of heaven or stain his reputation forever. The *vish*, the poison of the bard, was feared more than the sharpest sword; his verses could destroy honour, that most precious of all commodities.

Kishan Ram, a little put out by this diminishing of Banjara courage, tells a rather far-fetched story of his people's origins. 'It is said that we were once Rajputs. When they gave their women to the Mughals in marriage we were ashamed, and so we left and came to live in the jungle. *Ban* means forest, *jara* is a wanderer.'

But that is all in the past. Kishan Ram's eldest son is a doctor. 'He practices in Gwalior. My younger son is a basketball champion. He is currently doing his MA.' He sighs heavily. 'Both the boys have gone away from our society.'

A group of women standing outside a hut on the other side of the clearing gesticulate to me to join them. 'It would have been inappropriate for us to come to where the men are,' Jamuna says in explanation.

Jamuna is Kishan Ram's wife and the three other women with her are her daughters. Each is laden with clanking jewellery. I remark on this to Jamuna, and she summons her eldest daughter and shows me each piece. There is a two-kilo silver necklace around her neck, a girdle that weighs one kilo around her hips, anklets of one and a half kilos each, plus miscellaneous bangles, bracelets, rings and earrings! 'Contrary to what most people believe, jewellery is not purely decorative. The weight of an earring, girdle or anklet is believed to exert subtle pressure on the nerves which promotes the wellbeing of the body's internal organs.'

The young women do not travel with their husbands, as there are the fields to take care of. 'Surely your sons-in-law don't need to travel any more? The income from agriculture must be good,' I say to Jamuna, gesturing at the healthy crops that surround the settlement.

'Of course agriculture is profitable, the land is rich. But the men have travelled for so many generations. For them to stay in one place is to get claustrophobia of the soul.'

✧

We drive on deep into the interior, passing through wild but fertile country. I see fields girded by live cactus fences, and where there is water the crops are abundant. Vast areas of common land are liberally sprinkled with stunted trees, their contorted shapes replicating hidden root structures which probe in search of precious water. Dev has suggested a visit to a hamlet where Kalbelias have settled. These people are hard to define because their occupations have shifted with the centuries. They are itinerant entertainers, snake charmers, traders, mendicants and herbal healers, but also petty thieves. Naturally, they are nomadic.

We drive up to a small group of mud huts in a flurry of dust. The poverty is palpable. Some goats browse upon the bushes on the outskirts of the settlement, devouring every leaf in sight. A couple of donkeys stare sleepily into the distance, and men lounge on *charpoys* puffing contentedly on *bidis*.

'These people are expert hunters and trappers,' Dev tells me. 'And their dogs are particularly skilled in hunting.'

I look doubtfully at the bitch standing beside a man with an ancient muzzle-loader. She does have nice lines but stands legs splayed, ears and tail drooping, gazing in a sleepy, lackluster way at nothing in particular. The man catches my expression and grins, his eyes shifting quickly from the black bitch to me. He bends down to whisper something to her, and she pricks up her ears, muzzle twitching and alert eyes darting in every direction. At another quiet command she streaks out of the settlement, her long legs and streamlined body covering the distance rapidly.

The man laughs at my astonishment. 'We train our dogs to look stupid and lazy. They are among our most valuable assets, we never go anywhere without them.'

These Kalbelias used to sell the spindles they made, but few villagers spin their own thread these days and demand has fallen. A familiar theme. Now they travel from village to village selling various items of rural use: bamboo to support thatched roofs, grinding stones, red ochre for the paint which decorates many homes. They travel in large groups carrying their belongings on donkeys or in bullock carts, and while the men sell their wares their women sing and dance.

As with all nomadic tribes who wander among settled people, the Kalbelias are regarded as pariahs. Whenever there is a crime the police suspect them first. When Dev first came to this village, the Kalbelias thought he was from the police: the men vanished into the hills and the women locked themselves in their houses.

The women have gathered too and are listening into the conversation. Sita, a small, slender woman with a girl hanging on to her *lehanga,* joins in. 'Life is hard,' she says, 'but to be overcome by its difficulties is to be buried in misery. So, in the evenings when the moon is shining, we take out our drums and we sing and dance. We celebrate life.'

'After all,' says the man, 'we are *kal belia,* conquerors of time, of death.'

At the smallest prompting from me, a big drum is produced and tapped experimentally. Sita begins to sing a rather shrill song. Other women gather around her, clicking their fingers in time to the music. Unable to resist the rhythm, they begin to dance with graceful, flowing wrist movements and a rhythmic stamping of feet. Dust rises in great clouds, skirts swirl and the dance gathers momentum as more women and several little girls join in.

I have seen Kalbelias dance at stage-managed festivals or in hotels, their movements carefully choreographed; but nothing compares with the joyous spontaneity of this performance. If *I* was searching for the origin of the Gypsies, my money would be on these people rather than the Banjaras.

✧

On the way to Ghanerao the insistent rhythm of drums draws me to a small hamlet, a settlement of the Garasiya tribe, much to the disapproval of Udai Singh who is driving me around. 'They are a feckless people,' he says. 'They can't be relied upon, even as manual labourers, because as soon as they have enough to fill their bellies for the next couple of days, they stop work. Sing and dance, jumping around like monkeys – that is all they really like to do.'

I had seen a group of young Garasiya women near the temple at Ranakpur that morning. They were sitting on a wall, dangling their feet and laughing among themselves. They had radiated a feeling of festivity, of joy in life.

The small settlement is surrounded by fields and lit by a roaring fire. To the beating of drums, men and women dance together before the fire; it is an energetic yet sensual dance, with pronounced pelvic movements by the women and much posturing by the men. Full *lehengas* flare and the firelight gleams on the women's silver jewellery.

I get talking to a worker from Udaipur's Tribal Research Institute, who is a less than sympathetic spectator. 'I am working towards reforming these people,' Madan tells me with a troubled intensity. 'Their marriage customs are very disturbing. Boys and girls meet and mix freely at dances like this and they choose their own spouses. The girls are very forward and they initiate proceedings by offering the boy they like a small gift.'

If the boy is similarly inclined, they arrange to run away. They surface some days later, inform the parents on both sides and the boy pays a bride price to the girl's father – usually around two thousand rupees. If there is enough money to pay for a ceremony, a marriage takes place; if not, the couple live together until the boy can afford the ritual and feast that must follow.

'So what's wrong with that?' I ask. 'It seems a most sensible practice.'

'It is the lowest form of marriage. We call it marriage by capture,' Madan replies, outraged. 'And they don't value the marriage tie.

It's usually the woman who leaves; when she tires of a man, even if he is doing his best, she marries another. Only animals change their mates like this!'

Garasiya men, therefore, are very careful to keep their women happy and avoid offending them at all costs. Someone once said that the status of women is one of the best indicators of a progressive society – in which case, the Garasiyas win hands down.

As they dance, the young people sing about the beauties of nature, starry nights, the moon, the hills and the restless rivers. Movements become more languorous, and as we head back to the car I hear a peal of girlish laughter.

❖

We are on a narrow road outside Jodhpur leading to flat, open, sandy land. 'This is Bishnoi country,' my guide Mr Tak tells me. 'You can tell by the *khejri* trees in the fields, which unlike other areas have not been trimmed for fodder.'

Bishnois worship the *khejri*, and like so many other Indian beliefs, the tradition is based on sound commonsense. The deep-rooted *khejri*, one of the few species that survive in the desert, provides fodder for cattle and precious shade for houses. Its beans, *sangria*, are a nutritious food, and are dried for eating in summer when little else is available. The tree also binds the soil and absorbs some of the impact of the violent desert storms.

About 250 years ago, one of the maharajas of Jodhpur ordered that a certain number of *khejri* trees be cut for his furnace. The Bishnois opposed the felling, and many wrapped their arms around the trees and insisted that they would die to protect them. The maharaja's laboureres went ahead and cut down the trees, killing the 360 men and women who clung to them. An annual ceremony commemorates the sacrifice of these early conservationists.

Environmentalists the world over are now reaching similar conclusions to those arrived in the 5th century by Jambhaji, the founder of the Bishnois. The word *bishnoi* refers to the twenty *(bis)* proscriptions *(noi)* he established which included sacred prohibitions relating to the cutting of wood, the taking of any life, the gelding of bulls and the drinking of unfiltered water.

Bishnois fiercely protect their animals and birds and do not allow hunting. A memory surfaces of a trigger-happy teenaged cousin who, while driving through Bishnoi country, shot a brace of partridge for the pot. In seconds he was surrounded by an angry mob armed with staves and pitchforks.

A chinkara gazelle bounds across the road, followed by another dozen, wagging their tails in excitement. 'The Bishnois call them *cheenk* – sneeze,' Mr Tak tells me, 'because of their distinctive call.' Plump partridge peck in the sand, and a big blue bull stands among the trees on the side of the road a little further on. He bounds away in disapproval at our intrusion, followed by his harem that has been waiting in the undergrowth for him to signal that the coast is clear. Small herds of black buck leap through the fields of flowering mustard, their distinctive spiral horns laid flat across their backs and their dark upper bodies gleaming in the sun.

Mr Tak directs the driver onto a smaller track which leads to a cluster of huts surrounded by trees. The huts sit around a central clearing of packed mud, and the façade of each is washed with lime and decorated with paintings of birds and animals. Four women are sitting in the clearing, combing each others' hair. They welcome Tak Sahib as an old and favoured friend, smiling their pleasure. He hugs the youngest woman, pats another on the head and smiles happily. 'I love these people,' he tells me. 'I have been coming here before this one was born.' The girls are all very lovely, with clear, fair skins, well-defined features and large, luminous eyes.

One of the sons of the family, Jamua, returns. He shares the extreme good looks of his sisters, and a story I have heard about Bishnois comes to mind. In order to improve their stock, the Bishnois would choose a boy of about sixteen or seventeen with an outstanding physique, good looks, fair complexion and fine bones. He was called the *nassal sudhar*, the one who would improve the breed. All his sexual needs were taken care of by the village women, and when he left his shoes outside a hut, the woman's husband would graciously stay away. When a new bride came to the village, the *nassal sudhar* probably had first right.

The stud was killed at around the age of twenty-four, possibly with an overdose of opium, in order to avoid any subsequent paternity problems. The custom has, of course, long ceased, but its effects are visible in the good looks of most Bishnois, among whom there is still a relaxed attitude towards sexual morality. Even today, it is common for a man to come home and find a pair of shoes outside his front door, a signal for him to temporarily retire to another house.

If this handsome family is anything to go by, the Bishnois' racial engineering has been tremendously successful. We gather over the inevitable cup of tea, and I ask if their reverence for the *khejri* tree extends to replanting.

'During the mela that honours the martyrdom of our ancestors,' one of the girls, Koeli, explains, 'each Bishnoi must plant five *khejri* trees. The government supplies them to us free of cost. We plant some at the temple and the rest at home.'

Naturally, the *khejri* is never used for firewood. 'Earlier, there were fewer of us, so dried cow-dung cakes were sufficient for our fuel needs, supplemented by the odd dried tree,' Jamua explains. 'But now populations have grown, and we are forced to burn wood as well. But we only use useless species, the ones that don't allow grass to grow.'

'We also do not cut the *kair* bush,' Koeli adds, 'because from this we get the *kair* berry which we dry and cook with yoghurt. Nor do we cut the *rohira*, as it resists termites and can survive well in the desert which is the kingdom of the termites.'

I ask if there are any particular beliefs that impel them to protect the deer that I have noticed in such large numbers. 'According to our teachings,' Jamua explains, 'if you do good deeds, you will be reborn a deer.'

'That is why we treat the animals as our guests,' his mother adds. 'They eat almost half our crops, but what does that matter? We have the other half.'

'There is a song about it,' Koeli prompts her brother. Jamua obliges and recites some of it.

Oh God, after my death don't make me an ox or a horse, they have to work too hard.
Don't make me a frog either, or I'll have to spend my life croaking in a well.
Don't make me a dog, please, otherwise I'll be forced to roam the streets and bark.
Not a pig either, Lord, for pigs live in dirt.
Make me a deer, oh Lord, a free spirit of nature, but please, oh please, only near a Bishnoi village.

❖

Late one afternoon in Jodhpur, I decide on an impulse to take a drive into the countryside. I am not a city person and much as I enjoy Jodhpur, I feel stifled. I ask Udai Singh to take the same road I had been on with Mr Tak, and a group of women sitting by the side of the road wave us to stop. They are Rabaris, I gather from the white bangles one wears up to her armpit, and they want a lift home.

The three women, a mother around my age and her two daughters, hop happily into the car and squeeze onto the back seat together. The girls are around sixteen and eighteen, with glowing, flawless skins. They bounce excitedly on the seat, talking and giggling in shrill, high voices.

'They have never sat in any vehicle before,' Tungli, their mother, apologizes, 'not even a bus.'

Tungli's eyes contain all the browns of the earth: the sand, the camel, the gazelle, the fox. In addition to her arm bracelets, four sets of silver earrings dangle from her stretched ear lobes. Tattoo marks in elaborate designs that simulate jewellery are worked onto her wrists and the backs of her hands. What especially catches my fancy are the gold motifs embedded into her few remaining teeth.

I admire her ornaments and she smiles in pleasure. A bond forms between us that bridges the huge gap that separates our lives. The family have five goats, about twenty camels and 'six twenties' of sheep, she tells me. I am charmed by her ability to compensate for her ignorance of larger numbers, a skill I'm sure she applies with competence to the managing of her family's affairs.

Since the men are away for most of the year, Tungli copes entirely on her own. She sows and harvest the family's fields, and after putting aside enough to see the family through the year, markets the surplus produce. She deals with rapacious officials and lecherous upper-caste men who eye her daughters.

Tungli's hut sits in a small compound surrounded by a low mud wall. There are no windows, and the hut is thus insulated from Marwar's extreme climate. There is no chimney either, but the smoke from the wood fire that Tungli lights to makes us a cup of tea escapes through chinks in the thatch.

I ask Tungli if she has ever accompanied her husband on the annual migration. She used to, she tells me, but the situation has become difficult now. There are conflicts with farmers who now regard the Rabaris with antipathy; previously they would pay them to graze their herds in fallow fields because of the animals' rich droppings. There is also often trouble with the forestry department, which forbids entry into protected areas. And then there is harassment from government officials, because Rabaris now have to obtain permits to enter different states and pay a fee based on the size of their herd. The herdsmen frequently fudge their numbers and so there is more trouble.

'As a result of the many difficulties in migration,' she says, 'we have begun to realize that the old ways will soon cease altogether. So it is important that our children go to school, to prepare them for a different life. Which brings added importance to us women staying at home.'

Tungli has anticipated the future: Rabari men will probably get jobs with the Camel Corps of the Border Security Force. They are expert trackers, able to recognize and track individual animals by their hoof prints, and are also skilled rural vets. I think with sorrow of the inevitable cessation of their nomadism, which will change Rabari lifestyles and dilute their identity forever. I am reminded of the changes that I have constantly encountered in Rajasthan, of vanishing lifestyles that endured for centuries, and I fear the consequences of the settling of these people: more pressure on the existing land, more unemployment, more frustration. The price of progress.

◆

In Bikaner I enquire about the Siddh Naths, a religious sect whose incredible austerities are said to give them supernatural powers. Their fire dance is both a spectacular feat of endurance and a manifestation of this power.

I have heard strange stories about the Siddh Naths. Their cult is ancient and has been associated with occult practices. They performed miracles and attracted hordes of followers; they also foretold the future and wielded enormous temporal power through Rajas who were their devotees.

I discover that one of the secular heads of the cult lives in town and make an appointment to meet him. When I arrive at his home in a small dusty lane, I interrupt the women of the family at their morning meal. Sai Nath, the patriarch of the family, occupies a small room on the second floor of the house. A single bed and rows of book shelves are the only furniture; a folding chair has been set up for me. The old man sits cross-legged on his bed, wrapped in a blanket; he is a big man, physically powerful, with enormous hands. With him is his grandson, Yashpal, a bright-eyed ten-year-old.

'He too is a fire dancer, like myself,' says the old man. 'I used to be very good. I also developed some choreography for the dance to make it look more spectacular.'

The fire dance, according to Sai Nath, is performed only by those who have stilled the mind and achieved various powers, including a purity that protects them from fire. The lore of the Siddh Naths is replete with stories of the supernatural prowess of adepts who emerged unscathed from pits of flame, escaped from barred prisons and performed other feats to demonstrate the dominance of mind and the protection of the gods. Today's fire dance is a pale imitation of the real thing.

The children of the Siddh Naths are taught the technique from a very early age. 'The feet must be kept firm and tight, and only the soles should be in contact with the coals. Fire dancing is really a question of experience, balance and complete concentration. You must tread lightly on the fire, and it is essential that the feet be kept in constant motion. Even when the dancer is stationary, his feet must keep moving, even imperceptibly.'

A ring of wet soil is laid around the fire and kept damp. The dancers walk around the fire on this wet earth before treading on the fire, and the cold seeps deep into their bones to help them withstand the heat. On the opposite side of the fire hangs a pink flag with peacock feathers tied to it. 'We focus on this when we cross the embers,' the old man tells me.

The dancers are extremely careful about what they eat. All their food is cooked in the purest ghee, and they eat only the best quality vegetables and dals. On the day of the dance they eat only a *dal halwa* – food which gives them strength and contains nothing that could even minutely disrupt their equilibrium.

During the fire dance, the dancers sing songs based on mantras that induce a heightened state of being, and drums beat for added courage. Most dancers walk across the fire in a quick series of steps, but there are some who are able to stand for long periods among the flames. 'Even we are astonished,' Sai Nath says with reverence, 'we have to acknowledge that there is something extra at work. Something from the old days, some special power.'

✧

I've seized upon the idea of going to the desert around Tanot, a military outpost near the Pakistan border. My car has finally broken down, and it will take a few hours to repair it; and because Tanot is as close to the border as civilians are allowed to go, there is a curfew there at night. All things considered, it would be sensible to postpone the trip until the morning.

But I have the bit firmly in my teeth, and I am determined to go. I make several calls to various taxi drivers, and eventually an ancient jeep rolls up, with a driver of similar vintage. Udai Singh eyes the conveyance dubiously and writes down the registration number. 'If you are not back by nine,' he says loud enough for the other driver to hear, 'I'm coming to find you.'

It's a much longer drive than I had anticipated, but that's also because Rafique Mia, the driver, watches his speedometer carefully and keeps below the 40-km mark. I urge him repeatedly and politely to step on it; he nods sagely and continues at the same pace.

Rafique honks frequently as we pass the settlements, which are usually not much more than clutches of huts. 'I have friends in these places,' he explains, 'and it's important to stay in touch. If I have a breakdown on this long and lonely stretch, I'll have them to fall back upon for help.'

I scan the horizon eagerly for my first sight of sand dunes, and slowly the landscape begins to change. First hillocks and then great mountains of sand tower on both sides of the road and appear to stretch for miles. But every single one of the dunes has been planted. It would seem that the expanses of treeless sand I have seen pictured so many times are not in my karma. But my initial disappointment gradually gives way to the realization that before the planting, this must have been a terrifying land: the dunes would have shifted regularly; paths navigable one day would have vanished the next. And for those who survived the terrain, there were the bandits, whose own survival relied on looting and killing. There was never any romance – only incredible hardship, terror and death. I realize the foolishness of using a single photographic image as an icon for an entire geographical area; and what is more, I realize the stupidity of romanticizing such an image.

We drive on endlessly without passing a single person – an eerie feeling. The dunes are higher now, and as we reach the top of one of the highest, the landscape I've been searching for unfolds: for as far as the eye can see, there is nothing but an immensity of sand beneath a white sky. The sun is reflected off the sterile expanse, and the glare sears me, body and soul. The grand austerity of nature's bounty withdrawn cuts humanity down to size. I am intoxicated by the terrible beauty before me.

I think back to the nomads I have met on my travels, and their search for words to describe the desert. It is like the goddess, one of them had said, enormously beautiful but fierce and terrifying. Nothing could survive out here, and for the first time I truly appreciate the fortitude of the Rajputs. It was this harsh land that bred the endurance and courage they needed to conquer further handfuls of dust from which they could scratch a living.

We finally reach a small valley, with a temple and a tiny lake. Rafique grunts in satisfaction: 'We are getting close to Tanot now.'

My destination turns out to be a small settlement: just a few tents and a couple of barrack-type structures. Some soldiers are clustered around a tank near a small temple, sluicing off the day's dust before joining the evening worship. Their initial reticence disappears when I reveal my army background, and they slowly begin to tell me about their duties, which are largely concerned with preventing smuggling across the border.

'The problem is that the local people don't even think of their activities as smuggling,' says a man with sharp Rajput features and the usual handlebar moustache. 'They have carried goods back and forth across the desert for centuries. They've never thought of the desert as belonging to India or Pakistan: it is simply their homeland. The concept of a border means nothing to them.'

'The shepherds are big offenders,' adds another soldier, 'because they get excellent prices for their sheep and camels in Pakistan. And they often bring back opium and heroin. They have been involved in the opium trade for centuries.'

Suddenly, the temple bells ring out for the evening worship, and almost simultaneously the staccato chatter of rifle fire begins: a practice session has commenced nearby. The sun sinks slowly towards the horizon, and the sky is washed with saffron, the colour of renunciation, the colour worn by Rajput warriors to their final battle. The drab desert absorbs the radiant sunset, and I decide to head back to Jaisalmer before the indigo tones of twilight seep into the land.

On the final leg of our long drive we are cocooned in the velvety softness of the still night. Suddenly, in the distance, I see a collage of tiny pinpricks of light. We are not alone on the road anymore: hundreds of milling woolly black bodies block our path, and the silence is broken by the nasal whistle of the Rabari herdsmen who are trying to urge their flocks off the road.

As we draw closer, the melee of agitated shadows, surreal and elongated, is caught in the headlights of our jeep. The herdsmen are headed towards Tanot and beyond, and I am instantly caught up in the romance of their wandering lives. I wish I could cross the border with the herdsmen and see what lies on the other side. Once more I am seduced by nomadism: that fluid life, where it is possible to live out each fragment of time, each detour, without concern for conclusions.

11

THERE'S A SPARROW IN MY PURI!

Nilanjana S. Roy in Surajgarh

On the dusty road to Surajgarh, the tiny village from where one begins the journey into Rajasthan's Shekhavati region, I'm thinking of feasts past and present.

With the Surajgarh Fort opening its doors to guests, tourists jaded by camel safaris and an overdose of dal-baati have an unusual lure: a chance to sample royal dishes prepared by HRH Vikram Singh of Sailana, whose eldest daughter, Tikarani Shailija, manages the hotel along with her husband, Tikaraj Aishwarya.

Royal kitchens were the forerunners of today's massive restaurant chains and banquet halls, except that they had superior menus. If the pleasure-loving Kaiqabad could serve a thousand dishes at a feast in honour of his father, Maistre Chiquart would set down the basics necessary for feast preparation two centuries later in France: a hundred well-fattened cattle, a hundred and thirty sheep, a hundred and twenty pigs; and for each day during the feast, a hundred piglets, both for roasting and for other needs, and sixty salted large well-fattened pigs for larding and making soups. After this, suggested Chiquart, a good chef would turn his attention to kids, lambs, calves and 'two thousand head of poultry', an equal variety of fish and 'for each day of the said feast, six thousand eggs'.

And in China, the beautiful but gluttonous Lady Dai would have ample provisions buried with her so that she would never be hungry in death: pheasant bones, ox ribs, wheaten food, lotus root strips, cakes of sticky rice and ample wine and broth were found in her grave.

But Surajgarh's local population of cows, camels and goats seems to be safe enough. We arrived mid-week, and while the hotel has anywhere from forty to eighty-odd guests dropping by for the Sailana Food Festival on the weekends, it's fairly quiet at other times. The most raucous inhabitants at the hotel are a beautiful flock of Alexandrine parrots, who will spend the next two days supervising the cooking arrangements, like medieval courtiers offering up their "wah-wahs".

It takes me a while to register that the soft-voiced gentleman who asks anxiously whether our journey was comfortable and whether we'd like a little nimbu-pani is the Maharaja of Sailana himself. HRH has a tendency to wince if you call him by any of his royal titles, and has an absent-minded air that reminds you of Lord Emsworth of Blandings, but he sparkles on the subject of food.

The Sailana kingdom's fascination with good food stretches back for three generations. HH Vikram Singhji's grandfather, HH Sir Dilip Singhji, learned to cook late in life. 'The royal family had gone travelling, and there was some sort of muddle – the cooks got left behind on the road, so when they arrived at their destination, my grandfather discovered that not a single person in their entourage knew even the basics of cooking,' says Vikram Singhji. Sir Dilip Singhji was in his fifties then, but from that week, he taught himself how to cook – maharaja-style, as Vikram Singhji will demonstrate for us in the afternoon.

If you're a maharaja, you cook in much the fashion of a top professional chef. The actual preparation is carried out by the kitchen staff; a suitable balcony or verandah is located, and *sigris*, rugs, vessels, spices and key ingredients are brought out in procession while HH waits in royal splendour. He makes two relatively simple – but extraordinarily tasty – kababs for us, seated in the open-air courtyard at the top of Surajgarh fort while Naren, the head chef, watches and takes notes. The goolar kabab is made to resemble the shape of the local figs; a fish tikka is wonderfully light, with a crisp coating. These, it turns out, are just a taste of what we can expect.

As he makes arrangements for what seems to be a formidably elaborate dinner, Vikram Singhji discusses Sailana's legendary hospitality. His grandfather was famous for his banquets, which featured such *amuse-gueules* as puris of a certain thickness, cooked very rapidly: when the guest of honour punctured the top of a puri, a live sparrow would fly out. Sailana sat at the crossroads of Madhya Pradesh and Rajasthan, and Sir Dilip Singhji developed a fascination with the cuisine of other royal houses. The best-known legend about Sailana revolves around Sir Dilip Singhji's spice box and jewellers' scales. Knowing that the chefs who travelled with their royal patrons would never reveal the exact proportion and number of spices used in a particular dish, Sir Dilip Singhji would present them with his spice box and tactfully retreat from the kitchen. The chefs would finish their cooking, confident that they had revealed no secrets; but when the spice box went back, its contents were weighed on the jewellers' scales, and Sir Dilip Singhji had, by subtraction, the exact ingredients of the dish.

'I remember my father cooking in the evenings, on the verandah,' says Vikram Singhji as he inspects the jackfruit ('cut too thin, it won't absorb enough gravy') and checks on the marinade for the raan. Sir Digvijaya Singh, his father, inherited the family fascination with fine cuisine and compiled a cookbook – *Cooking Delights of the Maharajas* – where he pleaded with today's cooks and chefs to try the old recipes without taking shortcuts.

Some of what we're served for dinner sounds like the standard fare you'd find at any good North Indian restaurant, but here's the thing: food cooked by the hands of a maharaja really does taste different. Perhaps it's the obsession, carried out over three generations, with locating just the right version of the classic recipes, but the raan musallam is outstanding, more delicate and more intensely flavoured than anything I've come across in the great kitchens of India. There are little surprises: a classic lauki ka halwa, which transforms the humble bottle gourd into a dish you could serve at, well, a maharaja's table; though he doesn't serve the famous gulab jamuns made of mincemeat, or the meat cooked in sandalwood essence, scented by its very special aroma.

We'll see more of this playfulness over the next two days. An unusual mutton dahi bada brings a richness to this usually vegetarian dish; a gulab ki kheer, made with fresh rose petals, is astoundingly fresh on the palate; and Vikram Singhji's nargisi koftas are soft and tender, melting on the tongue. Between Sailana and Surajgarh, the two royal households are also trying to revive the art of making the old liqueurs – Vikram Singhji spends a day fussing over the cardamom and the rose liqueurs, adding more essence and fresh spices. It's lost on a non-drinker like me, but the two ladies from England assure me it has the kick and the freshness of Benedictine. And all the while, the Maharaja fusses over the presentation of his dishes and the service, adjuring the photographer to eat before the meal gets disastrously cold, explaining why one must eat each dish separately: 'Biryani should only be mixed with raita, eat the jackfruit before the murg musallam, or its flavours will overpower the vegetable.'

He is slightly wistful that he can't offer us any game. 'Soovar ki santh – a dish made of the fat of a freshly killed wild boar – is good for arthritic pains and rheumatism,' says Vikram Singhji. He thinks about it: 'It also tastes incredible.' Like many scions of royal houses, he is passionate about defending a certain kind of responsible *shikar*, where the royal hunt of the sun was a benevolent and necessary culling rather than a soulless bloodbath. But he laid down his gun many years ago after a bizarre incident.

'We were shooting fish – the really large ones you find only in certain streams. And I saw this huge fish leaping down the stream as though it had gone completely mad, its tail lashing out left and right,' he says. 'I sighted, and shot it. When we went down to the stream, we saw that it was a female ... and that about 200 of its babies were lying dead on the surface of the stream, killed by the blast from the gun. I felt terrible; she hadn't been mad, she had just been trying to protect her children. I've never shot since that day.'

As we settle down to yet another incredible meal, I'm glad that HH hung up his guns, but not his knives and cooking spoons. The Sailana Royal Food Festival has turned out to be an unexpected surprise – small and intimate, but offering the promise of truly rare dishes cooked by a passionate chef who happens to be a maharaja as well. There are no gimmicks served alongside HH of Sailana's feasts: just excellent food and recipes you won't get anywhere else.

The food festival is supposed to be an annual affair, but if you find yourself in Surajgarh when HH is not in residence, just ask Naren to hold the butter chicken and serve up some of the old Sailana classics instead. Yes, you'll gain several kilos if you eat like a maharaja, and yes, it'll need more than a light session of Pilates to work this off – but as I return, groaning and replete, back to Delhi, I know it's been worth every extra inch.

Here's the recipe of a favourite dish, from *Cooking Delights of the Maharajas* by HH Digvijaya Singh:

Mutton Dahi Bada

Preparation time: 30 min; cooking time: 1hr, 30 min; to serve: 10 persons

1/2kg minced lean mutton (keema) from leg or shoulder
12gm salt
12gm red chillies (powdered)
12gm coriander seeds (powdered)
3gm turmeric
3gm cumin seeds, whole
100gm onions, ground
12gm garlic, ground
12gm ginger, scraped and ground
60gm split gram (chana dal)
6gm garam masala powder
750gm curd, fresh and thick

6gm salt
18gm sugar, powdered
4gm fresh mint leaves, finely chopped
600ml sour buttermilk
Ghee for frying badas

Boil meat in about 4 cups of water along with salt, red chillies, coriander, turmeric, cumin seeds, onions, garlic, ginger and split grams. When tender, dry the liquids completely. Add garam masala powder. Grind the meat finely.

Divide into 20 equal parts. Flatten, wetting hands with a little water to give badas a smooth and even shape.

Heat ghee in a frying pan and shallow fry the badas, till dark brown in colour. Immediately put them in buttermilk. When they sink to the bottom, take them out and with both hands squeeze each of them gently to remove superfluous fat and water, taking care not to break them. Place them in a serving dish.

Sieve curd through muslin and mix into it salt, sugar and the mint leaves. Pour curd on badas and let them stand for about an hour. Serve cold.

Not to be put in the refrigerator as the badas lose their softness.

12

LOVE IN 'SWITCHERLAND'

Annie Zaidi in Mount Abu

I am so much of a child in the pictures that I can almost forgive myself for being her. The sickening embarrassment that once made me want to set fire to the album has receded now. But it has taken more than fifteen years for me to be able to turn the plastic pages of my childhood photo album to look at the Mount Abu set. I am wearing a maroon outfit with an orange cap and a veil on top. My head tilts to the side, one hand holding the neck of a metal pot, the other hand supporting the base of the pot. In another photograph, I have my hip out, a clumsy fist resting on the curve.

It was not that I wanted to be captured that way but the photographer had asked me to pose. This was his idea of a happy village belle. This was Bollywood's contribution to rustic romanticism – fair-skinned girls in colourful skirts with garish gold lace, heads covered, smiling, or singing as they fetch water from the river as if that was their life's sole ambition. The angles of arms and shoulders and neck are meant to be graceful, as if large metal pots full of water weigh nothing at all. This is how ordinary tunic-wearing schoolgirls got photographed in Mount Abu.

Photographers would rush up with an album full of photos of children and women in surreal costumes – velvet *lehengas* and tops that I have never again spotted in all my rural visits across north India over the last decade – with steel pots or plastic flowers. Soon, a young girl would be seduced by the idea of being transformed, at least in the pages of a photo album. Some girl like me would agree to pay for renting the clothes and props; she would lean against a tree or balance the pot on her head, and wait for the photographer to say 'smile'. He would offer to deliver the photos to the hotel.

It had seemed like a cool thing to do then. I was barely fifteen and though Sirohi, the township where I lived, was remote, it wasn't a village. We all wore tunics to school and frocks at home. We wore black buckled shoes or white canvas ones, and we all had one pair of "party" pumps that the girls called "bell-ee" for a reason I still cannot fathom.

Back then, I wore no jewellery except tiny gold hoops. I saw no movies except the old ones on Doordarshan, or the ones a travelling projectionist brought around once every two or three months, which were played on a white screen (or was it a bedsheet?) in an open field, assuming your parents let you carry out folding chairs and sit out in the dark night with the "workers". And for the summer vacation the only place we ever went to was Mount Abu.

Abu was where we went for school picnics. At cultural events, we sang folk songs about it: *Mor bole, Abu re pahaad sunhane* (The peacock sings, the hills of Abu are lovely). Abu was where we went for field trips. Abu was where we took the rare visitor who cared enough to trek down to a dusty colony carved into the southern Aravallis. Abu was where the Ladies Club group went for picnics. Abu was our only reference point, the only way we could explain ourselves to cousins, co-passengers, strangers.

When I was little, if I tried to tell an outsider that I lived in Sirohi, he would frown: 'Where's that?' Even if he was Rajasthani, he wouldn't have heard of that tiny township. Outside of Rajasthan, nobody had heard of Sirohi district. The only place through which I could identify myself was Mount Abu, a two hour drive away.

I don't remember my first few visits to Abu, except for the fact that I threw up a lot. I used to get car sick and the hill roads wound up, up, up. Within the first half hour, I would have thrown up once. Perhaps twice, if I was unlucky. Going to Abu meant packing a towel and lots of water in large plastic water bottles. It meant eating a cautious breakfast and taking Avomine. If I threw up anyway, it meant having the terrible powdery bitter taste of Avomine mixed with vomit on my tongue. It meant distracting myself by looking outside the window but seeing nothing except winding roads and other cars and jeeps and buses, from the windows of which somebody's head would often be poking out, sending back a stream of vomit into the cool air, splashing against the sides of the bus.

Going with other kids meant watching out for the heads that poked out and shutting your window in time, so that the vomit didn't streak backwards to slap your face. If you went in a jeep, it meant choosing your spot well. Preferably at the back, which was open, so you could just lean over and puke without causing everyone the inconvenience of stopping the bus. But usually, there would have to be a few stops along the way because you weren't the only one; many kids had to puke. One by one, we would urgently tell the teacher, who would ask the driver to stop. Somebody or the other would squat on the side of the road, head bowed, wanting to weep. The biology teacher would jokingly recall a particularly memorable field trip as the "vomit trip" because so many stops had to be made not just while going up but also while coming down.

On those trips I could hardly be expected to notice whether Abu was beautiful or not. I know there was a picnic spot, perhaps Trevor's Tank, with a warning sign: "Swimming strictly prohibited. Survivors shall be prosecuted."

For me and my brother, that was a singular source of excitement – looking at the sign and imagining what might happen if you tried to wade into the waters. Crocodiles? Suppose you did meet a crocodile in the water and you somehow escaped its yawning jaws, when you emerged on dry land, you would find cops waiting for you. Imagine being arrested and being hauled off to court to appear in front of a magistrate, still wet and shivering. It was a hilarious idea.

The other memorable thing was Dilwara, a set of temples of which my first memory is befuddlement. I remember seeing white all around except it wasn't solid white like the whitewashed walls of our house. The carved white marble seemed semi-solid to me. I remember padding about on the cold, clean floor in my socks, feeling silence slither down from white ceilings on white walls and pillars. There was no visible flaw in the body of those Jain temples. I do not remember feeling pious but the quiet got inside of me.

Nobody gave me the history of the place or even its mythology. Nobody mentioned the myth of sage Vashisht in connection with

Abu, or the Gurjars or Rajput clans. I think there was a fort in the area but we never visited it. We did go to Gurushikhar and Nakki Lake. The former was a temple set high up on a hill and the excitement of climbing so many stairs carried me up the first couple of times. The latter was doomed to turn into a picnic area, as most water bodies in Indian towns are.

There was a myth associated with the lake – a powerful sage ran his nails down the surface of the earth and the furrow filled up with water. Hence, "nakki" lake. I always thought it was a demon, though, because he had to be some kind of *raakshas* to have nails that size. I have a vague memory of the whole enterprise having to do with an unfortunate princess in love. But princesses in love are always unfortunate, so that part of the story did not seem very remarkable. Besides, it is hard to think of princesses, when all you see are families milling around with squalling children in polyester blend sweaters.

But when I was fifteen, my relationship with Abu changed. I was studying at a tiny school affiliated to the Central Board of Secondary Education. The school, of which my mother was the principal, had serious difficulties. Teachers were hard to find in this remote hilly corner of Rajasthan. The few who came and stayed were sometimes talented and patient, and sometimes not.

The result was that many parents sent their children to study elsewhere – to Mayo College, if they were ambitious; or to one of cool boarding schools in Mussoorie or Dehradun or Ooty if they could afford it; or even just to Jaipur or Kota. As a result, the senior section of the school had a population crisis. My brother's batch had only four students in Class X. The batch ahead of me had only one student. My class was crowded, with ten students.

Such pitiful numbers meant that the board exams could not be conducted in our school. In fact, the CBSE board exams were not conducted even in the district headquarters in Sirohi. The nearest exam center was in – yes, you guessed right – Mount Abu.

So there we were, anxious students who had never lived away from our parents for more than a day, being hauled off to live in Abu for the duration of the exams. My batch had seven girls and three boys and we were all staying in a hotel that overlooked a main street that led to a park.

Despite the exams, and despite not having access to radio or television (we hadn't even heard of the Internet) and despite not doing any of the things cousins in bigger towns like Jaipur or Lucknow did, we were never bored here. As we leaned over the balcony at the hotel, one of my classmates would stare at the honeymooners walking past and say – 'The exam centre should not be held in a place like Abu. How can anyone study here?'

We were distracted by the honeymoon-y atmosphere, shy newlyweds – women with their hands full of red and white plastic bangles; men in shiny polyester coats and brown lace-ups. They held hands. They caused us to giggle.

Oddly enough, Abu was also full of Brahmkumaris – women wearing pure white sarees, like nuns or widows. They were another source of fascination. It was the first time in my brief life that I was seeing so many women moving about on their own, minus children, husbands, fathers or other male escorts. They seemed fairly independent, and they never did things other women do in public spaces – buying vegetables, shopping for clothes, waiting for someone. And when they smiled, their vagueness suggested that if we were made of wood and had cabbages for heads, they would still be smiling the same detached smiles.

I did not know much about them, but I knew they were out of the pale of society as I knew it. I also had the impression that adults did not want us to talk to the Brahmkumaris much. At fifteen, I had learnt only one thing – these women never married. Never ever, ever. I would often search their faces, look at their neat plaits, their firm arms, their feet, looking for a clue to some question, except that I didn't know what the question was. Did they really never, ever, ever?

On days we had exams, we were bundled into jeeps and taken to large schools with low ceilings and a distinct smell of usage – the smell of old walls, feet, socks, damp chalk, furniture that had not seen sunshine for years, scarred and inked with the secret sufferings of hearts that are too young to break.

All this was new to me. Since my school suffered a reverse crisis of numbers in the senior section, we often persuaded teachers to let us carry our desks outside so they would teach us under the winter sun. Also, our personal crises usually unraveled in a public way. In tiny classes, it is impossible to mimic joy, or to carve desks without others noticing. It is also impossible for young people to hold hands.

That must have been why we found it impossible to tear our eyes away from those honeymooning couples in Abu. We went out to eat in restaurants. This was an event because where we lived, there were no restaurants. Still in our school uniforms, we would agonize over where to go. Finally, the teacher would choose a place that offered Jain fare, because a few of the students were Jain. I would inevitably order Maggi because I disliked most things on the menu. Other students were encountering things like finger bowls for the first time. One of my classmates picked up the slice of lemon floating in the warm water, squeezed it into his glass and drank it! He had no idea it was meant to clean his greasy fingers.

In restaurants, we found more couples to ogle at. Leaning across the table towards each other, or sitting beside each other on a sofa, probably holding hands or rubbing knees under cover of the table cloth. We would drink in the strangely open smiles of the women, the vulnerability of the mustachioed men.

Sometimes, in gardens, we'd catch "uncle-ji" holding women with bright red or maroon lipstick. These women would invariably flash a part-embarrassed, part-gratified smile that seemed to eat up nearly all their faces. The men never looked back at us.

In Sirohi where I lived, nobody held hands in public, except with a friend of the same sex. Even married couples did not hold hands. I spent my entire childhood and most of my teens there but I do not recall any couples touching each other. Even on New Year's Eve, when the men were drunk and the women perfumed, and everyone was encouraged to go and give a "happy new year" hug to their friends – even then, the couples did not hug each other, only their children.

Thus, at fifteen, in Abu, I came to the conclusion that this holding of hands thing was clearly a honeymoon activity – a getaway thing, a thing couples did when their families, neighbours and colleagues were not watching. Now, having lived in metropolises, I realize the rule still holds. In Delhi, you go to public parks so you may lie with your head in the lap of a lover. In Bombay, you go to Carter Road or Bandstand to kiss or neck amongst the tetrapods.

It never occurred to me then that perhaps these couples were not actually married. I never thought to look for the telltale signs – the red and white bangles, the *mangalsutra*, the *sindoor*. There must have been some university students from southern Rajasthan who had stolen away for a day but back then, it seemed an impossibility. Surely, the whole town would guess at once if you weren't married? Surely, your body and face would give you away?

In a way, it did too. The obviously married couples hardly ever talked to each other. The men in their shirts and pants and V-neck sweaters in dull blues and greys and ochres; the women in polyester sarees, tightly pleated and pinned high up on the shoulder so that their large stomachs were left exposed, the loose end of the saree wound around oiled, plaited heads. They sat sulkily on the shores of Nakki Lake. If they ventured into boats, they paddled about in a desultory fashion, not looking at each other. If they went to restaurants, they glowered at the *thali*. If we made too much noise, they looked like they wanted to drown us in Nakki Lake. Most of the time, though, they contented themselves with saying something forbidding to their kids.

The other place for visitors to go to was a garden, the name of which I have forgotten. Perhaps it was Gandhi Park. Or Shaitan Singh Park, for I have a dim memory of wondering why a garden was named after such a ferocious-sounding person. Who would give their child the name of the devil?

At any rate, it was a park where tourists went and where photographers lurked with their albums and rented costumes. Mostly the girls who would deign to be shot in heavy velveteen *ghaghras* were honeymooning brides. Sometimes wistful mothers would dress up their little girls and get them to pose mock-seductively. There was, of course, a sprinkling of oddballs like me – schoolgirls who volunteered.

For years, the photos have embarrassed me – the terrible clothes, the stupid plasticky flowers, the pose right out of one of those cheap pseudo-Rajasthani paintings dominated by buxom women carrying pots. But most embarrassing of all was my desire to be photographed as something other than myself – my pink smile as I posed, confident that I was being transformed into somebody lovable; my small town heart's faith in the easy seductions of glamour, my inability to see an empty promise.

Now, years after I left Rajasthan, I look the place up on the Internet. I read descriptions – the government website describes it as the "Switcherland of Rajasthan". It feels strange. The words "Nakki" and "Dilwara" and "Trevor's Tank" sound familiar but the photos don't look familiar. This feels like a place I have never been to. There is too much colour. The hills are too blue. The lake froze over last winter. A website mentions the photographers who will click pictures of you in costumes you can rent.

I went back to look for my fifteen-year-old self in the album then. I had wanted to tear up those photos for the longest time. But I am glad they are there. I still wonder what made me do it, though. Why, in a velvet skirt edged with cheap golden lace, was I smiling right down to my eyes in Mount Abu?

13

IN SEARCH OF KIKA RANA

Rajesh Mishra in Udaipur, Haldighati and Kumbhalgarh

As a young boy growing up south of the Vindhyas, my dad, then serving as an officer in the Indian Army, regaled us with stories from history and his early tenures. His stint at the border posts of Jaisalmer, Bikaner and Jodhpur in the mid-1960s had left him with fond memories. 'Whenever we travelled across rural Rajasthan in convoys there were two constants in the theme of folk songs that one heard en route. In lieu of a little rum and food local singers from nearby villages would entertain us with song and dance in the evenings. And invariably they sang of Rana Pratap and Mira Bai.' Tales from Rana Pratap's life soon became some of my most cherished bedtime stories. Mewar, in my mind back then, seemed a far off place tucked away in some deep recess. I'd always wanted to see the place of the celebrated warrior-king's birth, the place where he fought and the hills he roamed.

'Window seat' I remember saying at the Jaipur bus ticket counter. Once on the bus I waited in anticipation to catch a glimpse of Chittor fort en route to Udaipur. Through my growing years in the 1970s, whenever I'd thought of the Rajputs, a frame of Chittor fort from the Amar Chitra Katha comics invariably came to mind. After crossing Bhilwara, I often looked out from the bus window. I didn't want to miss a single frame. Finally, when the moment came, it surpassed my expectation. Sitting high above the surrounding plains, on the crest of an Aravalli outcrop, stood that magnificent emblem of the Rajputs.

I visualized Rana Pratap, surrounded by his trusted Bhils, looking at the hill fort from a vantage point in the surrounding forests. Winning back the fort from the clutches of the Mughal Emperor Akbar had been one of the main objectives of his life. The kingdom of Mewar that he had inherited was in dire straits. The Mughal forces had wrested its capital, Chittor, along with much of the fertile plains around. Rana Pratap's father, Rana Udai Singh, had been forced to retreat into the Aravalli hills surrounding Udaipur. He'd been pushed back from his hitherto forward position in the plains. Akbar had isolated Mewar by surrounding it from all sides. Apart from Malwa to the east and Gujarat to the south, fellow Rajput kingdoms around Mewar such as Amber, Bikaner, Marwar and Bundi had already become vassals of the Mughals. Mewar was getting strangulated from all sides. So deep ran the influence of the Mughals that two of Rana Pratap's estranged brothers were serving in the Mughal courts. It was against this backdrop that Rana Pratap took charge. The odds were stacked heavily against him.

The bus was now moving through the hill stretch leading into Udaipur. With Udaipur as my base I hoped to visit Kumbhalgarh and Haldighati, the latter being the site of the famous battle between Rana Pratap's and Akbar's forces led by the Kachhwaha

Rajput prince of Amber, Man Singh. My first visit to Udaipur had been a business trip during which I had sensed that in the hearts of the people of Mewar he continued to reign supreme. Apart from the fact that the airport had been named after him, his statues dotted the city. Even his horse Chetak seemed to be more celebrated than many of the other rulers of Mewar. I had seen little of the city back then, so here I was again, this time to retrace his footsteps.

My quest led me to the 17th generation descendants of Rana Pratap's younger brother – Veeram. Veeram was an important cog in Rana Pratap's administrative set up. While Rana Pratap was busy planning his offensive and defensive moves against the Mughals for much of his adult life, Veeram played an active part in the day-to-day affairs of the kingdom. What is it that makes Rana Pratap stand out? I asked the Rajput couple who'd spent their working years in the tea and coffee estates of Assam, West Bengal and Coorg before settling down in their home town, Udaipur. 'Personal sacrifice and upholding the spirit of independence throughout his life,' said the gentleman. After being crowned king, Rana Pratap vowed that he would not sleep on a bed and that he would lead a frugal life until he regained Mewar's lost ground from Akbar. 'It was a tremendous oath coming from a king. For someone born into luxury to take such a pledge gives you an insight into the character of the man,' said the lady. The couple's sentiment was largely in line with that of the common man on the streets of Udaipur. For a moment I drew a parallel between Pratap and Gandhi. Their methods might have been different, but in spirit they were united.

From Udaipur I took a ride to Haldighati with Mr Paliwal, a Brahmin from the nearby town of Pali. Do tourists visiting Udaipur include Haldighati in their itinerary? I asked him. 'Some domestic tourists do. But increasingly such things are receding from people's mind,' he said. 'Very few care about history anymore.' The traffic of Udaipur was giving way to small villages and a sparsely populated countryside. We were off the beaten track now. I asked Mr. Paliwal, 'Do *you* feel proud of Rana Pratap today?' His serious demeanour gave way to a gentle smile. 'No Mewari worth his salt can ever forget him. His sacrifice continues to inspire us.'

Haldighati was the site of medieval Rajasthan's most talked about battle. On June 18, 1576, Rana Pratap's forces took on Akbar's vastly superior (in numbers and weaponry) army in a narrow valley a little ahead. After the initial burst in the valley, the battle spread out on to the open area around village Khamnor, a few kilometers down the road. It marked the beginning of a two-decade long tussle between the two illustrious foes. One was fighting for the independence of his kingdom; the other trying to stamp his imperial command. This was one of the early battles in recorded Indian history that brought guerilla warfare tactics to the fore. The Maratha, Shivaji almost a century later employed similar tactics to devastating effect against Aurangzeb's forces in the Sahyadri ranges. Rana Pratap was the forerunner of a tactic made famous in modern world history by the likes of Mao Zedong, Ho Chí Minh and Simón Bolívar.

In commemoration of the epic battle the state government set up a museum complex called the Maharana Pratap Haldighati Museum in 2003. A series of dioramas depicting the battle and a film are the focal points. A touristy book-cum-curio shop and a food court lend a picnic-like atmosphere to the place. It didn't whet my curiosity. Often very interesting chapters of our history get buried under the weight of tourism. What's the solution? You want to attract a larger audience but not at the cost of diluting the experience, the seriousness of the subject. How can government agencies walk this fine line? Involving the private sector perhaps, contemporary museum experts? A similar memorial to Rana Pratap at Moti Magri in Udaipur seems to me to have been better conceived.

Further down the road from the museum lies the resting ground of Chetak, Rana Pratap's favourite horse. On account of its surroundings this place is ideal for a cenotaph. Neatly landscaped, the ASI monument complex harnesses the hill slope. It seems an apt resting place – by the temple of Pashupatinath or "Lord of the Animals". The twittering of birds, the occasional vehicle passing by, and the locked Shiva shrine lend to the place a contemplative air. Shiva, or Eklingji, incidentally, is the family deity of the Ranas of Mewar.

Enjoying a quiet moment I noticed something incongruous. The plaque indicates June 21, 1576 as the day Chetak died. If the horse was "fatally" injured on the day of the battle – June 18 – how did it survive the next three days? K.S. Gupta, retired history professor from Udaipur came to my rescue the following day. 'There's some controversy over the exact date of the Battle of Haldighati. The more established version is June 18, based on Persian records of the Mughal court and tallying them with local versions of Rajputana. The battle was fought on a Monday, in the season of Asadh Krishna, 7 Samvat 1633, which matches with the date Abul Faz'l records in the *Akbar Nama* based on the Islamic calendar. But in the conversion of the above two versions into the universal calendar followed today, there is scope for variation. While the state government has gone with historian G.N. Sharma's date of June 21 as the date of the battle (and hence Chetak's death), the popular and more accepted date is June 18.

I encountered a similar predicament over the breed of Chetak. The official version is that he was of Arab stock, while another puts him down as the hardy local breed called the "Marwari". Horse lovers the world over are familiar with the prowess of the former, but the latter is little known beyond the boundaries of Rajasthan. The Rajputs used the Marwari horse extensively in warfare, and the breed is known for its alertness, endurance and stamina, and much like the Rajputs the breed is hot blooded and fiercely loyal. Whatever be its breed, Chetak is one of the best remembered horses in the annals of Indian history. From Chetak Helicopters used by the Indian Armed Forces to the endurance of Bajaj Chetak scooters, the horse has created a niche in local folklore and invariably comes into the frame at any mention of Rana Pratap. While in Udaipur, there's no missing Chetak Circle. Rarely does one see a solitary horse occupy such a pride of place in a contemporary city's landscape.

On the hill above Chetak's resting ground and the Maharana Pratap Haldighati Museum, stands the statue of Pratap astride Chetak, a lovely manicured memorial. It offers a vantage point to observe the surrounding hills and valleys. The place lifted my spirits after the less than satisfactory experience of the museum below. I had the entire hill-top memorial to myself save the solitary *mali* going about his job in the mellow afternoon sun and a gentle breeze for company. One of the reasons for such quiet could have been that a cricket match was on in a nearby city. I walked around taking in the picturesque setting. It was tailor made for guerilla warfare. The advantage of a large army with elephants and heavy artillery would be offset by skilled cavalrymen on swift horses especially if they knew the topography well.

In the run up to the day of the battle, the opposition armies were engaged in a battle of wits. Akbar had played his cards well. He had appointed Man Singh, the Kachhwaha Rajput prince of Amber (Jaipur), as the commander of his army knowing fully well that the Kachhwaha Rajputs in his army might not be motivated enough to give their best against a fellow Rajput, albeit from Mewar, under a Muslim commander with origins in Central Asia! But for their young prince, Man Singh, they would willingly fight until death. Akbar was all too aware of this situation. Furthermore, Akbar knew that the young prince was still smarting under the snub subjected on him when he had gone for a dialogue with the idea of urging Rana Pratap to become a vassal of the Mughals. Besides, Mewar and Amber were rivals of sorts. Both had been vying for supremacy in Rajputana. From the days of Rana Kumbha (Rana Pratap's forefather) Mewar had got the better of Amber. Akbar sought to exploit this sentiment as well. This was Man Singh's chance to get back at the Sesodia kings from Mewar.

Man Singh had been camping in the plains fully aware of Rana Pratap's prowess in guerilla tactics. He had been biding his time for two months in the hope that Pratap would lose his patience and make the charge into the plains. But Rana Pratap knew with the approaching monsoon that it was a matter of time before Man Singh made his move.

Here it would be worthwhile to note that it was not a communal battle, but a fight for freedom. In these times of polarized politics the world over, it is a fact that could do with reiteration. The social context and composition of the opposition armies spells it out. While Hindu Rajputs from Amber were fighting for Akbar, Afghan Hakim Khan Sur, a Muslim, and his troops were leading one of the three divisions in Rana Pratap's offensive formation.

Hakim Khan Sur was part of the battle to extract revenge from the Mughals for the defeat of Sher Shah Suri, his forefather. The Bhil king of Merpur, Rana Punja (also called Bhiloo Rana, for he hailed from the Bhil tribe) and Rana Pratap himself were on the forefront in the other two.

In the wee hours of the eventful day, Rana Pratap's advance Bhil pickets noticed movement towards the narrow valley. The stage was set. Rana Pratap's troops were ready and waiting despite being numbered in a ratio of 1:3 (some sources put it at 1:4). In the initial skirmishes in the narrow valley, Rana Pratap's tactics worked well. The battle then moved on to the plains near village Khamnor. Man Singh, mounted on an elephant, was at the centre of the formation guarded by elite horsemen.

After knocking over Qazi Khan and his group in the front formation, Rana Pratap in a daredevil move went for the heavily guarded central formation with Man Singh at the helm. If he scalped the commander of the army the troops would be demoralized, was his logic. He also had a personal score to settle. Through a hail of swords and arrows Rana Pratap reached Man Singh's elephant. The ensuing fight is visually captured by artists and is the defining image of the Battle of Haldighati, with Chetak's forelegs on the elephant and Pratap releasing his lance aimed at Man Singh. The lance hit the mahout instead and Man Singh managed to escape while Rana Pratap battled opposition cavalry men who came from all directions. Chetak's hind legs had been badly wounded by Man Singh's tusker but he carried on. Rana Pratap, unaware of his horse's condition battled on till a tactical decision was taken by the strategists in his team that it was time for the Rana to retreat into the jungles to fight another day. By then Mihtar Khan, a trusted aid of Akbar, had brought in another reserve of soldiers to bolster the sagging morale of Akbar's forces. The Rana's forces were now heavily outnumbered. Jhala Maan and his band of fighters covered Rana Pratap's retreat as he melted into the forests in the hills. En route Rana Pratap noticed the limp in his redoubtable horse's rear leg. Dismounting, he took Chetak to a small Shiva temple by a waterbody. A four-pillared cenotaph today stands in poignant silence at the site.

James Tod famously called the Battle of Haldighati the "Thermopylae of Mewar". Thermopylae, like Haldighati, is a narrow passage where heavily outnumbered Greeks took on the Persians in 480 BCE. The former comprised 300 crack soldiers from Sparta under the inspirational leadership of Leonidas fighting for the cause of the Greeks against the much larger Persian army of Xerxes. The episode gained further popularity through the Hollywood film "300".

By now the *mali* tending to the flower beds was within earshot. I asked for the precise direction of Khamnor to get a geographical perspective to the battle scenes that had been running through my mind. Tulsiram had been working as the *mali* since the memorial's inauguration in 2003. Do Bhils still inhabit these parts? 'Yes. You'll find them in village Balicha below.' During his two-decade long struggle, Rana Pratap fought most of his battles with the support of tribes comprising largely Bhils and to a lesser extent the Meenas. One of the earliest tribes to inhabit the subcontinent, the Bhils continue to live along the areas where Rajasthan, Madhya Pradesh and Gujarat share boundaries. This roughly translates to the hills of the southern Aravallis, western Vindhyas and the valley of the Narmada river. Recognizing their contribution to the cause of Mewar, the royal insignia shows a Rajput and a Bhil. It was a combination that served Rana Pratap well!

Rana Pratap has often been referred to as "Kika Rana" by chroniclers – both Indian and Persian. It is a word used by the Bhils. "Kika" means "child". To the Bhils, Rana Pratap was their child. He was adoringly referred to as "Kika Rana" by them. Five centuries on, he is very much "Kika Rana" in Mewar in particular and across Rajasthan in general.

What do you make of Rana Pratap? I asked Tulsiram as a parting question. 'There is not a single man like him in the whole of Rajputana today,' was his reply.

Most of the Rajput kingdoms were either vassals of Akbar or were too tiny to demand any attention from the great Mughal. Mewar under Rana Pratap stood out like the final frontier that never caved in during his lifetime. Akbar sent as many as six diplomatic missions to lure and persuade Rana Pratap to recognize him as the Emperor of India. Had he wanted, Rana Pratap could have led a life of luxury like Man Singh. But he never accepted Akbar as the ruler of India. For him Akbar was the Turk. I thought to myself, What if the Rajputs under Rana Pratap had formed a united front against the Mughals? Would the history of India have read a little different? Under Rana Sanga, a Rajput confederacy of sorts had challenged Babur but the superior artillery of the Mughals had won the day against the cavalry charges of the Rajputs.

The historian James Tod never hid his appreciation for such commitment to a cause: ' ... the moral effect of history depends on the sympathy it excites, the annals of these states possess commanding interest. The struggle of a brave people for independence during a series of ages, sacrificing whatever was dear to them for the maintenance of the religion of their forefathers, and sturdily defending to the death, and in spite of every temptation, their rights and national liberty, forms a picture which is difficult to contemplate without emotion.'

The following day I made my way to Kumbhalgarh. Tucked deep in the hills, Kumbhalgarh had always been one the strongholds of the Mewar kings. Built by Rana Kumbha, it forms part of the highest plateau in the Aravalli ranges. At a little over 3,500 feet above sea level, this was the ultimate bastion of Mewar. It was here that Rana Pratap, eldest son of Rana Udai Singh, was born. On his deathbed at the nearby Gogunda Fort, Udai Singh anointed one of his younger sons – Prince Jagmall – as his successor. This was against the established order of the eldest son taking over, and more importantly, against popular sentiment. Pratap was loved and revered by the people at large, and the noblemen of the court decided that he was the best man to rule Mewar in their moment of crisis. And thus Pratap became the Rana of Mewar. A disgruntled Jagmall went and joined Akbar's court.

The highest point on the palace terrace commands a magnificent view of the surrounding terrain. But it is its sprawling ramparts that Kumbalgarh is most famous for. Ascending the fort from the exterior I walked for a kilometer taking in the vista. After the Great Wall of China this is said to be the second largest continuous fortified wall, covering 36 km. What an effort it must have been building this fortress! In its history the fort fell only once to opponents. Soon after the Battle of Haldighati, Man Singh's forces captured Gogunda and a year later Shahbaz Khan of the Mughal army managed to breach the defenses of Kumbhalgarh. The former was won back by Rana Pratap within days of the Battle of Haldighati. The latter took a bit longer. By 1580 it was back in Rana Pratap's control. Before he died in 1597 at Chavand, he had won back all of Mewar's forts under the Mughals save Chittorgarh and

Mandalgarh. The last decade of Rana Pratap's life was relatively peaceful as Akbar realized the futility in pursuing him. And until his death Rana Pratap kept his vow of not sleeping on a bed and of leading a frugal life.

'You must watch the sound and light show at Kumbhalgarh,' my host at Udaipur had recommended. It turned out to be a worthwhile suggestion. Fully utilising the scale and height of the fort and its ramparts, it lived up to its billing. Spanning the history of Mewar from the time of Bappa Rawal, first of the Sesodia rulers of Mewar, the show highlighted the contribution of Rana Kumbha (who built the fort and after whom it is named) and Rana Sangha (who took on Babur). The poignant tale of Panna Dai, who sacrificed her own son to save the crown prince Udai Singh, visibly moved the audience. The section on Rana Pratap hit a dramatic high, indicative of where he stands in the pantheon of Mewar's rulers. The last line in the narration sounded improbable to me, however: 'Akbar had tears in his eyes on hearing of Rana Pratap's death.' I knew that Akbar was never vindictive with Rana Pratap's admirers in his court. And there were a few. He was particularly fond of a Rajput scholar-poet named Prithviraj Rathore from Bikaner, an unabashed Pratap admirer. The two often shared friendly banter over Rana Pratap. But for Akbar to have shed a tear seemed an exaggeration!

Through my early years, in trying to instill a sense of history in me, my father would tell me about the impact Rana Pratap had beyond the borders of Rajputana. He used to recall a story about the legendary warrior-king from his Class VIII text book, written by a Godavarish Mishra. Indeed, stories of the Rana inspired many through India's freedom struggle. In the aftermath of the First War of Independence in 1857, when the spirit of the nation was down, writers from Bengal such as Dwijendralala Rai (better known as D.L. Roy) and Rabindranath Tagore wrote about Rana Pratap and Mewar to inspire people. Likewise he is celebrated in Hindi, Gujarati, Marathi, and Telugu literature. Rana Pratap epitomized the spirit of freedom and he became a rallying point for India's quest for Independence. Soon after Independence, when certain princely states such as Hyderabad were dilly-dallying about joining the Indian Union, Sardar Vallabhbhai Patel held Mewar as an example. 'If any ruler in India had any right to claim independence it was Mewar, which has gladly and readily merged with the Indian Union.' Today Rana Pratap mounted on Chetak with his trusted fighters Jhala Maan, Bhiloo Rana, Bhama Shah and Hakim Khan Sur proudly graces the space in front of Parliament House in New Delhi.

Walking has always been my preferred way of experiencing a city. Back in Udaipur I walked to Saheliyon ki Bari from the Sardarpura locality where I was based. Built in the 18ᵗʰ century, the garden was designed for the relaxation of ladies from the royal family. Two centuries on, it retains much of its charm. Seated on a bench with the gentle strains of water sprinklers and the distant view of a hill top temple, I chalked my final walking trail. I'd begin the day by walking to Suraj Pol, the throbbing heart of Udaipur, and then on to the vintage car museum, catch a glimpse of the iconic Taj in the middle of Lake Pichola, walk through the old quarter and on to Moti Magri, a multi-dimensional memorial dedicated to Rana Pratap.

It's not difficult to see why Udaipur consistently features among the most romantic cities worldwide. Laid out over gentle rolling hills of the Aravallis, every now and then you catch sight of a hill top, and from the hill top the lakes and gardens below are mesmerizing. But most importantly its rich history has instilled a quiet pride and grace among the locals. It is unmistakable when you walk the streets of Udaipur, in the way people address you with the traditional "Hukum", in the way a young guide engages European tourists about details of the impressive vintage cars from the king's stable, in the way the roadside artist explains the finer nuances of the Mewar school of miniature painting.

Towards evening I reached Moti Magri via Chetak Circle. It had been a day-long walk, rich in sights and sounds. Overlooking Fateh Sagar Lake, I savoured my final moments at the hill top memorial to my childhood icon. And then I remembered my own five-year-old son's query the day we picked up his copy of Amar Chitra Katha on Rana Pratap. 'Who is the bad man out of the two?' The cover had Rana Pratap on Chetak attacking Man Singh on an elephant.

One day I hope to revisit Mewar with my father and son together. With them for company, I might even think of negotiating the 36-km ramparts of Kumbhalgarh fort. I hear it is a two day trek ....

14

MAPPINGS

James Tod in the Aravallis
1829

On the 12th *October,* at five a.m. our trumpet sounded to horse, and we were not slow in obeying the summons; the "yellow boys" with their old native commandant looking even more cheerful than usual as we joined them. Skinner's Horse wear a jamah or tunic of yellow broadcloth, with scarlet turbans and cincture. Who does not know that James Skinner's men are the most orderly in the Company's service, and that in every other qualification constituting the efficient soldier, they are second to none? On another signal which reverberated from the palace, where the drums announced that the descendant of Surya was no sluggard, we moved on through the yet silent capital [Oodipoor] towards the gate of the sun, where we found drawn up the quotas of Bheendir, Dailwarra, Amait, and Bansi, sent as an honorary guard by the Rana, to escort us to the frontiers. As they would have been an incumbrance to me and an inconvenience to the country, from their laxity of discipline, after chatting with their leader, during a sociable ride, I dismissed them at the pass, with my respects to the Rana and their several chieftains. We reached the camp before eight o'clock, the distance being only thirteen miles. The spot chosen (and where I afterwards built a residence) was a rising ground between the villages of Mairta and Toos, sprinkled with trees, and for a space of four miles clear of the belt of forest which fringes the granite barriers of the valley. It commanded an entire view of the plains in the direction of Cheetore, still covered, excepting a patch of cultivation here and there, with jungle. The tiger-mount, its preserves of game, and the smouldering hunting-seats of the Rana and his chieftains, were three miles to the north; to the south, a mile distant, we had the Beris River, abounding in trout; and the noble lake whence it issues, called after its founder the Oody Sagur, was not more than three to the west. For several reasons it was deemed advisable to choose a spot out of the valley; the health of the party, though not an unimportant, was not a principal motive for choosing such a distance from the court. The wretchedness in which we found it rendered a certain degree of interference requisite, and it was necessary that they should shake this off, in order to preserve their independence. It was dreaded lest the aid requested by the Rana, from the peculiar circumstances on our first going amongst them, might be construed as a precedent for the intrusion of advice on after occasions. The distance between the court and the agent of the British Government was calculated to diminish this impression, and obliged them also to trust to their own resources, after the machine was once set in motion. On the heights of Toos our tents were pitched, the escort paraded, and St. George's flag displayed. Here camels, almost wild, were fitted for the first time with the pack-saddle, lamenting in discordant gutturals the hardship of their fate, though luckily ignorant of the difference between grazing whither they listed in the happy valley, and carrying a load in "the region of death," where they would only find the thorny *mimosa* or prickly *phok* to satisfy their hunger.

NAT'HDWARA – *October* 14. – Marched at day-break, and found the route almost impracticable for camels, from the swampy nature of the soil. The country is much broken with irregular low ridges of micaceous schist, in the shape of a chine or hog's back, the crest of which has throughout all its length a vein of quartz piercing the slate, and resembling a back-bone; the direction of these veins is uniformly N.N.E., and the inclination about 75 degrees to the east. Crossed the Nat'hdwara ridge, about four hundred feet in height, and, like the hills encircling the valley, composed of a brown granite intersected with protruding veins of quartz, incumbent on blue compact slate. The ascent was a mile and a half east of the town, and on the summit, which is table-land, there are two small lakes, whence water-courses conduct streams on each side of the road to supply the temple and the town. There are noble trees planted on either side of these rivulets, forming a delightful shade. As we passed through the town to our encampment on the opposite side of the Bunas River, the inhabitants crowded the streets, shouting their grateful acknowledgments to the power which had redeemed the sacred precincts of Kaniya from the scenes of turpitude amidst which they had grown up. They were all looking forward with much pleasure to the approaching festival of Anacuta.

October 15. – Halted to allow the baggage to join, which, partly from the swamps and partly from the intractable temper of the cattle, we have not seen since we parted company at Mairta. Received a visit from the mookhia of the temple, accompanied by a pilgrim in the person of a rich banker of Surat. A splendid quilted cloak of gold brocade, a blue scarf with a deep border of gold, and an embroidered band for the head, were brought to me as the gift of the god through his high-priest, in testimony of my zeal. I was also honoured with a tray of the sacred food, which consisted of all the dried fruits, spices and aromatics of the East. In the evening I had a portion of the afternoon repast, consisting of a preparation of milk; but the days of simplicity are gone, and the Apollo of Vrij has his curds adulterated with rose-water and amber. Perhaps, with the exception of Lodi, where is fabricated the far-famed *Parmasan*, whose pastures maintain forty thousand kine, there is no other place known which possesses more than the city of the Hindu Apollo, though but a tenth of that of Lodi. But from the four thousand cows, the expenditure of milk and butter for the votaries of Kaniya may be judged. I was entertained with the opinions of the old banker on the miraculous and oracular power of the god of Nat'hdwara. He had just been permitted to prostrate himself before the car which conveyed the deity from the Yamuna, and held forth on the impiety of the age, in withholding the transmission of the miraculous wheels from heaven, which in former days came once in six months. The most devout alone are permitted to worship the chariot of Kaniya. The garments which decorate his representative are changed several times a day, to imitate the different stages of his existence, from the youthful Bala to the conqueror of Kansa; or, as the Surat devotee said in broken English, 'Oh, sir, he be much great god; he first of all; and he change from de baluk, or child, to de fierce chief, with de bow and arrow a hees hands;' while the old mookhia, whose office it is to perambulate the whole continent of India as one of the couriers of Kaniya, lifted up his eyes as he ejaculated, 'Sri Kishna! Sri Kishna!' I gave him a paper addressed to all officers of the British Government who might pass through the lands of the church, recommending the protection of the peacocks and peepul trees, and to forbear polluting the precincts of the god with the blood of animals. To avoid offending against their prejudices in this particular, I crossed the river, and killed our fowls within our own sanctuary, and afterwards concealed the murder by burying the feathers.

October 18. – Marched at daybreak to Sumaicha. Again found our advanced elephant and breakfast-tent in a swamp: halted to extricate him from his difficulties. The road from Nat'hdwara is but a footpath, over or skirting a succession of low broken ridges, covered with prickly shrubs, as the Khyr, the Khureel, and Babool. At the village of Gong Goorah, midway in the morning's journey, we entered the alpine valley called the Shero Nullah. The village of Goorah is placed in the opening or break in the range through which the river flows, whose serpentine meanderings indicate the only road up this majestic valley. On the banks, or in its bed, which we frequently crossed, lay the reminder of this day's march. The valley varies in breadth, but is seldom less than half a mile, the hills riding boldly from their base; some with a fine and even surface covered with mango trees, others lifting their splintered pinnacles into the clouds. Nature has been lavish of her beauties to this romantic region. The *goolur* or wild fig, the *sitaphal* or custard-apple, the peach or *aroo boddam* (almond-peach), are indigenous and abundant; the banks of the stream are shaded by the withy, while the large trees, the useful mango and picturesque tamarind, the sacred peepul and burr, are abundantly scattered with many others, throughout. Nor has nature in vain appealed to human industry and ingenuity to second her intents. From the margins of the stream on each side to the mountain's base, they have constructed a series of terraces rising over each other, whence by simple and ingenious methods they raise the waters to irrigate the rich crops of sugar-cane, cotton, and rice, which they cultivate upon them. Here we have a proof that ingenuity is the same, when prompted by necessity, in the Jura or the Aravulli. Wherever soil could be found, or time decomposed these primitive rocks, a barrier was raised. When discovered, should it be in a hollow below, or on the summit of a crag, it is alike greedily seized on: even there water is found, and if you leave the path below and ascend a hundred feet above the terraces, you will discover pools or reservoirs dammed in with massive trees, which serve to irrigate such insulated spots, or serve as nurseries to the young rice-plants. Not unfrequently, their labour is entirely destroyed, and the dykes swept away by the periodical inundations; for we observed the high-water mark in the trees considerably up the acclivity. The rice crop was abundant, and the *joar* or maize was thriving, but scanty; the standard autumnal crop which preceded it, the *makhi*, or "Indian corn", had been entirely devoured by the locust. The sugar-cane, by far the most valuable product of this curious region, was very fine but sparingly cultivated, from the dread of this insect, which for the last three years had ravaged the valley. There are two species of locusts, which come in clouds, darkening the air, from the desert: the *farka* and the *teeri* are their names; the first is the great enemy of our incipient prosperity. I observed a colony some time ago proceeding eastward with a rustling, rushing sound, like a distant torrent, or the wind in a forest at the fall of the leaf. We have thus to struggle against natural and artificial obstacles to the rising energies of the country; and dread of the *farkas* deters speculators from renting this fertile tract, which almost entirely belongs to the fisc. Its natural fertility cannot be better demonstrated than in recording the success of an experiment, which produced *five crops, from the same piece of ground, within thirteen months.* It must, however, be understood that two of these are species of millet, which are cut in six weeks from the time of sowing. A patch of ground, for which the cultivator pays six rupees rent, will produce sugar-cane six hundred rupees in value: but the labour and expense of cultivation are heavy, and cupidity too often deprives the husbandman of the greater share of the fruits, ninety rupees having been taken in arbitrary taxes, besides his original rent.

The air of this elevated region gave vigour to the limbs, and appetite to the disordered stomach. There was an exhilarating *fraicheur,* which made us quite frantic; the transition being from 96 degrees of Fahrenheit to English summer heat. We breakfasted in a verdant spot under the shade of a noble fig-tree fanned by the cool breezes from the mountains.

October 20. – Halted till noon, that the men might dress their dinners, and prepare for the descent into "the region of death," or Marwar. The pass by which we had to gain it was represented as terrific; but as both horse and elephant, with the aid of the hatchet, will pick their way wherever man can go, we determined to persevere. Struck the camp at noon, when the baggage filed off, halting ourselves till three; the escort and advanced tents, and part of the *cuisine* being ordered to clear the pass, while we designed to spend the night midway, in a spot forming the natural boundary of Mewar and Marwar, reported to be sufficiently capacious. Rumour had not magnified the difficulties of the descent, which we found strewed with our baggage, arresting all progress for a full hour. For nearly a mile there was just breadth sufficient to admit the passage of a loaded elephant, the descent being at an angle of 55 degrees with the horizon, and streams on either side rushing with a deafening roar over their rugged beds. As we gained a firmer footing at the base of this first descent, we found that the gallant Manika, the gift of my friend the Boondi prince, had missed his footing and rolled down the steep, breaking the cantle of the saddle; a little further appeared the cook, hanging in dismay over the scattered implements of his art, his camel remonstrating against the replacing of his *cujavas* or panniers. For another mile it became more gentle, when we passed under a tower of Komulmer, erected on a scarped projection of the rock, full five hundred feet above us. The scenery was magnificent; the mountains rising on each side in every variety of form, and their summits, as they caught a ray of the departing sun, reflecting on our somber path a momentary gleam from the masses of rose-coloured quartz which created them. Noble forest trees covered every face of the hills and the bottom of the glen, through which, along the margin of the serpentine torrent which was repeatedly crossed, lay our path. Notwithstanding all our mishaps, partly from the novelty and grandeur of the scene, and partly from the invigorating coolness of the air, our mirth became wild and clamorous: a week before, I was oppressed with a thousand ills; and now I trudged the rugged path, leaping the masses of granite which had rolled into the torrent.

There was one spot where the waters formed a pool or *de*. Little Cary determined to trust to his pony to carry him across, but deviating to the left, just as I was leaping from a projecting ledge, to my horror, horse and rider disappeared. The shock was momentary, and a good ducking the only result, which in the end was the luckiest thing that could have befallen him. On reaching the Hattidurra, or "barrier of the elephant" (a very appropriate designation for a mass of rock serving as a rampart to shut up the pass), where we had intended to remain the night, we found no spot capacious enough even for a single tent. Orders accordingly passed to the rear for the baggage to collect there, and wait the return of day to continue the march. The shades of night were fast descending, and we proceeded almost in utter darkness towards the banks of the stream, the roar of whose waters was our guide, and not a little perplexed by the tumultuous rush which issued from every glen, to join that we were seeking. Towards the termination of the descent the path became wider, and the voice of the waters of a deeper and hoarser tone, as they glided to gain the plains of Marwar. The vault of heaven, in which there was not a cloud, appeared as an arch to the perpendicular cliffs surrounding us on all sides, and the stars beamed with peculiar brilliancy from the confined space through which we viewed them.

October 29. – Camp at Eendurra. This small town, placed on the north bank of one of the nameless feeders of the "salt river", is the boundary of Godwar; here the reign of the yellow *aonla* terminates, and here commences *Maroost'hali,* or "the region of death". The transition is great. We can look back upon fertility, and forward on aridity, which does not, however, imply sterility: for that cunning artist, nature, compensates the want of verdure and foliage to the inhabitants of the desert, by many spontaneous bounties. An entire race of cucurbitaceous plants is the eleemosynary equivalent for the mango and exotics of the commercial sons from Osi, Palli, and Pokurna, to bring wealth from the Ganges and the Kistna, to the Looni, or to the still more remote oasis, Jessulmer. From Eendurra everything assumed a new character: the sand, of which we had before scarcely a springling, became occasionally heavy; the shallow beds of the numerous streams were white with saline incrustations; and the vegetable creation had been gradually diminishing, from the giant race of the sacred fig-tree with leaf "broad as Amazonian targe," to the dwarfish shrubs of the desert. At once the satiric stanza of the bard of a more favoured region was brought to my mind, and as I repeated it to my old friend the Rana's envoy, he enjoyed the confession, and afresh urged his wish that nature should decide the question of their boundaries:

> *Ak ra jhopra,*
> *Phok ra bdr,*
> *Bajra ra rooti,*
> *Mot'h ra dal,*
> *Dekho ho Raja, teri Marwar.*

> 'Huts of the ak,
> Barriers of thorns,
> Bread of maize,
> Lentils of the vetch,
> Behold Raja, your Marwar!'

The villages are of a construction totally distinct from anything we have seen, and more approaching the wigwam of the western world. Every commune is surrounded with a circumvallation of thorns, *kanta ka kote,* and the stacks of *bhoos,* or "chaff", which are placed at intervals, give it the appearance of a respectable fortification.

These *bhoos* stacks are erected to provide provender for the cattle in scanty rainy seasons, when the parched earth denies grass, or full crops of maize. They are erected to the height of twenty or thirty feet, coated with a cement of earth and cow-dung, and with a sprinkling of thorns, to prevent the fowls of the air from reposing in them. In this manner, with a little fresh coating, they will exist ten years, being only resorted to on emergencies, when the kine may be said to devour the village walls. Their appearance is a great relief to the monotony of the march through the desert; which, however, cannot strictly be said to commence till you cross the Looni.

November 28. – Camp at Jhirrow, five cos (11 miles). We this day altered our course from the N.N.E., which would have carried us, had we pursued it, to the Imperial city, for a direction to the southward of east, in order to cross our own Aravulli and gain Ajmer. The road was excellent, the soil very fair; but though there were symptoms of cultivation near the villages, the wastes were frightfully predominant; yet they are not void of vegetation: there is no want of herbiage or stunted shrubs. The Aravulli towered majestically in the distant horizon, fading from our view towards the south-east, and intercepted by rising grounds.

We had a magnificent *mirage* this morning: nor do I ever recollect observing this singularly grand phenomenon on a more extensive scale, or with greater variety of form. The morning was desperately cold; the thermometer, as I mounted my horse, a little after sunrise, stood at 32 degrees, the freezing point, with a sharp biting wind from the north-east. The ground was blanched with frost, and the water-skins, or *behishtis masheks,* were covered with ice at the mouth. The slender shrubs, especially the milky ak, were completely burnt up; and as the weather had been hitherto mild, the transition was severely felt, by things animate and inanimate.

It is only in the cold season that the *mirage* is visible; the sojourners of Maroo call it the *see-kote,* or "castles in the air." In the deep desert to the westward, the herdsmen and travelers through these regions style it *chittram,* "the picture"; while about the plains of the Chumbul and Jumna they term it *dessasur,* "the omen of the quarter." This optical deception has been noticed from the remotest times. The prophet Isiah alludes to it when he says, 'and the parched ground shall become a pool'; which the critic has justly rendered, 'and the *sehrab* shall become real water.' Quintus Curtius, describing the *mirage* in the Sogdian desert, says that 'for the space of four hundred furlongs not a drop of water is to be found, and the sun's heat, being very vehement in summer, kindles such a fire in the sands, that everything is burnt up. There also arises such an exhalation, that the plains wear the appearance of a vast and deep sea;' which is an exact description of the *chittram* of the Indian desert. But the *sehrab* and *chittram,* the true *mirage* of Isiah, differ from that illusion called the *see-kote;* and though the traveller will hasten to it, in order to obtain a night's lodging, I do not think he would expect to slake his thirst there.

December 1. – Lake of Poshkur, four coss: the thermometer stood at the freezing-point this morning – heavy sands the whole way. Crossed the Sarasvati near Naund; its banks were covered with bulrushes, at least ten feet in height – many vehicles were lading with them for the interior, to be used for the purposes of thatching – elephants make a feast among them. We again crossed the Sarasvati, at the entrance of the valley of Poshkur, which comes from Old (*boora*) Poshkur, four miles east of the present lake, which was excavated by the last of the Puriharas of

Mundore. The sand drifted from the plains by the currents of air has formed a complete bar at the mouth of the valley, which is about one mile in breadth; occasionally the *teebas,* or sand-hills, are of considerable elevation. The summits of the mountains to the left were sparkling with a deep rose-coloured quartz, amidst which, on the peak of Naund, arose a shrine to "the Mother". The hills preserve the same character: bold pinnacles, abrupt sides, and surface thinly covered. The stratification inclines to the west; the dip of the strata is about twenty degrees. There is, however, a considerable difference in the colour of the mountains: those on the left have a rose tint; those on the right are of grayish granite, with masses of white quartz about their summits.

Poshkur is the most sacred lake in India; that of Mansurwar in Thibet may alone compete with it in this respect. It is placed in the centre of the valley, which here becomes wider, and affords abundant space for the numerous shrines and cenotaphs with which the hopes and fears of the virtuous and the wicked amongst the magnates of India have studded its margin. It is surrounded by sand-hills of considerable magnitude, excepting on the east, where a swamp extends to the very base of the mountains. The form of the lake may be called an irregular ellipse. Around its margin, except towards the marshy outlet, is a display of varied architecture. Every Hindu family of rank has its niches here, for the purpose of devotional pursuits when they could abstract themselves from mundane affairs. The most conspicuous are those erected by Raka Maun of Jeipoor, Ahelya Bae, the Holkar queen, Jowahir Mull of Bhurtpoor, and Beejy Singh of Marwar. The cenotaphs are also numerous. The ashes of Jey Appa, who was assassinated at Nagore, are superbly covered; as are those of his brother Suntaji, who was killed during the siege of that place.

By far the most conspicuous edifice is the shrine of the creator Brimha, erected, about four years ago, by a private individual, if we may so designate Gocul Pauk, the minister of Sindia; it cost the sum of 130,000 rupees (about 15,000 pounds), though all the materials were at hand, and labour could be had for almost nothing. This is the sole tabernacle dedicated to the ONE GOD which I ever saw or have heard of in India. The statue is quadrifrons; and what struck me as not a little curious was that the *sikra*, or pinnacle of the temple, is surmounted by a cross. Tradition was here again at work. Before creation began, Brimha assembled all the celestials on this very spot, and performed the *Yuga*; around the hallowed spot walls were raised, and sentinels placed to guard it from the intrusion of the evil spirits. In testimony of the fact, the natives point out the four isolated mountains, placed towards the cardinal points, beyond the lake, on which, they assert, rested the *kanats*, or cloth-walls of inclosure. That to the south is called *Rutnagir*, or "the hill of gems", on the summit of which is the shrine of Sawuntri. That to the north is *Nilagir*, or "the blue mountain". East, and guarding the valley, is the *Kutchactar Gir*; and to the west, *Sonachooru*, or "the golden". Nanda, the bull-steed of Mahadeva, was placed at the mouth of the valley, to keep away the spirits of the desert; while Kaniya himself performed this office to the north. The sacred fire was kindled: but Sawuntri, the wife of Brimha, was nowhere to be found, and as without a female the rites could not proceed, a young Goojari took the place of Sawuntri; who, on her return, was so enraged at the indignity, that she retired to the mountain of gems, where she disappeared. On this spot a fountain gushed up, still called by her name; close to which is her shrine, not the least attractive in the precincts of Poshkur. During these rites, Mahadeva, or, as he is called, *Bhola Nath*, represented always in a state of stupefaction from the use of intoxicating herbs, omitted to put out the sacred fire, which spread, and was likely to involve the world in combustion; when Brimha extinguished it with the sand, and hence the *teebas* of the valley. Such is the origin of the sanctity of Poshkur. In after ages, one of the sovereigns of Mundore, in the eagerness of the chase, was led to the spot, and washing his hands in the fountain, was cured of some disorder. That he might know the place again, he tore his turban into shreds, and suspended the fragments to the trees, to serve him as guides to the spot – there he made the excavation. The Brahmins pretend to have a copper-plate grant from the Purihara prince of the lands about Poshkur; but I was able to obtain only a Persian translation of it, which I was heretical enough to disbelieve. I had many grants brought to me, written by various princes and chiefs, making provision for the prayers of these recluses at their shrines.

The name of Beesildeva, the famed Chohan king of Ajmer, is the most conspicuous here; and they still point out the residence of his great ancestor, Aja Pal, on the *Nag-pahar,* or "serpent-rock" directly south of the lake, where the remains of the fortress of the Pali or Shepherd-king are yet visible. Aja Pal was, as his name implies, a *goatherd,* whose piety, in supplying one of the saints of Poshkur with daily libations of goats' milk, procured him a territory. Satisfied, however, with the scene of his early days, he commenced his castle on the serpent-mount; but his evil genius knocking down in the night what he erected in the day, he sought out another site on the opposite side of the range; hence arose the far-famed Aja-mer.

December 2. – Ajmer, three coss. Proceeded up the valley, where lofty barriers on either side, covered with the milky toor (cactus), and the "yellow aonla of the border", showed they were but the prolongation of our own Aravulli. Granite appeared of every hue, but of a stratification so irregular as to bid defiance to the geologist. The higher we ascended the valley, the loftier became the sand-hills, which appeared to aspire to the altitude of their granite neighbours. A small rill poured down the valley; there came also a cold blast from the north, which made our fingers tingle. Suddenly we changed our direction from north to east, and ascending the mountain, surveyed through a gap in the range the far-famed Dhar-ool-Khyr. The view which thus suddenly burst upon us was magnificent. A noble plain, *with trees,* and the expansive lake of Beesildeva, lay at our feet, while "the fortress of the goatherd" crowned the crest of a majestic isolated hill. The point of descent affords a fine field for the mineralogist; on each side, high over the pass, rise peaks of reddish granite, which are discovered half-way down the descent to be reposing on a blue micaceous slate, whose inclination is westward, at an angle of about 25 degrees with the horizon. The formation is the same to the southward, but the slate there is more compact, and freer from mica and quartz. I picked up a fragment of black marble; its crystals were large and brilliant.

Passed through the city of Ajmer, which, though long a regal abode, does not display that magnificence we might have expected, and, like all other towns in India, exhibits poverty and ease in juxtaposition. It was gratifying to find that the finest part was rising, under the auspices of the British Government and, the superintendent of the province, Mr. Wilder. The main street, when finished, will well answer the purpose intended – a place of traffic for the sons of commerce of Rajast'han, who, in a body, did me the honour of a visit: they were contented and happy at the protection they enjoyed in their commercial pursuits. With the prosperity of Bhilwara, that of Ajmer is materially connected; and having no interests which can clash, each town views the welfare of the other as its own: a sentiment which we do not fail to encourage.

Breakfasted with Mr. Wilder, and consulted how we could best promote our favourite objects – the prosperity of Ajmer and Bhilwara.

Ajmer has been too long the haunt of Moguls and Pat'hans, the Goths and Vandals of Rajast'han, to afford much scope to the researches of the antiquary. Whatever time has spared of the hallowed relics of old, bigotry has destroyed, or raised to herself altars of materials, whose sculptured fragments serve now as disjointed memorials of two distinct and distant eras: that of the independent Hindu, and that of the conquering Mahomedan, whose eedgas and mosques, mausoleums and country-seats, constructed from the wrecks of aboriginal art, are fast mouldering to decay. The associations they call forth afford the only motive to wish their preservation; except one "relic of nobler days and noblest arts", which, though impressed with this double character, every spectator must desire to rescue from the sweeping sentence – an ancient Jain temple, a visit to which excited these reflections. Let us rather bless than execrate the hand, though it be that of a Turk, which has spared, from whatever motive, one of the most perfect, as well as the most ancient monuments of Hindu architecture. It is built on the western declivity of the fortress, and called *Urai din ca jhopra*, or "the shed of two and a half days", from its having occupied (as tradition tells) its magical builders only this short period. The skill of the Pali or Takshac architect, the three sacred mounts of these countries abundantly attest: nor had he occasion for any mysterious arts, besides those of masonry, to accomplish them. In discussing the cosmogony of the Hindus, we have had occasion to convert their years into days; here we must reverse the method, and understand (as in interpreting the sacred prophecies of Scripture) their days as meaning years. Had it, indeed, been of more humble pretensions, we might have supposed the monotheistic Jain had borrowed from the Athenian legislator Cecrops, who ordained that no tomb should consist of more work than ten men could finish in *three days*; to which Demetrius, the Phalerian, sanctioned the addition of a little vessel to contain the ghost's victuals.

I have already mentioned the lake, called after the excavator, the Beesil Talab. It is about eight miles in circumference, and besides the beauty it adds to the vale of Ajmer, it has a source of interest in being the fountain of the Looni, which pursues its silent course until it unites with the eastern arm of the Delta of the Indus: the point of outlet is at the northern angle of the *Doulut Bag'h*, "the gardens of wealth", built by Jehangir for his residence when he undertook to conquer the Rajpoots. The water is not unwholesome, and there are three outlets at this fountain-head for the escape of the water fitting its periodical altitudes. The stream at its parent source is thence called the Sagur-Mati. It takes a sweep northward by Bhowtah and Pisangun, and close to where we crossed it, at Govindgurh, it is joined by the Sarasvati from Poshkur; when the united waters (at whose *sangum*, or confluence, there is a small temple to the *manes*) are called the Looni.

The gardens erected on the embankment of the lake must have been a pleasant abode for "the king of the world", while his lieutenants were carrying on the war against the Rana: but the imperial residence of marble, in which he received the submissions of that prince, through his grandson, and the first ambassador sent by England to the Mogul, are now going fast to decay. The walks on which his majesty last paraded, in the state-coach sent by our James the First, are now over grown with shrubs.

The stratification of the rock, at the point of outlet, would interest the geologist, especially an extensive vein of mica, adjoining another of almost transparent quartz.

Eastward of this lake about a mile, is another named the *Anah-sagur*, after the grandson of Beesildeo, who has left the reputation of great liberality, and a contrast with Visala. The vestiges of an island are yet seen in the lake, and upon its margin; but the materials have been carried away by the Goths. There are two small buildings on the adjacent heights, called "the annulets of Khwaja Kootub", and some other saint.

December 9. – Bhilwara. – I encamped about half a mile from *our* good town of Bhilwara, which was making rapid strides to prosperity, notwithstanding drawbacks from sectarian feuds; with which, however, I was so dissatisfied, that I refused every request to visi: the town until such causes of retardation were removed. I received a deputation from both parties at my tents, and read them a lecture for their benefit, in which I lamented the privation of the pleasure of witnessing their unalloyed prosperity. Although I reconciled them to each other, I would not confide in their promises until months of improvement should elapse. They abided by their promise, and I fulfilled mine when the death of the Boondi prince afforded an opportunity, *en route* to that capital, to visit them. My reception was far too flattering to describe, even if this were the proper place. The sentiments they entertained for me had suffered no diminution when Bishop Heber visited the town. But his informant (one of the merchants), when he said it ought to have been called *Tod-gunj*, meant that it was so intended, and actually received this appellation: but it was changed, at my request, and on pain of withdrawing my entire support from it. The Rana, who used to call it himself in conversation *"Tod Sahib ca bustee"*, would have been gratified; but it would have been wrong to avail myself of his partiality. In all I was enabled to do, from my friendship, not from my official character, I always feared the dangers to his independence from such precedent for interference.

December 11. – Poor'h. – This is one of the oldest towns of Mewar, and if we credit tradition, anterior in date to Vicrama. We crossed the Kotaserri to and from Mandel, passing by the tin and copper mines of Dureeba, and the Poorawut estate of Peetawas. *Poor'h* means *par eminence*, "the city," and anciently the title was admissible; even now it is one of the chief fiscal towns.

About a mile east of Poor'h there is an isolated hill of blue slate, in which I found garnets imbedded. I have no doubt persevering adventurers would be rewarded; but though I tried them with a hammer, I obtained none of any value.

December 12. – Rasmi, on the Bunas river. – We had a long march through the most fertile lands of Mewar, all belonging to the Rana's personal domain. The progress towards prosperity is great; of which Rasmi, the head of a tuppa or subdivision of a district, affords evidence, as well as every village. On our way, we were continually met by peasants with songs of joy, and our entrance into each village was one of triumph. The patels and other rustic officers, surrounded by the ryots, came out of the villages; while the females collected in groups, with brass vessels filled with water gracefully resting on their heads, stood at the entrance, their scarfs half covering their faces, chanting the *suhailea*; a very ancient custom of the Hindu cultivator on receiving the superior, and tantamount to an acknowledgment of supremacy. Whether vanity was flattered, or whether a better sentiment was awakened, on receiving such tokens of gratitude, it is not for me to determine: the sight was pleasing, and the custom was general while I travelled in Mewar. The females bearing the *kullus* on their heads, were everywhere met with. These were chiefly the wives and daughters of the cultivators, though not unfrequently those of the Rajput sub-vassals. The former were seldom very fair, though they had generally fine eyes and good persons. We met many fragments of antiquity at Rasmi. Captain Waugh and the doctor were gratified with angling in the Bunas for trout; but as the fish would not rise to the fly, I set the net, and obtained several dozens: the largest measured seventeen inches, and weighed nearly two pounds.

December 16. – Mairta. – After an absence of two months, we terminated our circuitous journey, and encamped on the ground whence we started, all rejoiced at the prospect of again entering "the happy valley." We made four marches across the *do-ab*, watered by the Beris and Bunas rivers; the land naturally rich, and formerly boasting some large towns, but as yet only disclosing the germs of prosperity. There is not a more fertile tract in India than this, which would alone defray the expenses of the court if its resources were properly husbanded. But years must first roll on, and the peasant must meet with encouragement, and a reduction of taxation to the lowest rate; and the lord-paramount must alike be indulgent in the exaction of his tribute. Our camels were the greatest sufferers in the march through the desert, and one-half were rendered useless.

15

THE SONG OF FAMINE

Pierre Loti in Jaipur and Amber
1901

To hear the full blast of this dread song, one must travel towards the north-west, towards the land of the Rajput, where men die by thousands for want of the little rice which no one sends them. In this land the forests are dead, the jungle is dead, everything is dead.

The beautiful rose-coloured city

The avenues leading to the crenellated walls and arched gateways of the city are thronged by white-robed cavaliers, by women wrapped in long red and yellow veils, by ox carts, and by strings of camels decked in gay accoutrements. Surely the times of plenty could not show a more dazzling display of life and colour!

But what can be the meaning of those miserable heaps of rags lying at the foot of the ramparts? There are human shapes hidden under them. What can all these people be doing on the ground? Are they ill, or are they drunk? Ah! These are heaps of bones, or the withered and mummified carcasses of the dead. No, it cannot be that, for there are some who still move, their eyelids tremble and they can see, and there are some who can even stand on the tottering bones that serve as legs.

After we have passed the first gate another is seen, cut through an inner wall which is painted in rose colour up to its jagged crests, a bright rose colour so regularly flecked with white flowers as to resemble a piece of chintz. The tatters of humanity are there also, but the dark forms wallowing in the dust look more frightful close to the charming rose colour of the flower-spangled wall. They look like skeletons with leather overdrawn, and their bones stand out with horrible precision. Elbows and knee-caps make great swellings like the knots upon a stick, and the thighs, which have only one bone, are thinner than the legs which have two. Some are grouped in families, but others are abandoned and alone; some lie extended on the ground, almost at the point of death, whilst the rest sit huddled in crouching attitudes of stupid immobility, with grinning teeth and eyes which sparkle with fever. In one corner a fleshless old woman, who appears to be alone in the world, weeps silently upon her rags.

What an enchanting surprise awaits us as we pass through the second gate and behold the interior of the town!

What an astonishing and kingly caprice it must have been that planned a whole rose-coloured city where all the houses, ramparts, palaces, towers, balconies and temples are of one colour, evenly diapered with similar posies of white flowers. One might almost think that all the walls had been hung with an antique chintz of floral design, or that the town had been hewn out of onyx in the style of the old cameos of the eighteenth century. It is so different from anything that we have seen elsewhere, and the whole effect is one of complete and charming improbability.

There are streets laid out in straight lines, some almost a mile long and twice as broad as our boulevards. These are flanked by high palaces, the facades of which display an endless succession of Oriental fantasies. I have never seen such extravagant luxury of colonnades, of festooned arches, towers, windows, and balconies. All, too, of the same tint, a rosy tint whose colour is that of a flower or of an old silk, and even the tiniest moulding or the tiniest arabesque is outlined by a white thread graven in relief. It almost looks as if a delicate tracery of white lace had been nailed over the pieces of sculpture. On the flat surfaces, however, the decoration which resembles chintz with old-fashioned posies is again to be seen.

A seething crowd fills the whole length of the streets with a dazzling and ever-changing play of colour. Each side of the pavement is encumbered by merchants who have spread out their wares of cloth, copper, and arms on the ground before them. Wandering amongst the crowd are busy throngs of women, who are decked in muslins emblazoned with all manner of fantastic designs, whose naked arms are encircled with bracelets which go right up to their shoulders.

In the middle of the street there is an unending procession of armed horsemen bestriding gorgeous saddles, of long strings of camels, and of elephants with gilded robes whose trunks have been ornamented with complicated networks of coloured patterns. Dromedaries, on which two people ride one behind the other, also pass by with ambling gait and outstretched necks like those of running ostriches. Nude fakirs, covered with white powder from head to foot, walk past, and palanquins and chairs that are borne on men's shoulders are carried along; an Oriental fairland parading in all its splendour in a setting of rosy magnificence inconceivable in its beauty.

Servants lead tamed cheetahs belonging to the King through the streets. These are led on slips so that they may become accustomed to crowds. They wear little embroidered caps tied under their chins with a bow, and they pace along, putting down each velvet paw with infinite precaution as though stepping over eggs laid on the ground. For greater security they are also held by their ringed tails, and four attendants always walk behind. But there are also many hideous vagrants – graveyard specters like those lying at the rampart gates. For these have actually dared to enter the rose-coloured city and to drag their skeletons through the streets. There are more of them than I should have thought possible. Nor are those who wander tottering and with haggard eyes through the streets the only ones. There are horrible heaps of rags and bones lying on the pavements hidden amongst the gay booths of the merchants, and people have to step aside so as not to tread upon them. These phantoms are peasants who used to live in the surrounding districts. They have struggled against the droughts which have brought destruction to the land, and their long agony is imprinted on their incredibly emaciated bodies. Now all is over; their cattle have died because there was no more grass, and their hides have been sold for a mere trifle. The fields which they have sown are only steppes of dusty earth where nothing can grow, and they have even sold their rags and the silver rings that they used to wear on their arms and ankles so that they might buy food. They starved for months, till at last famine definitely appeared, hideous famine which filled the villages with the reek of a charnel house.

They are hungry and they wish to eat, that is why they have come into the city. They thought that people would take pity on them, and would not let them die, and they had heard that food and grain were stored here, as if to resist a siege; they had heard too, that every one in the city had something to eat.

Even now carts and strings of camels are constantly bringing sacks of rice and barley that the King has procured from distant lands, and people are piling them up in the barns, or even on the pavements, in dread of the famine which threatens the beautiful city on every side.

But though there is food it cannot be had without money. It is indeed true that the King gives food to the poor who dwell in his capital, but, as to helping the peasants who die by thousands in the surrounding fields, how can that be done if there is not sufficiency? So all heads are turned aside from the poor wretches who wander through the streets, and who haunt the places where people eat, still hoping that a few grains of rice may be thrown to them, till at length the time comes when they must lie down anywhere, even on the stones of the street, to wait for death's deliverance.

At this very moment they are piling hundreds of sacks, which the camels have brought, on to the pavements: room cannot be found in the barns – so three starved and naked children, whose ages range from five to ten years, must be driven from the place where they had sought a rest.

A woman who is standing by tells us that they are three brothers and that their parent, who brought them here, is dead (of hunger, I suppose): that is why they are here and they stay because they have nowhere else to go.

The woman appears to see nothing unusual in all this, yet she does not seem heartless or unkind. My God! What sort of folk are these? What can be the material from which the souls of these people are fashioned? People who would not kill a bird, but who feel no compunction when little children are left to die upon their doorsteps?

The tiniest of the three children seems to be almost dead, for he is motionless and has no longer strength enough to drive away the flies that cling to his closed eyelids: his belly is so empty that it resembles the carcass of an animal that has been drawn for cooking, and he has dragged himself along the ground so long that at last his hip bones have rubbed through the skin.

But they must move on elsewhere so that there may be room for the sacks of grain that have been brought here. The tallest of them gets up and takes the little child tenderly to his bosom, and after giving a hand to the other brother, who can still walk, he silently moves away.

The eyes of the little one open for a moment. Oh! What a look of unspeakable anguish is written on the face of this innocent martyr! What an expression of reproach, of astonishment, of surprise that anyone could be so unhappy, and be left to linger in such suffering! But the dying eyes are soon closed; the flies return to settle there, and the poor little head falls back on the wasted shoulder of the elder brother.

With a wonderful look of resignation and childish dignity the small elder brother totters forward with his charges, but he neither murmurs nor sheds a tear, for is he not now the head of the family? Then after having made sure that he is far enough off not to be in the way, he lays his brothers very gently on the ground and stretches himself out by their side.

The wonderful luxury of the city attains its most curious effects in the open space from which the principal streets diverge. There the pyramids of the Brahmin temples are coloured pink up to their extremities, and, rising through flights of black crows into their dusky sky, give us the impression of rosy yew trees dotted with flowers. The façade of the King's palace is also rose, overlaid with white flowers: this building even surpasses in height the fronts of our cathedrals, and is composed of an endless repetition of kiosks placed one above the other. Each kiosk is like the one below it, and each has the same colonnades, the same lattice-work and the same complicated domes, whilst on the topmost pinnacles are royal standards whose coloured bannerets flap in the parching wind. Rose are the palaces, rose are the houses lining the streets that lead on all sides into the dusty distances.

In the central square the crowds are more animated and more noisy, and many jewels sparkle amidst the dazzling diversities of colour that the revelers wear. The spectres of famine are more numerous too – especially the shadowy forms of little children who are drawn hither by the smell of the rice-cakes and the sweets of honey and sugar that are being cooked in the middle of the open space. Of course, no one gives them away, but they stay on all the same, their dilated eyes sparkling with a fevered longing, even though they can hardly stand on their trembling legs.

And the invasion of these hunger-smitten ones increases rapidly. It is like a ghastly tide that flows from the country towards the town, and the roads leading across the plains are strewn with the corpses of those who have died before reaching the city gates.

A woman has just stopped to beg at the stall of a bracelet-seller, who is even now eating hot and savoury pancakes. The woman is a mere spectre, who clasps to her bony bosom and withered breasts the skeleton of a child. No, the trader will give her nothing; he does not even deign to look at her. Then the mother, whose breasts are dried up and whose child must die, flies into fury and the cry of a maddened she-wolf hurls itself forth through her unclenched teeth. She is quite young, and was doubtless beautiful; youth still glimmers in her ravaged cheeks, indeed she is almost a child and can hardly have seen more than sixteen years. But at last she understands that no one will take pity on her and that she is doomed. Then her despairing wail rises into the yell of a hunted beast that knows that its pursuers are at hand. Meanwhile the huge and pampered elephants walk past with heavy tread, munching the costly forage which has been brought from distant lands.

The outcries of the crows which swarm in thousands on the roofs and in the air can ever be heard rising above the clamouring of the crowd. This eternal and perpetual croaking, that dominates all other Indian sounds, here swells into a mighty crescendo, into a scream of delirious ecstasy, for the times of famine, when the odour of death is rife in the land, are the times of plenty for the crows, the vultures, and the flies.

It is now time to feed the royal crocodiles that live in the shadow of high walled gardens.

The kingly palace is almost a world in itself, with its endless dependencies, its stables for elephants and for horses. In order to reach the artificial lake where the crocodiles are to be found, we must pass through many doors bristling with iron, and through many courtyards broad as those of the Louvre. All these courtyards are flanked by sullen-looking buildings whose windows are barred with iron. Naturally, their walls are painted in rose colour and scattered over with nosegays of white flowers. Today these quarters are crowded, and the roll-call is being read out. It is payday, and soldiers of barbaric aspect and superb bearing are waiting with standards and lances in their hands. They are paid in heavy coins of the olden time, in round pieces of silver or in squares of bronze.

We pass through a marble hall, with arches and columns sculptured into arabesques. Here a cloth of purple is stretched over a gigantic loom, and dozens of workmen are occupied in covering the surface with raised flowers of gold embroidery. This is only a new trapping for one of the favourite elephants.

The gardens, by dint of laborious watering, have been kept almost green so that they seem a wondrous oasis in the midst of the parched land. A crested wall, some fifty feet in height, encloses vast and park-like slopes over which a gentle melancholy broods. There are cypresses and palms and little woods of orange trees and many roses that load the air with fragrance. There are marble seats where one may rest in the shade, kiosks of marble, and marble basins where princes may bathe. There are peacocks and monkeys, and occasionally the furtive muzzles of jackals peer out from under the orange trees.

At last we reach the formidable walls which surround the great pond, and at once see that its waters have almost disappeared through the long drought. Enormous old crocodiles, that look like rocks, slumber in the mud. Soon, however, a white-haired old man advances and stations himself on the steps leading down to the water's brink, singing as he walks in the high falsetto voice of a muezzin calling to prayer, and as he sings he waves his arms as if to call the slumbering reptiles. Then the crocodiles awake, and their first slow and indolent movement gives way to a fearful agility and suppleness of motion. They approach quickly, swimming across the pond, accompanied by great greedy tortoises who have also heard the call and wish to be fed too. All now form a circle at the foot of the steps on which the old man stands with his serving-men, who carry baskets of meat. The livid and viscous jaws now distend cavernously in readiness to swallow the goat's flesh, the logs of mutton, and the lungs and entrails which are thrown to them.

Yet outside in the streets no one, with muezzin's call, summons the starving to come and be fed. Those who have just arrived still wander about with outstretched hands, tapping, should any one chance to look their way, upon their hollow bellies. The rest, who have lost all hope, lie down anywhere, even under the feet of the crowd and in the track of the horses.

A French stranger has ordered his carriage to stop at a crossing where two of the avenues of rosy palaces and temples join, a spot much thronged by merchants, horsemen, and women in gay muslins. Here he alights and advances towards one of these dreadful, inert heaps of starving human beings and stoops down to place pieces of money into their lifeless hands.

Immediately it is as though a horde of mummies had suddenly risen from the dead. Heads emerge from the rags that covered the heap, and withered and bony forms rise slowly from the ground. 'What! He is giving money! We can buy something to eat!' The ghastly resurrection suddenly extends to other heaps lying hidden behind the piles of merchandise, the crowds and the furnaces of the pastrycooks. Then a swarm of phantoms advances with faces of dead men, with horrible, grinning teeth, with eyes whose lids have been eaten away by the flies, with breasts that hang like empty bags on their hollow chests, and with bones which rattle as they walk. Instantly the stranger is encircled by these spectres of the charnel house. They throng round him, they seize on his clothes, and try to snatch the money from his hands with finger nails which look like claws. And all the while their poor pleading eyes seem to ask pardon and forgiveness for their importunity.

Then silently the phantoms melt away. One of the spectres who was too weak to stand tottered and fell, causing the spectre nearest to him to fall also. This one in his fall brought others to the ground, but as each one in tumbling over clung to his neighbour, all gradually collapsed, fainting and exhausted, into the dust, from which they had no longer strength to rise, like a troupe of marionettes or like a set of ninepins that are bowled over.

Now the sound of approaching music is heard, and I can see an agitated crowd. It is a religious procession that has been sent out to announce that a festival will be held on the morrow in the Temple of Brahma. One of the attendants, whose duty it is to keep the road clear, notices that an old woman has fallen on her face into the roadway, so he picks her up and throws her back on to the pavement out of the way, where she lies bruised and groaning.

The passing procession is one of great beauty. A black elephant, ornamented with designs in gold, leads the way; behind him musicians walk, playing a solemn air in the minor mode on their bagpipes and their copper instruments.

Then four gray elephants advance, bearing on their backs young men adorned like gods. These graceful youths wear tall tiaras on their heads, and throw perfumed and coloured powders over the people standing beneath them. These powders are so light and subtle that it almost looks as if they were scattering clouds. Gradually too, the colours of green, violet, yellow, and orange settle on the elephants and tinge them with strange fantastic tones. The joyous youths throw the scented dust by handfuls, and the robes and turbans of the crowd are coloured at their will. Even the little, starving children, who look up from the ground on which they lie, are covered with the sandal-scented powder, and often their eyes are filled, for the motions of their enfeebled hands are too slow to shield them.

Now the day suddenly declines and a universal pallor seems to irradiate from the rose-coloured walls. Overhead the sky is blue, but the air is so charged with dust that the moon looks wan. Flocks of black-winged birds swoop down to roost, and crows and pigeons nestle so closely together on the cornices that the rosy palaces are outlined by strings of somber hue. Vultures and eagles still swoop in wheeling circles through the air, and the monkeys, who live freely on the house-tops, grow lively as the night comes, and chase each other with nimble feet: strange little shadows running with lifted tails along the edges of the roofs.

Below, the streets grow empty, for there is no night life in Eastern cities.

One of the tame cheetahs, who is on her way back to the palace to sleep, has seated herself on her haunches near the corner of a street. Just now she is on her best behaviour and with her cap all awry ·vears an expression of well-fed contentment. Her attendants have seated themselves in like fashion around her, though one of them still holds her by the tail. The cheetah's mystic eyes of pale green jade are fixed on some of the starving children who lie panting on the ground, only a few steps away from her.

The merchants hasten to fold up their many coloured stuffs and to pack their plates, vases, and vessels of copper into baskets. Then they retire to their houses, leaving more heaps of starving wretches, who had been hidden amidst their gay merchandise, exposed to view. Soon these will be the only human beings to be seen, and during the night they will be the masters of the pavement.

Gradually the heaps of death-smitten wretches become more clearly defined, and they are more numerous than I could have fancied. The square becomes deserted, and these rigid forms and hideous heaps of rags will soon be left to the loneliness of the night.

In the deserted country outside the city walls all the trees swarm with life in this twilight hour. Eagles, vultures, and splendid peacocks flock there in troops, each forming a little colony on the slender and leafless branches. Gradually their outcry ceases, and the stillness is only broken by intermittent calls which soon become less frequent. The complaining voices of the peacocks still linger in the evening air; then, as night comes on, the mournful cries of the jackals take up the song. It is ten o'clock, a late hour for the city whose life almost ceases with the day. The country around has become exquisitely silent. A mist seems to veil the distance, but it is only the dust rising from the parched land. The pale moonlight glistens in the white and dusty ground, the dead trees, and thorny cactus plants. Night has brought a sudden chill, and we seem to see the snows of winter. How cold it will be for the poor children who are lying naked and starving on the ground! The silence of the desert has now penetrated within the walls, and nothing can be heard but the rumbling of muffled music issuing from the depths of the Brahmin temples. A few white-robed men still move up and down the lofty staircases, which are flanked by elephants of stone. No one else can be seen, and the streets are quite deserted – those long, straight streets that seemed broader and larger now that they are no longer thronged with people and equipages. The beauty of the palaces, their fretted windows, seem even more imposing in the calm moonlight, and the rose-coloured city is still rosy in the whiteness of the moon.

But the black and sinister heaps are still there, those horrible piles of panting rags, those starving herds which have collapsed by the side of the sacks of corn that have been piled hastily on the pavement, and which are now being guarded by men armed with bludgeons.

Now we are able to see many niches of stone that were hidden during the day by the teeming multitudes. Each one shelters a god, may be the elephant-headed Ganesa, or may be Siva, the king of Death, but each idol is decked with flowers, and each has his little lamp which will burn till dawn comes.

Soon the heaps of rags become transformed into dark shapeless masses, patches of black which befleck the rosy gray of the enchanted city; but ever and anon a cough or a groan may be heard, and sometimes a leg or an arm protrudes from the ragged heap and stretches itself quiveringly into the air. To those who lie on the ground what matters the joyous day, the calm night, or the radiant dawn? No one will pity them; they have lost all hope, and they know that their weary heads must remain where they have fallen, and that they have naught to expect but the last pangs which will end all.

The terrace on which the councils were held by moonlight

The pale, full moon that hangs in the twilight sky has not yet commenced to shed its wan light over the masses of ruins that stretch out beneath my feet, and though the sun has sunk behind the mountains more than an hour ago, these ruins are still irradiated by its yellow glow. I am stationed on the lofty terraces of the dwelling of the ancient kings, a sort of formidable and unapproachable eyrie standing in the midst of a great abandoned town. Once it was filled with priceless treasures, but now it is empty, save for the few serving-men who have charge of it.

I am already at a great height, and if I lean over the luxuriantly carved granite slabs that serve as balustrades to these terraces, I overlook abysses, at the bottom of which lie the remains of houses, temples, mosques, and other splendours. I am already at a great height, and yet I am overlooked on all sides, for the rocks on which the palace is built stand encircled by mountains that are still more lofty. Around me are great pointed peaks of reddish stone rising almost vertically into the air, whose topmost summits are crested by ramparts, the jagged edges of which are outlined against the yellow sky. The towering wall is one of those ancient works whose audacity and enormity fill us with perplexity, for it is built of huge blocks poised on almost inaccessible mountain peaks, and it encloses a circle of several miles. It seems, too, to rise so loftily and with such confidence into the air that I can hardly look at it without a feeling of giddiness. Surely the people of olden times could hardly have imagined a more wonderful defence for the now decayed palace where I am standing, for they have transformed the summits of the whole encircling chain of mountains into one huge fortress. And there is but one entrance into the forbidden circle, a sort of natural cleft, through which I can see distant deserts that look as if they had been ravaged by fire.

The sun was declining as I set out for the ancient capital of Amber, whose ruins now lie beneath my feet, a capital replaced nearly two centuries ago by the town of Jeypore, which I have lately quitted. I was accompanied by guides and horses, placed at my disposal by the Maharajah of the beautiful rosy city, the successor of the kings who formerly inhabited this palace of Amber, on whose terraces I now stand. I had hastened to make my escape from the fairy splendours and the Dantesque horrors of Jeypore, and was glad to reach the open plains, where at least all the agonies would be over and the silence of death would reign.

Yet I knew through what regions of terror I should have to pass directly I left the rampart gates: it would be like a battlefield over which a conquering enemy had long since swept. Withered corpses would lie in the parching sun, and these corpses would breathe, and some even would be able to rise and follow me or seize me with their poor bony hands in supreme and despairing appeal.

Yes, indeed, I found all that awaiting me.

Amongst the dreadful heaps of bones and rags were many old women whose descendants had probably perished of hunger: abandoned grandmothers who lay there, calmly waiting for their turn to come. They did not beg, nor even move, though their great eyes expressed an infinitude of despair. Above their heads multitudes of crows, perched on the branches of the dead trees, were keeping anxious watch until the time should come.

But children were even more numerous than on the previous days. Oh! the little faces that seemed astonished at so much misery and destitution, and that looked at us so appealingly from the ground. We got down and stopped before some of the most emaciated, though we could not stop before them all, for they were legion. Poor, little, weary heads, attached to skeletons that could no longer support them. We lifted them up gently, but they fell back confidingly into our arms, and the eyes closed as if they would sleep under our protection. Sometimes we see that the succour we have brought comes too late, but often the tiny spectres get up and take the piece of money that we have given them to the merchants who sell rice.

My God! It would cost so little to keep these infants from starvation! The frugal nourishment of an Indian costs about three half-pence a day.

After issuing from the rosy gates we had to pass through two miles of ruins before the open country was reached. The gardens that adjoined the road were filled with dead trees and with interminable suites of cupolas and carved stone kiosks, now only inhabited by monkeys, crows, and vultures. The outskirts of all the towns of this country resemble each other in that they are crowded with burying places and with vast relics of former civilization.

It is needless to say that there are no signs of cultivation, and that no living person can be seen in the villages, which swarm with flies.

When at last we reached the foot of the mountains, it seemed as if the regions of reddish stone in which we found ourselves were heated by some artificial means. Even in the shade each gust of dry and dusty wind seemed like a breath of flame. The only vegetation of this neighbourhood consisted of great plants of dead cactus. These still remained standing, and all the surrounding rocks bristled with their thorny spears. My two guides rode on horseback with bucklers by their sides, carrying their lances erect, just as the soldiers of kings may have done in the olden times.

The declining rays of the evening sun were flashing in our eyes as we at last saw the narrow cleft which gives access to the enclosed valley of Amber. A formidable door barred the only entrance, but, when we passed through it, the ancient capital lay before us.

We ascended by paved slopes, on which our horses could scarcely find foothold, to that kingly palace of stone and marble, so proudly enthroned on the rocks that overlook the other ruins.

Close by the entry, near one of the first windings of the ascending road, we came upon a black and evil-looking temple, the floor of which was stained with pools of blood, and which reeked with the stench of a slaughter-house. In a niche at the back, the fearful Dourga lives. She is quite little and almost shapeless, and has the look of a malevolent gnome cowering under a heap of red rags. At her feet lies a tom-tom, almost as large as a tower. For centuries past a goat has been slaughtered here each morning at daybreak to the sound of the enormous tom-tom. Then the priests offer the warm blood to the goddess in a cup of bronze, and place the horned head before her on a plate. How can the goddess have slipped into the Brahmin Pantheon even under the title of Spouse of the God of Death, this Dourga, this fearful Kali, who is so greedy of blood that even human sacrifices were formerly offered to her in the very land where for ages all slaughter has been forbidden?

Where can she have come from with her red cloak, from what dark ages, and from what gloomy night?

At different points on our route, heavily studded bronze gates have been thrown open for us, but at last we had to leave our horses and continue our ascent on foot, through courtyards and gardens and winding staircases. We pass through marble halls, whose thickset pillars are decorated with tiny designs of barbaric taste. The vaulted arches were once clothed with glittering mosaics, and patches of shining looking-glass still shimmer under the damp incrustations that make the walls resemble the sides of a stalactite cave. The doors, too, were of sandalwood inlaid with ivory. As we climb higher we see baths hollowed out of the rock in which the ladies of the harem used to bathe. In the central space there is a cloistered, hanging garden, from which the rooms of the queens, princesses, and beauties of former days opened out. As I passed through on my way to the topmost terraces, the air was scented with the perfume of ancient orange trees, but the old guardian complained bitterly of the monkeys who now seemed to think themselves masters of the place, and were even bold enough to gather the oranges.

Now that I had reached the topmost terraces, I waited for the night to come. The ancient kings had built these places and surrounded them by rich balustrades so that they might give audiences or hold councils there by moonlight, and I had wished to see these terraces at their allotted hour, under the moonlight which will soon pour down upon them.

The eagles, vultures, peacocks, turtle-doves, and swallows have now retired for the night, and the abandoned palace seems doubly abandoned in the pervading silence. The sun has been hidden from me for a long time by the lofty mountains, but it must have set by now, for on the terrace below me I can see the Mussulman guardians, who ever wait for the holy hour of Moghreb, turn towards Mecca, and say their evening prayers.

Just at this moment a hollow sound reaches me from the blood-stained temple. It is the Brahmin hour of prayer also, and the tom-tom commences to roar, the tom-tom of the witch-like goddess with the scarlet cloak.

These heavy and resounding blows are but the prelude of, and signal for, an orgy of savage sounds. Groaning bagpipes and iron cymbals join in, and a horn howls unceasingly on two ever repeated notes, which swell and fall and become blurred in their passage through the hollow and empty rooms on which these terraces are built. Suddenly an answering peal of bells floats through the air. It is the little temple of Siva whence this insistent ringing comes, a little chapel perched on the top of the pointed peaks which surround me, a temple leaning against the lofty wall whose crests stand out against the evening sky like the teeth of a black comb.

I had not expected to hear so much clamour amidst these ruins, but in India the destruction of a town and the decay of its sanctuaries does not prevent the performance of the sacred rites, and the gods still continue to receive service in the midst of the most deserted regions.

For the last few moments my eyes have been turned towards the little temple from which the pealing bells resound, and when I next look towards the ground, I am almost shocked to see my shadow suddenly and sharply defined there. Instinctively I turn to see whether someone has not lighted a strangely bright lamp behind me, or whether an electric search-light has not enveloped me in its wan rays. But no, it is the great full moon, the moon of royal audiences that I had quite forgotten, but which has already commenced its nightly offices, almost without any intervening twilight, so quickly in this country do the days make haste to die.

Other shadows, the shadows of motionless things, are now thrown everywhere in alarming contrast with spectral brightness, but the terrace of the moonlight audiences is bathed in the full white glory of the moon.

I shall descend when the clanging music has ceased, for I should hardly care to traverse so many narrow staircases and passages whilst it lasts, or to walk alone at this late hour through the palatial halls that must now be given up to wraiths and monkeys.

But the music lasts a long while, so long that I can count the kindling stars.

How commanding and yet how hidden the place is, and what kings of fantasy these sovereigns must have been who planned these moonlight terraces!

In about half an hour the sounds of the tom-toms and the howls of the sacred horns become less deafening and less frequent. Their vibrations linger and grow feeble, and their outbursts of renewed and desperate frenzy are of ever diminishing duration. I feel that the sounds express a lingering agony, and that they are dying of exhaustion. At last silence comes back again, and from the bottom of the valley, where the ruins of Amber lie, I can hear the melancholy flute-like voice of wandering jackals.

It is not really dark in the stairways and the low halls of the palace as I make my way down. Everything seems bathed in moonbeams of bluish whiteness, and silvery rays enter through festooned windows and cast the charming outlines of the pointed arches on to the pavement: the faded mosaics on the walls glow with new life, so that the halls seem studded with gems or sparkling drops of water. As I passed through the gardens, now heavy with the scent of flowers, the upper branches of the orange trees became all alive with the agitated and noisy awakening of the monkeys.

My guides await me at the lower doors, where, after the freshness of the terraces, the air seems hot and stifling. They are already in the saddle, and carry their lances in their hands. We trot tranquilly through the night towards the city of Jeypore, which I am leaving for good tomorrow.

I have decided to avoid Beckanire, a town lying a hundred leagues further north. I had intended to visit it, but I have heard that the horrors of the famine culminate there, and that the streets are lined with corpses. Alas! No! I have seen enough. So I shall take the road that leads back to less desolate lands, to places where, being near to the sea of Bengal, life can still thrive.

16

THE PLEASURES OF LOAFERDOM

Rudyard Kipling in Chitor
1891

To enjoy life thoroughly, haste and bustle must be abandoned.
Ram Baksh has said that Englishmen are always bothering to
go forward, and for this reason, though beyond doubt they pay
well and readily, are not wise men.

There is a certain want of taste, almost an actual indecency, in seeing the sun rise on the earth. Until the heat-haze begins and the distances thicken, Nature is so very naked that the Actaeon who has surprised her dressing, blushes. Sunrise on the plains of Mewar is an especially brutal affair.

The moon was burnt out and the air was bitterly cold, when the Englishman headed due east in his tonga, and the patient sowar behind nodded and yawned in the saddle. There was no warning of the day's advent. The horses were unharnessed, at one halting-stage, in the thick, soft shadows of night, and ere their successors had limped under the bar, a raw and cruel light was upon all things, so that the Englishman could see every rent seam in the rocks around. A little further, and he came upon the black bulk of Chitor between him and the morning sun. It has already been said that the Fort resembles a man-of-war. Every distant view heightens this impression, for the swell of the sides follows the form of a ship, and the bastions on the south wall make the sponsons in which the machine-guns are mounted. From bow to stern, the thing more than three miles long, is between three and five hundred feet high, and from one-half to one-quarter of a mile broad.

There was an elephant at Chitor to take birds of passage up the hill, and she – she was fifty-one years old, and her name was Gerowlia – came to the dak-bungalow for the Englishman. Let not the word dak-bungalow deceive any man into believing that there is even moderate comfort in Chitor. Gerowlia waited in the sunshine, and chuckled to herself like a female pauper when she receives snuff. Her *mahout* said that he would go away for a drink of water. So he walked, and walked, and walked, till he disappeared on the stone-strewn plains, and the Englishman was left alone with Gerowlia, aged fifty-one. She had been tied by the chain on her near hind leg to a pillar of the verandah; but the string was coir, and more an emblem of authority than a means of restraint. When she had thoroughly exhausted all the resources of the country within range of her trunk, she ate up the string and began to investigate the verandah. There was more coir string, and she ate it all, while the carpenter, who was repairing the dak-bungalow, cursed her and her ancestry from afar. About this time the Englishman was roused to a knowledge of the business, for Gerowlia, having exhausted the string, tried to come into the verandah. She had, most unwisely, been pampered with biscuits an hour before. The carpenter stood on an outcrop of rock, and said angrily: 'See what damage your *hathi* has done, Sahib.' 'Tisn't my *hathi*,' said the Sahib, plaintively. 'You ordered it,' quoth he, 'and it has been here ever so long, eating up everything.' He threw pieces of stone at Gerowlia, and went away. It is a terrible thing to be left alone with an unshackled elephant, even though she be a venerable spinster. Gerowlia moved round the dak-bungalow, blowing her nose in a nervous and undecided manner, and presently found some more string and thatch, which she ate. This was too much. The Englishman went out and spoke to her. She opened her mouth and salaamed; meaning thereby 'biscuits.' So long as she remained in this position she could do no harm.

Imagine a boundless rock-strewn plain, broken here and there by low hills, dominated by the rock of Chitor, and bisected by a single metre-gauge railway track running into the Infinite, and unrelieved by even a way-inspector's trolly. In the foreground put a brand-new dak-bungalow, furnished with a French bedstead, and nothing else; in the verandah place an embarrassed Englishman, smiling into the open mouth of an idiotic female elephant. But Gerowlia could not live on smiles alone. Finding that no food was forthcoming, she shut her mouth, and renewed her attempts to get into the verandah, and ate more thatch. To say 'Hi!' to an elephant is a misdirected courtesy. It quickens her pace, and if you flick her on the trunk with a wet towel, she curls the trunk out of harm's way. Special education is necessary. A little breechless boy passed, carrying a lump of stone. 'Hit her on the feet, Sahib,' said he; hit her on the feet.' Gerowlia had by this time nearly scraped off her pad, and there were no signs of the *mahout*. The Englishman went out and found a tent-peg, and returning, in the extremity of his wrath smote her bitterly on the nails of the forefoot.

Gerowlia held up her foot to be beaten, and made the most absurd noises – squawked in fact, exactly like an old lady who has narrowly escaped being run over. She backed out of the verandah, still squawking, on three feet, and in the open held up near and off forefoot alternately to be beaten. It was very pitiful, for one swing of her trunk could have knocked the Englishman flat. He ceased whacking her, but she squawked for some minutes and then fell placidly asleep in the sunshine. When the *mahout* returned, he beat her for breaking her tether exactly as the Englishman had done, but much more severely, and the ridiculous old thing hopped on three legs for fully five minutes. 'Come along, Sahib,' said the *mahout*. 'I will show this mother of bastards who is the driver. Fat daughter of the Devil, sit down. You would eat thatch, would you? How does the iron taste?' And he gave Gerowlia a headache, which affected her temper all through the afternoon. She set off, across the railway line which runs below the rock of Chitor, into broken ground cut up with *nullahs* and covered with low scrub, over which it would have been difficult to have taken a sure-footed horse, so fragmentary and disconnected was its nature.

❖

The Gamberi River – clear as a trout-stream – runs through the waste round Chitor, and is spanned by an old bridge, very solid and massive, said to have been built before the sack of Ala-ud-din. The bridge is in the middle of the stream – the floods have raced round either end of it – and is reached by a steeply sloping stone causeway. From the bridge to the new town of Chitor, which lies at the foot of the hill, runs a straight and well-kept road, flanked on either side by the scattered remnants of old houses, and, here and there, fallen temples. The road, like the bridge, is no new thing, and is wide enough for twenty horsemen to ride abreast.

New Chitor is a very dirty, and apparently thriving, little town, full of grain-merchants and sellers of arms. The ways are barely wide enough for the elephant of dignity and the little brown babies of impudence. The Englishman went through, always on a slope painfully accentuated by Gerowlia who, with all possible respect to her years, must have been a baggage-animal and no true *Sahib's* mount. Let the local Baedeker speak for a moment: 'The ascent to Chitor, which begins from within the south-east angle of the town, is nearly a mile to the upper gate, with a slope of about 1 in 15. There are two zigzag bends, and on the three portions thus formed, are seven gates, of which one, however, has only the basement left.' This is the language of fact, which, very properly, leaves out of all account the Genius of the Place who sits at the gate nearest the new city and is with the sightseer throughout. The first impression of repulsion and awe is given by a fragment of tumbled sculpture close to a red daubed *lingam*, near the Padal Pol or lowest gate. It is a piece of frieze, and the figures of the men are worn nearly smooth by time. What is visible is finely and frankly obscene.

The road is protected on the cliff side by a thick stone wall, loopholed for musketry, one aperture to every two feet, between fifteen and twenty feet high. This wall is being repaired throughout its length by the Maharana of Udaipur. On the hillside, among the boulders, loose stones, and *dhak*-scrub, lies stone wreckage that must have come down from the brown bastions above.

As Gerowlia laboured up the stone-shod slope, the Englishman wondered how much life had flowed down this sluice of battles, and been lost at the Padal Pol – the last and lowest gate where, in the old days, the besieging armies put their best and bravest battalions. Once at the head of the lower slope, there is a clear run down of a thousand yards with no chance of turning aside either to the right or left. Even as he wondered, he was brought abreast of two stone chhatris, each carrying a red daubed stone. There were the graves of two very brave men, Jeemal of Bedmore, and Kalla, who fell in Akbar's sack fighting like Rajputs. Read the story of their deaths, and learn what manner of warriors they were. Their graves were all that spoke openly of the hundreds of struggles on the lower slope where the fight was always fiercest.

At last, after half an hour's climb, the main gate, the Ram Pol, was gained, and the Englishman passed into the City of Chitor and – then and there formed a resolution, since broken, not to write one word about it for fear that he should be set down as a babbling and a gushing enthusiast. Objects of archæological interest are duly described in an admirable little book of Chitor which, after one look, the Englishman abandoned. One cannot "do" Chitor with a guide-book. The Chaplain of the English Mission to Jehangir said the best that was to be said, when he described the place three hundred years ago, writing quaintly: 'Chitor, an ancient great kingdom, the chief city so called which standeth on a mighty high hill, flat on the top, walled about at the least ten English miles. There appear to this day above a hundred churches ruined and divers fair palaces which are lodged in like manner among their ruins, as many Englishmen by the observation have guessed. Its chief inhabitants to-day are Zum and Ohim, birds and wild beasts, but the stately ruins thereof give a shadow of its beauty while it flourished in its pride.'

Gerowlia struck into a narrow pathway, forcing herself through garden-trees and disturbing the peacocks. An evil guide-man on the ground waved his hand, and began to speak, but was silenced. The death of Amber was as nothing to the death of Chitor – a body whence the life had been driven by riot and the sword. Men had parcelled the gardens of her palaces and the courtyards of her temples into fields; and cattle grazed among the remnants of the shattered tombs. But over all–over rent and bastion, split temple-wall, pierced roof, and prone pillar–lay the 'shadow of its beauty while it flourished in its pride.' The Englishman walked into a stately palace of many rooms, where the sunlight streamed in through wall and roof, and up crazy stone stairways, held together, it seemed, by the marauding trees. In one bastion, a wind-sown peepul had wrenched a thick slab clear of the wall, but held it tight pressed in a crook of a branch, as a man holds down a fallen enemy under his elbow, shoulder, and forearm. In another place, a strange uncanny wind sprung from nowhere, was singing all alone among the pillars of what may have been a Hall of Audience. The Englishman wandered so far in one palace that he came to an almost black-dark room, high up in a wall, and said proudly to himself: 'I must be the first man who has been here'; meaning no harm or insult to any one. But he tripped and fell, and as he put out his hands, he felt that the stairs had been worn hollow and smooth by the tread of innumerable naked feet. Then he was afraid, and came away very quickly, stepping delicately over fallen friezes and bits of sculptured men, so as not to offend the Dead; and was mightily relieved when he recovered his elephant and allowed the guide to take him to Kumbha Rana's Tower of Victory.

This stands, like all things in Chitor, among ruins, but Time and the other enemies have been good to it. It is a Jain edifice, nine stories high, crowned atop – was this designed insult or undesigned repair? – with a purely Mahometan dome, where the pigeons and the bats live. Excepting this blemish, the Tower of Victory is nearly as fair as when it left the hands of the builder whose name has not been handed down to us. It is to be observed here that the first, or more ruined, Tower of Victory, built in Alluji's days, when Chitor was comparatively young, was raised by some pious Jain as proof of conquest over things spiritual. The second tower is more worldly in intent.

Those who care to look, may find elsewhere a definition of its architecture and its more striking peculiarities. It was in kind, but not in degree, like the Jugdesh Temple at Udaipur, and, as it exceeded it in magnificence, so its effect upon the mind was more intense. The confusing intricacy of the figures with which it was wreathed from top to bottom, the recurrence of the one calm face, the God enthroned, holding the Wheel of the Law, and the appalling lavishness of decoration, all worked toward the instilment of fear and aversion.

Surely this must have been one of the objects of the architect. The tower, in the arrangement of its stairways, is like the interior of a Chinese carved ivory puzzle-ball. The idea given is that, even while you are ascending, you are wrapping yourself deeper and deeper in the tangle of a mighty maze. Add to this the half-light, the thronging armies of sculptured figures, the mad profusion of design splashed as impartially upon the undersides of the stone window-slabs as upon the door-beam of the threshold – add, most abhorrent of all, the slippery sliminess of the walls always worn smooth by naked men, and you will understand that the tower is not a soothing place to visit. The Englishman fancied presumptuously that he had, in a way, grasped the builder's idea; and when he came to the top story and sat among the pigeons his theory was this: To attain power, wrote the builder of old, in sentences of fine stone, it is necessary to pass through all sorts of close-packed horrors, treacheries, battles, and insults, in darkness and without knowledge whether the road leads upward or into a hopeless *cul-de-sac*. Kumbha Rana must many times have climbed to the top story, and looked out toward the uplands of Malwa on the one side and his own great Mewar on the other, in the days when all the rock hummed with life and the clatter of hooves upon the stony ways, and Mahmoud of Malwa was safe in hold. How he must have swelled with pride – fine insolent pride of life and rule and power–power not only to break things but to compel such builders as those who piled the tower to his royal will! There was no decoration in the top story to bewilder or amaze – nothing but well-grooved stone slabs, and a boundless view fit for kings who traced their ancestry –

> From times when forth from the sunlight, the
> first of our Kings came down,
> And had the earth for his footstool, and wore
> the stars for his crown.

The builder had left no mark behind him – not even a mark on the threshold of the door, or a sign in the head of the topmost step. The Englishman looked in both places, believing that those were the places generally chosen for markcutting. So he sat and meditated on the beauties of kingship and the unholiness of

Hindu art, and what power a shadowland of lewd monstrosities had upon those who believed in it, and what Lord Dufferin, who is the nearest approach to a king in this India, must have thought when aide-de-camps clanked after him up the narrow steps. But the day was wearing, and he came down – in both senses – and, in his descent, the things on every side of the tower, and above and below, once more took hold of and perverted his fancy, so that he arrived at the bottom in a frame of mind eminently fitted for a descent into the Gau-Mukh, which is nothing more terrible than a little spring, falling into a reservoir, in the side of the hill.

He stumbled across more ruins and passed between tombs of dead Ranis, till he came to a flight of steps, built out and cut out from rock, going down as far as he could see into a growth of trees on a terrace below him. The stone of the steps had been worn and polished by the terrible naked feet till it showed its markings clearly as agate; and where the steps ended in a rock-slope, there was a visible glair, a great snail-track, upon the rocks. It was hard to keep safe footing upon the sliminess. The air was thick with the sick smell of stale incense, and grains of rice were scattered upon the steps. But there was no one to be seen. Now this in itself was not specially alarming; but the Genius of the Place must be responsible for making it so. The Englishman slipped and bumped on the rocks, and arrived, more suddenly than he desired, upon the edge of a dull blue tank, sunk between walls of timeless masonry. In a stabbed-in recess, water was pouring through a shapeless stone gargoyle, into a trough; which trough again dripped into the tank. Almost under the little trickle of water, was the loathsome Emblem of Creation, and there were flowers and rice around it. Water was trickling from a score of places in the cut face of the hill; oozing between the edges of the steps and welling up between the stone slabs of the terrace. Trees sprouted in the sides of the tank and hid its surroundings. It seemed as though the descent had led the Englishman, firstly, two thousand years away from his own century, and secondly, into a trap, and that he would fall off the polished stones into the stinking tank, or that the Gau-Mukh would continue to pour water until the tank rose up and swamped him, or that some of the stone slabs would fall forward and crush him flat.

Then he was conscious of remembering, with peculiar and unnecessary distinctness, that, from the Gau-Mukh, a passage led to the subterranean chambers in which the fair Pudmini and her handmaids had slain themselves. And, that Tod had written and the Stationmaster at Chitor had said, that some sort of devil, or ghoul, or Something, stood at the entrance of that approach. All of which was a nightmare bred in full day and folly to boot; but it was the fault of the Genius of the Place, who made the Englishman feel that he had done a great wrong in trespassing into the very heart and soul of all Chitor. And, behind him, the Gau-Mukh guggled and choked like a man in his death-throe. The Englishman endured as long as he could – about two minutes. Then it came upon him that he must go quickly out of this place of years and blood – must get back to the afternoon sunshine, and Gerowlia, and the dak-bungalow with the French bedstead. He desired no archæological information, he wished to take no notes, and, above all, he did not care to look behind him, where stood the reminder that he was no better than the beasts that perish. But he had to cross the smooth, worn rocks, and he felt their sliminess through his boot-soles. It was as though he were treading on the soft, oiled skin of a Hindu. As soon as the steps gave refuge, he floundered up them, and so came out of the Gau-

Mukh, bedewed with that perspiration which follows alike on honest toil or – childish fear.

'This,' said he to himself, 'is absurd!' and sat down on the fallen top of a temple to review the situation. But the Gau-Mukh had disappeared. He could see the dip in the ground and the beginning of the steps, but nothing more.

Perhaps it was absurd. It undoubtedly appeared so, later. Yet there was something uncanny about it all. It was not exactly a feeling of danger or pain, but an apprehension of great evil.

If any man doubt this, let him sit for two hours in a hot sun on an elephant, stay half an hour in the Tower of Victory, and then go down into the Gau-Mukh, which, it must never be forgotten, is merely a set of springs 'three or four in number, issuing from the cliff face at cow-mouth carvings, now mutilated. The water, evidently percolating from the Hathi Kund above, falls first in an old pillared hall and thence into the masonry reservoir below, eventually, when abundant enough, supplying a little waterfall lower down.' That, Gentlemen and Ladies, on the honour of one who has been frightened of the dark in broad daylight, is the Gau-Mukh, as though photographed!

The Englishman regained Gerowlia and demanded to be taken away, but Gerowlia's driver went forward instead and showed him a new Mahal just built by the present Maharana. Carriage drives, however, do not consort well with Chitor and the 'shadow of her ancient beauty.' The return journey, past temple after temple and palace upon palace, began in the failing light, and Gerowlia was still blundering up and down narrow by-paths – for she possessed all an old woman's delusion as to the slimness of her waist – when the twilight fell, and the smoke from the town below began to creep up the brown flanks of Chitor, and the jackals howled.

Then the sense of desolation, which had been strong enough in all conscience in the sunshine, began to grow and grow.

Near the Ram Pol there was some semblance of a town with living people in it, and a priest sat in the middle of the road and howled aloud upon his gods, until a little boy came and laughed in his face and he went away grumbling. This touch was deeply refreshing; in the contemplation of it, the Englishman clean forgot that he had overlooked the gathering in of materials for an elaborate statistical, historical, geographical account of Chitor. All that remained to him was a shuddering reminiscence of the Gau-Mukh and two lines of the Holy Grail,

And up into the sounding halls he passed,
But nothing in the sounding halls he saw.

Post Scriptum. — There was something very uncanny about the Genius of the Place. He dragged an ease-loving egotist out of the French bedstead with the gilt knobs at head and foot, into a more than usually big folly – nothing less than a seeing of Chitor by moonlight. There was no possibility of getting Gerowlia out of *her* bed, and a mistrust of the Maharana's soldiery who in the daytime guarded the gates, prompted the Englishman to avoid the public way, and scramble straight up the hillside, along an attempt at a path which he had noted from Gerowlia's back. There was no one to interfere, and nothing but an infinity of pestilent nullahs and loose stones to check. Owls came out and hooted at him, and animals ran about in the dark and made uncouth noises. It was an idiotic journey, and it ended – Oh, horror! in that unspeakable Gau-Mukh – this time entered from the opposite or brushwooded side, as far as could be made out in the dusk and from the chuckle of the water which, by night, was peculiarly malevolent.

Escaping from this place, crab-fashion, the Englishman crawled into Chitor and sat upon a flat tomb till the moon, a very inferior and second-hand one, rose, and turned the city of the dead into a city of scurrying ghouls – in sobriety, jackals. The ruins took strange shapes and shifted in the half light and cast objectionable shadows.

It was easy enough to fill the rock with the people of old times, and a very beautiful account of Chitor restored, made out by the help of Tod, and bristling with the names of the illustrious dead, would undoubtedly have been written, had not a woman, a living breathing woman, stolen out of a temple – what was she doing in that galley? – and screamed in piercing and public-spirited fashion. The Englishman got off the tomb and departed rather more noisily than a jackal; feeling for the moment that he was not much better. Somebody opened a door with a crash, and a man cried out 'Who is there?' But the cause of the disturbance was, for his sins, being most horribly scratched by some thorny scrub over the edge of the hill – there are no bastions worth speaking of near the Gau-Mukh – and the rest was partly rolling, partly scrambling, and mainly bad language.

When you are too lucky sacrifice something, a beloved pipe for choice, to Ganesh. The Englishman has seen Chitor by moonlight – not the best moonlight truly, but the watery glare of a nearly spent moon – and his sacrifice to Luck is this. He will never try to describe what he has seen – but will keep it as a love-letter, a thing for one pair of eyes only – a memory that few men today can be sharers in. And does he, through this fiction, evade insulting, by pen and ink, a scene as lovely, wild, and unmatchable as any that mortal eyes have been privileged to rest upon?

An intelligent and discriminating public are perfectly at liberty to form their own opinions.

Contributors

Annie Zaidi

As her piece "Love in Switcherland" shows, Annie Zaidi tried very hard to grow up in Sirohi, Rajasthan. She went to college at Sophia, Ajmer, before studying communications in Mumbai. She is the author of *Known Turf: Bantering with Bandits and Other True Tales*. She has worked as a journalist for over a decade and as a poet for longer. A collection of illustrated poems, *Crush*, was published in 2006. More work has been published in journals like *Pratilipi*, *The Little Magazine*, *The Raleigh Review* and *Desilit*. *The Bad Boy's Guide to the Good Indian Girl*, a series of interlinked narratives written with Smriti Ravindra, is due to be published soon.

Bittu Sahgal

Bittu Sahgal is the Editor of *Sanctuary Asia* magazine. A natural affinity for nature, borne of frequent treks and camping trips to the Indian wilderness over a decade, saw him start *Sanctuary Asia* and *Cub Magazine* in the early eighties. To communicate the rationale for conservation to as wide an audience as possible, he has used the medium of film, having produced over 30 conservation-oriented documentaries that were aired over India's national television network. Sahgal's columns on environmental and development issues appear in a number of English and regional language publications in India. A journalist-writer, he has been closely involved with several national campaigns and is an active member on a range of government and non-government organization boards and committees. He initiated and currently helps run Kids for Tigers, a school outreach conservation programme that hopes to explain the rationale of biodiversity protection to children around the country. He is a trustee of the Wildlife Conservation Trust, India, and his key involvements focus around campaigns to save the tiger and to highlight the connection between human rights, biodiversity conservation, deforestation, ecosystem values and climate change.

Gayatri Devi (1919-2009)

Gayatri Devi was the daughter of the Maharaja of Cooch Behar and the third wife of Maharaja Sawai Man Singh II of Jaipur. In the manner of all Rajput royalty, she loved horses, polo, cars and *shikar* but at the same time, moving much beyond the conventional role of a Rajput princess, she became a champion of women's rights, shocking the conservative Rajasthan of her time by condemning the *purdah* system. In 1943 she established the Maharani Gayatri Devi Girls' Public School in Jaipur. To her credit also goes the revival and promotion of the dying art of blue pottery. Following Independence and the abolition of the princely states, she took to politics, with a landslide victory in the 1962 parliamentary elections.

James Tod (1782-1835)

Lieutenant-Colonel James Tod joined the East India Company as a cadet in the Bengal army at the age of eighteen. In 1805 he was assigned the command of the suite of Graeme Mercer, Agent of Sindhia's court and remained associated with Sindhia's court till 1818, with his final appointment being as Political Agent for western Rajasthan. During this period Tod not only conciliated warring chieftains and settled their feuds but painstakingly collected staggering amounts of geographical, topographical and historical data on Rajasthan. His two valuable works on which rests his abiding place of honour in the field of historical writing are the *Annals and Antiquities of Rajasthan* and *Travels in Western India*, the latter being published posthumously. A remote village in Rajasthan where he began compiling his notes and data to form the *Annals* was re-named Todgarh in his honour.

Jug Suraiya

Described by Khushwant Singh as India's Art Buchwald, Jug Suraiya is perhaps best known for his free-wheeling column, "Jugular Vein", which appears every Friday on the editorial page of *The Times of India*. He also writes a weekly contrarian column on topical issues, called "Second Opinion", which appears every Wednesday, also on the editorial page of *The Times of India*, in which he deals with social, literary and political themes. Among his many avatars, he is – together with artist Neelabh Banerjee – the co-creator of the comic strip "Duniya Ke Neta", which appears daily in *The Times of India*. A separate collaboration with cartoonist Ajit Ninan has seen the creation of "Like That Only", a twice-weekly cartoon commenting on our life and times, also featured in *The Times of India*. He is the author of several books and his previous titles include *Mind Matters*, a collection of editorial page articles; *Juggling Act*, an anthology of humorous writings; *Calcutta: A City Remembered*; and *A Tika for Jung Bahadur*, a collection of short stories. An inveterate traveller, Jug Suraiya is the first Asian to have won the Grand Prize for Travel Writing awarded by the Pacific Area Travel Association (PATA).

Nilanjana Roy

Nilanjana S. Roy is a literary columnist who also writes on gender issues. Her columns currently appear in the *Business Standard* and the *International Herald Tribune*. She has spent several decades working extensively in publishing and the media; she was Senior Features Editor at the *Business Standard*, has been a consulting editor with *Outlook* and with *Man's World*, and was chief editor at the publishing house Westland/ Tranquebar. Her work has appeared in most of India's leading publications; she has also been published in *Le Monde, Guernica* and *Publishers Weekly*. She is a recipient of the Human Rights Press Award for her journalism on gender issues. She is the editor of Penguin India's anthology of food writing, *A Matter of Taste*, and is working on a collection of essays on reading, *How to Read in Indian*, to be published soon by HarperCollins India. Her favourite T-shirt slogan, "Will Travel For Free", was far too literally interpreted by *Outlook Traveller*, but as stories like "There's a sparrow in my puri!" demonstrate, she doesn't really mind.

Pierre Loti (1850-1923)

Pierre Loti, pseudonym of Julien Viaud, was a novelist and a naval officer. It was his fellow naval officers who persuaded him to turn into a novel certain passages in his diary, eventually published as *Aziyade*. His second book, *Rarahu*, inspired the opera "Lakme" by Leo Delibes. Loti went on to publish an astonishing number of books, with his *Pecheur d'Islande* becoming a classic of French literature. It was in 1899 that Loti visited India and described the horrors of what he saw, a sample of which is included in this anthology. Henri Rousseau painted a portrait of Pierre Loti in in 1891, and one of Loti's great admirers was Marcel Proust. Loti's house in Rochefort is preserved as a museum.

Pradip Krishen

Pradip Krishen directed feature films in the eighties (*Massey Sahib*, *In Which Annie Gives It Those Ones*, and *Electric Moon*) before he became a naturalist in 1995. He began the project of identifying and photographing Delhi's trees in 1997, walking extensively through the city and on the Ridge. He published *Trees of Delhi: A Field Guide* in 2006 which quickly became a benchmark for nature field-guides in this country. Today he divides his time between growing and photographing native plants and writing about them. Since 2006, he has worked as Director/Curator of the Rao Jodha Desert Rock Park in Jodhpur that is devoted to growing plants native to rocky parts of the Thar desert. He is close to publishing his second book, *Jungle Trees of Central India*, based on extensive travelling in Madhya Pradesh where his interest in wild trees and plants was first kindled.

Prem Shankar Jha

After working for five years for the United Nations Development Programme in New York and Damascus, Prem Shankar Jha returned to India to pursue a career in journalism. He has been Editor of the *Economic Times*, the *Financial Express*, Economic Editor of *The Times of India* and Editor of the *Hindustan Times*. Jha has been a visiting scholar at the Indian Institute of Management, Calcutta; Nuffield College, Oxford; Weatherhead Centre for International Studies, Harvard; and the Fairbank Center for East Asian Research, Harvard. He has also been a Visiting Professor at the University of Virginia and the first holder of the chair on the Indian Economy at Sciences-Po in Paris. He has been a member of the Energy Panel of the World Commission on Environment and Development. In 1987 he received the Energy Journalist of the Year award from the International Association of Energy Economics.

He is the author of several books including *India – A Political Economy of Stagnation; Twilight of the Nation State – Globalisation Chaos and War; Crouching Dragon, Hidden Tiger: Can China and India dominate the world?* and *A Planet in Peril: The race against global warming.*

Rajesh Mishra

Growing up in army cantonments, Rajesh Mishra was exposed to India's cultural and geographical diversity early in life. Comings and goings, separations and new beginnings have been an intrinsic part of his life, with journeys continuing to be at the core of his being. Rajesh began his career as a features writer with *Society* magazine. Since then his articles and photographs have been published in *The Times of India, Hindustan Times, India Today, Verve, Man's World* and *Swagat,* among others. He has many cover stories to his credit, with his travel feature based on a nine-day visit to Pakistan in the summer of 2004 titled "Love in the time of cricket" gaining much appreciation. Rajesh's travel assignments with acclaimed photographer S. Paul on Kerala and Chilika Lake, likewise, were well received. In his writings, Rajesh has approached travel from a variety of perspectives – from a biking story in the Indo-Tibetan border in Kumaon, to community portraits of the Parsis and the Anglo Indians, to travelling on the Konkan Kanya Express from Ratnagiri to Madgaon for a piece on the Konkan region. He has trekked in high altitude Ladakh and scuba-dived in the coral rich waters around Havelock Island in the Andaman archipelago, but even though he has in a manner of speaking "been there, done that" every time the prospect of a journey presents itself he struggles to reign in the excitement.

Royina Grewal

Royina Grewal wrote journals since childhood, filled with jottings of places visited and things that caught her attention. These later translated into a multitude of interests. Travel and the writing of travelogues was an obvious favourite. Wildlife and nature followed closely, articulated in work for a magazine on environment. Concerns about the condition of lesser known monuments evolved into research on how to combine the imperatives of cultural conservation and development, manifest in her monographs on *Chanderi*, an early and definitive case study of its kind in India, followed by *Mandav*. These were accepted towards a PhD in architectural conservation at York, making Royina, at that stage, the only non-architect to have been admitted. A curiosity about the past developed into a series of Son et Lumiere productions, conceived, scripted and directed by her. She also created India's first audio guide. In between these various endeavours she wrote, *Travels along the Narmada*; *In Rajasthan*; *The Book of Ganesha*; and *In the Shadow of the Taj*. Royina has just completed her first novel based on the life of Babur. She lives between Delhi and an organic farm in Rajasthan.

Rudyard Kipling (1865-1936)

Rudyard Kipling, poet, short story writer, and novelist, was born in Mumbai. His very early years in India seem to have been idyllic but at the age of six, he was left in a foster home in England where he was severely bullied. This left him with deep psychological scars, and in his autobiography that was published some sixty-five years later, he recalls that time with horror, wondering whether it might have hastened the onset of his literary life. In 1882 he returned to India where he spent the next seven years working as a journalist and editor. This was when he also began to write about India. His short stories and verses gained both popular and critical acclaim in the late 1880s in England where he was hailed as a literary heir to Charles Dickens. In 1907 he received the Nobel Prize for Literature. He died at the age of seventy and his ashes are buried in the Poet's Corner at Westminster Abbey.

Sanjay Singh Badnor

Sanjay Singh Badnor hails from an aristocratic family of Rajasthan that traces its ancestry to the Rathore rulers of Marwar. He was educated at Mayo College, Ajmer, and St Stephens College, Delhi, after which he acquired a degree in Hotel Management from the Taj Group. Aborting midway a career in hoteleering he decided to pursue his passion for photo-journalism and travel writing. He has been a stringer for *The Times of India*, Ajmer, and has over the years contributed to leading newspapers, magazines, guide books such as the Lonely Planet series, travel websites and visual books, with his book on the Ajmer *dargah* being widely received. He has also authored a coffee-table book on Rajasthan. He was a stills photographer for "Beyond the Royal Veil", an Australian television documentary on Indian royalty. Although he has travelled throughout the country, Sanjay confesses to a decided passion for his native desert state of Rajasthan. Photographing people and in particular, royalty, is his forte.

William Dalrymple

William Dalrymple was born in Scotland and brought up on the shores of the Firth of Forth, but has lived in Delhi on and off for the last twenty-five years. He is the author of seven books about India and the Islamic world, all of which have won major literary awards, including *City of Djinns* (Thomas Cook Travel Book Award and Sunday Times Young British Writer of the Year Prize), *White Mughals* (Wolfson Prize for History and SAC Scottish Book of the Year Prize), *The Last Mughal* (Duff Cooper Prize and Crossword Vodafone Award for Non-Fiction) and *Nine Lives: In Search of the Sacred in Modern India* (Asia House Literary Award). He has also written and presented a number of prize-winning radio and TV documentaries, among them "The Long Search" (Stanford St Martin Prize) and "Indian Journeys" which won the Grierson Award at BAFTA. He is one of the founders and a co-director of the annual Jaipur Literary Festival, and has honorary doctorates of letters from the universities of St Andrews, Aberdeen and Lucknow.

Acknowledgements

Every reasonable effort has been made to trace copyright holders of material reproduced in this book, but if any have been inadvertently overlooked the publishers would be glad to hear from them.

"Going home" by Amrita Kumar © is adapted from the novel *Damage*, published by Harper Collins India and is reproduced by permission of the publisher; "The Singer of Epics" by William Dalrymple © is extracted from the book *Nine Lives*, published by Bloomsbury and is reproduced by permission of the author and the publisher; "Bury my heart at Rambagh" by Gayatri Devi © is extracted from the book *A Princess Remembers*, published by Rupa & Co. and is reproduced by permission of the publisher; "Where on earth am I?" by Jug Suraiya © is extracted from the book *"Where on earth am I?"* published by Penguin Books India and is reproduced by permission of the author; "When I saw Laxmi" by Bittu Sahgal © was first published as "Ranthambhore Tiger Reserve" in the book *India Naturally*, published by Sanctuary Asia and is reproduced by permission of the author and the publisher; "Fate in the balance" by Prem Shankar Jha, apart from the postscript, was first published as "Death of a sanctuary" in *Outlook Traveller* and is reproduced by permission of the author and the publisher; "The nowhere people" by Royina Grewal © is extracted from the book *In Rajasthan* published by Lonely Planet and is reproduced by permission of the author; "There's a sparrow in my puri!" by Nilanjana Roy was first published as "Royal Repast" in *Outlook Traveller* and is reproduced by permission of the author and the publisher; "Mappings" by James Tod is extracted from the book *Annals and Antiquities of Rajasthan,* published by Rupa & Co. and is reproduced by permission of the publisher; "The song of famine" by Pierre Loti is extracted from the book *India,* published by Rupa & Co and reproduced by permission of the publisher; "The pleasures of loaferdom" by Rudyard Kipling is extracted from the book *Rajasthan Stories,* published by Rupa & Co. and is reproduced by permission of the publisher.

The photographs in "Through a glass, darkly" are by Sanjay Singh Badnor © except for the following: The photograph of Gayatri Devi is printed here with the permission of Maharaj Devraj Singh Jaipur; the photographs of vintage cars and the interior of Shah Niwas are courtesy "Eternal Mewar".

A special word of thanks is due to Aman Nath and to Sanjay Singh Badnor for their advice and help with the project.